PALMERSTON AND
OF FOREIGN POLICY
1846–55

MANCHESTER
UNIVERSITY PRESS

PALMERSTON AND THE POLITICS OF FOREIGN POLICY 1846–55

David Brown

MANCHESTER UNIVERSITY PRESS

Manchester and New York

distributed exclusively in the USA by Palgrave

The right of David Brown to be identified as the author of this work has been asserted by him in accordance with the Copyright, Designs and Patents Act 1988

Published by Manchester University Press
Oxford Road, Manchester M13 9NR, UK
and Room 400, 175 Fifth Avenue, New York, NY 10010, USA
www.manchesteruniversitypress.co.uk

Distributed exclusively in the USA by
Palgrave, 175 Fifth Avenue, New York, NY 10010, USA

Distributed exclusively in Canada by
UBC Press, University of British Columbia, 2029 West Mall, Vancouver, BC, Canada V6T 1Z2

British Library Cataloguing-in-Publication Data
A catalogue record for this book is available from the British Library

Library of Congress Cataloging-in-Publication Data applied for

ISBN   0 7190 6199 7   *hardback*
       0 7190 6392 2   *paperback*

First published 2002

10 09 08 07 06 05 04 03 02   10 9 8 7 6 5 4 3 2 1

Typeset in Monotype Bell
by Carnegie Publishing, Chatsworth Rd, Lancaster
Printed in Great Britain
by Bell & Bain Ltd, Glasgow

To my parents

Contents

Preface

This book began as a doctoral thesis at Southampton University and along the way I have accumulated many debts. Firstly, I would like to thank those who have allowed me to use copyright material, especially the Trustees of the Broadlands Archives; the Earl of Clarendon; Lord Howick of Glendale; the Controller of Her Majesty's Stationery Office; the Bodleian Library, Oxford; the British Library; the University of Nottingham Department of Manuscripts and Special Collections; the National Library of Scotland; and the Public Record Office. I am indebted to the staff of the libraries and record offices visited in the course of this research and in particular would like to thank Chris Woolgar and the staff of the Department of Manuscripts and Special Collections at Southampton University Library whose advice and assistance have been invaluable. I am also grateful to the Parliamentary History Yearbook Trust for permission to reproduce material first published in my article in *Parliamentary History* (October 2001). Much of the research for this book was funded initially by a Southampton University Archive Research Studentship and also a number of smaller awards from the School of Research and Graduate Studies in the Faculty of Arts. In Manchester University Press, I have been fortunate to have an extremely efficient and accommodating publisher.

This book could not have been written without the friendship and support of a number of people, in particular Donald Bloxham, Polly Clark, Richard King, Nick Kingwell, Tony Kushner, John Oldfield and all members of the Cavaliers Cricket Club. John Charmley first introduced me to the world of Palmerstonian politics and Muriel Chamberlain encouraged me to pursue my work on Palmerston further. Peter Gray read earlier versions of this work and his comments have saved me from many errors. I am grateful to Richard Davis for his observations on a version of what became chapter 5. Angus Hawkins has taken a kind interest in this work and I have greatly valued his comments and suggestions. Above all, I must record my debt to Paul Smith who, as supervisor and friend, has been a constant source of encouragement and inspiration and whose close reading of my work has been greatly to its advantage. I hope I have made good use of the advice I have been given but I am, of course, responsible alone for any errors that remain.

Most importantly, I could not have completed this work without the love and support of my parents.

D.B.

1

Introduction

Lord Palmerston, variously regarded as a Tory, Liberal Tory, Canningite, Whig and Liberal; successively a Junior Lord of the Admiralty, Secretary at War, Foreign Secretary, Home Secretary and Prime Minister, left an indelible mark on the history of Victorian politics. From the 'last candle of the Eighteenth Century'[1] to the possessor of a 'genius for adaptation' whose governments were a 'conscious introduction to the new era' of democratic politics,[2] Palmerston's career spans an important transitional period in British politics while in many ways also shaping that change. His career and interests, at least after 1830, were concerned primarily with foreign policy yet through this specific and in certain senses peculiar and unique area of public business, he contributed to the evolution of a new style of government and to the refining of ideas of the political nation. Heretofore, however, studies of Palmerston have tended to focus almost exclusively on a 'high political' approach to his career, that is studying his ministerial and diplomatic involvements, or have covered only his life down to 1841.[3] The approach taken by Kenneth Bourne in his *Palmerston: The Early Years, 1784–1841* represents a break with this tradition in seeking to place Palmerston's career in a much broader personal and private context, yet, unfortunately, this volume concludes with the end of Palmerston's second term as Foreign Secretary and Bourne was unable to complete the projected second volume which would have taken the analysis down to 1865.[4] More recent writing on Palmerston has sought to develop an understanding of his career as Prime Minister from 1855 until, with only a brief hiatus in 1858–59, his death in 1865, focusing in particular on Palmerston's relationship with liberalism and the Liberal party.[5] There remains, however, a noticeable lack of work for the 1840s and early 1850s. With the exception of those studies which treat of Palmerston's whole career generally, primarily in the work of Bell, Southgate, Ridley and Chamberlain, attention to Palmerston or Palmerstonism for these years is scarce, perhaps the most important exception being Kingsley Martin's study of public opinion leading up to the Crimean War.[6]

Between the fall of Melbourne's government in 1841 and the creation of Lord John Russell's in 1846, Palmerston was not idle, although more so than at any other time in his career (at least since 1830) his energies were devoted to affairs of a non-political nature. He continued to contribute to debates on questions of foreign policy, notably that relating to the Ashburton-Webster treaty,[7] but it was, as one biographer observes, 'Palmerston's longest "holiday"'.[8] During the decade between 1846 and the establishment of his first government, however, Palmerston did much to place himself at the forefront of political life, forging a reputation which would allow him to face down opponents and install Palmerstonism as a distinct political creed.

From the bureaucrat of Bourne's *Early Years*, Palmerston emerged in the later 1850s and early 1860s as 'the defining political personality of his age'.[9] In large part this rested upon his achievements and conduct immediately preceding his accession to the premiership. This book seeks to elucidate the key features of that period, by examining the politics of foreign policy, in order to establish quite how Palmerston managed to carve out a specific role in politics and, against the odds, rise to the highest office in government at the age of seventy. In so doing, the book is concerned with questions of constitutional practice and theory, for in large part Palmerston's strength derived from constituencies traditionally seen as operating beyond the pale of the constitution, in particular the unenfranchised, as well as from among the increasingly politically important middle classes. To some extent this was a condition of the particular area of politics with which Palmerston pre-occupied himself, foreign affairs, yet also it was grounded in a view of the potential for invigorating a new force in government and politics. Palmerston's mobilisation of popular support for political ends during this period does more than hint at a Canningite legacy, it suggests an important element in the conception of the Victorian constitution – that is, the growing role and use of public opinion –

with repercussions for ministers, the people, and the monarchy. This present study, then, is not a textbook on British foreign policy, nor, strictly, a biographical treatment of Palmerston. Rather, it seeks to examine the conception of the political nation and the use and manipulation of public opinion with particular reference to the formulation and execution of Palmerstonian foreign policy.

Whig orthodoxy was suspicious of monarchical authority and trusted to the benevolence of a parliamentary government which included some measure of accountability. Palmerston had been schooled in the Whig tradition of political economy at Edinburgh under Professor Dugald Stewart, but ultimately his political philosophy was conditioned by a diverse range of influences. Simultaneously radical and reactionary, Palmerston's outlook boiled down, ultimately, to a belief in pragmatism above abstract principle, or as has been observed of his later years as Prime Minister, that politics was 'largely a matter of getting from Monday to Friday without conspicuous damage'.[10]

Above all, however, Palmerston regarded foreign policy as an issue of exclusively national importance, as operating beyond party, although differences could well still exist in terms of the execution of that policy. Thus, foreign policy was to be constructed with reference not only to Parliament, the Cabinet and the Crown, but also the 'nation'. In an age of growing national consciousness (and indeed coherence), Palmerston, if not the disciple of Canning, at least the heir to his legacy, followed his erstwhile mentor in grounding the moral justification for his foreign policy in the weight of popular approbation. In part this was a political tactic – to counterbalance opposition to his policy in the Government – but it was also indicative of a sincere perception of ministerial responsibility to conduct affairs of state in the interest of the nation as a whole, as he perceived it. If, as David Steele suggests, it appeared to contemporary observers that Parliament in this period between the Reform Acts had become virtually the representative chamber of not only the enfranchised but also the unenfranchised, then it was the responsibility of the politicians, so they believed, to articulate such views as were thus representative.[11] To the Chartists this would have appeared a curious judgement, yet with regard to foreign affairs, as David Urquhart's ultimately unsuccessful attempts to

channel Chartist forces towards a credible and consistent critique
of Palmerston's foreign policy illustrated, the proposition carries
some force. Even the unenfranchised and generally exploited members of society still seemed capable of feeling part of the nation
when it came to dealing with the foreigner, as Dickens illustrated
in his portrayal of the inhabitants of Bleeding Heart Yard in *Little
Dorrit.*

This argument assumes too readily, however, the existence of
a uniform extra-parliamentary view of foreign policy, whereas such
interest was, typically, much more inconsistent; but it helps explain
not only Palmerston's courting of popular support – playing up to
the public gallery as some contemporaries observed scathingly –
but his continued political potency: the 'People's Minister' (as the
Mayor of Southampton described him) [12] had a vital role to play if
this was to be the People's Parliament. Necessarily, however,
Palmerston's conduct of policy and his so-called popular appeal are
not to be taken as representative of a comprehensive conception of
the 'nation' and of all the elements which constituted the nation.
Palmerston's foreign policy reinforced certain specific characteristics of the 'national' character. He was 'the most English Minister'
(as Russell dubbed him), and not, significantly, the most British.
The ambiguities of this were little explored at the time, but 'Englishness' in the nineteenth century was not confined exclusively by the
boundaries of England. He represented strong, masculine qualities,
he embodied Protestant godliness: the British Foreign Secretary
was the true English patriot. [13]

Palmerston's popular maverick reputation should not be taken
as indicative of an absence of reason. The origins of his political
philosophy are to be found in his undergraduate days at Edinburgh.
Dugald Stewart, a former student of Adam Smith, held the Chair
in Moral Philosophy at Edinburgh from 1785 until 1810 and oversaw the education of many future prominent Whigs, including many
subsequent writers for the *Edinburgh Review.* Palmerston appears
to have taken well to Stewart's teaching, [14] and much of what Stewart
taught the young Palmerston provided an intellectual rationale for
the latter's future career.

During Palmerston's time as a lodger in Stewart's house in
1802 and 1803, Stewart's lectures on political economy focused
primarily on population, the theory of national wealth, free trade

and the circulation of money, the poor law and education of the lower classes. Most important were Stewart's views on constitutional responsibilities. The stability of modern government, Stewart believed, depended 'on the coincidence between [government] measures and the tide of public opinion', yet significantly this was a tide and thus not static; therefore the modern government should be prepared for 'gradual and prudent accommodation of established institutions to the varying opinions, manners, and circumstances of mankind'. This was a period of increased enlightenment, Stewart argued, and his work demonstrated a belief in the 'possible attainments of mankind' fulfilling their potential through the 'general and infallible progress of human reason'.[15] This was not the prologue to a belief in democracy, however.[16] Stewart advocated a kind of virtual representation: 'the most perfect Democracy which can be realized,' he maintained, 'must admit of certain delegations of power to select councils, or to individual magistrates'.[17] The 'happiness of mankind depends,' he argued, 'not on the share which the people possess, directly or indirectly, in the enactment of laws, but on the equity and expedience of the laws that are enacted'.[18] After all, as Stewart pointed out approvingly in a lecture on forms of government, '"It was one great fault," says Montesquieu, "in most of the ancient Republics, that the people had a right to influence immediately the public resolutions; – a thing of which they are absolutely incapable. They ought to have no hand in the government but for the choosing of representatives"'.[19] Furthermore, and importantly, Stewart also spoke of 'patriotic exertion' on behalf of the common good.[20] If he took nothing else from Edinburgh, then, Palmerston had at least been exposed to notions of responsible (paternalist) government and of this combining with national or patriotic honour and duty. Palmerston's view of public opinion, however, was to be tempered in later life by a practical understanding of, and familiarity with, the nature of society at mid-century.

Thus, public opinion, or more specifically, popular approval, would supply moral legitimacy for government action. Later commentators such as Walter Bagehot and John Stuart Mill would ascribe to such support constrictive qualities,[21] yet Palmerston followed Canning in a belief that careful manipulation of public opinion would ensure that it fulfilled the political economists' prescription of advancing society, and that through an abdication of

authority in favour of a governing class or elite, responsible government would prevail. More importantly, establishing a control over
that opinion and containing its excesses underpinned Palmerstonian
notions of political stability.

During his 'political apprenticeship', however, in the Tory ministries of Spencer Perceval and Lord Liverpool, Palmerston
displayed little inclination to put such principles into practice. He
had become an early adherent to the teaching of Pitt to whom he
had been introduced in 1799 by his father, and Palmerston's political
patrons, particularly the first Earl of Malmesbury, all sprang from
the Tory ranks. Palmerston's own desire to spend time acquiring
experience rather than glory combined with a growing alienation
from his earlier patrons, however, hindered the development of a
significant parliamentary career.[22] He was increasingly linked to no
special Tory faction, he socialised with Whigs but was not one of
them; until William IV ascended the throne he enjoyed little or no
royal support and in short, therefore, Palmerston found no-one willing to take a leading part in the development of his parliamentary
career.[23]

Palmerston the bureaucrat, an efficient but uninspired Junior
Lord of the Admiralty (1807–09) and later Secretary at War (1809–
28), attended to public office more in the fashion of a manager than
an innovator. He had, after all, as much interest in the charms of
society as the draw of politics, and was content to remain in his
relatively junior post gaining experience and biding his time, even
if, by the time he turned 44 he still appeared destined for an
undistinguished public career.[24] Work on his Irish estates occupied
as much of Palmerston's time in the early 1820s as did his parliamentary duties and there seemed no obvious way out of the political
rut in which he was mired.

Unlike his contemporary, Lord John Russell, Palmerston was
not part of the Whig 'great grandmotherhood' and his Whig education was not consolidated at one of the great Whig salons of the
day. Consequently, in these early years, political issues rarely
inspired Palmerston – even over Catholic emancipation, for example,
Bourne argues that political expediency probably played as great a
part as any other consideration in determining Palmerston's
course [25] – and he displayed none of the particular interest in foreign
policy which characterised his later career. Only after 1827 when

he entered the Cabinet and its meetings brought him into regular contact with such questions did diplomacy begin to fire his imagination. Significantly, his interest in foreign policy evolved just as George Canning's career was at its zenith. As Foreign Secretary 1822–27 and then serving a very short-lived premiership between April and August 1827, Canning succeeded in establishing certain principles or practices in foreign policy which Palmerston's own later handling of foreign policy was to mirror, or at least invoke. Not only did Canning's 'English' policy represent a positive alternative to the 'European', or supposedly unduly conciliatory approach of Castlereagh, but his view of the use and foundation of such policy arguably echoed in some respects Palmerston's Edinburgh schooling. While serving in Tory ministries Canning stood on the liberal wing (which ultimately saw his adherents break ranks and defect to an alliance with the Whigs in 1830) and indeed in many ways has been seen as establishing a distinct liberal strand in the politics of this period.[26] Significantly, if Canningism meant anything it represented a contribution to the understanding of the political importance and indeed influence of the people. In more ways than one did he call the new world into existence to redress the balance of the old.[27]

Palmerston very quickly adopted a Canningite line and in his first significant parliamentary speech on foreign affairs he demonstrated clearly his belief in the strength and value of popular support. 'There is in nature no moving power but mind,' he argued, 'all else is passive and inert; in human affairs this power is opinion; in political affairs it is public opinion; and he who can grasp this power, with it will subdue the fleshly arm of physical strength, and compel it to work out his purpose'. Thus, he continued, the statesmen who found the means by which to harness such opinion exercised a 'sway over human affairs, far out of all proportion greater than belong to the power and resources of the state over which they preside'.[28]

Canningism did not entail subservience to a popular will at all costs, however. Public opinion and popular support were instruments of government or symbols of moral strength; the initiative for policy still lay within government, although good government would act in accord with such opinion blurring these distinctions. According to Jonathan Parry, Canning established three liberal principles: that the state was no longer oligarchical but rested on public opinion; that public opinion was Protestant, patriotic and liberty loving; and that open government which sought to liberate public energies would make great progress. Yet this popular role in government was in no sense substantial: operating under an unreformed electoral system, the best that Canning could do was to flatter public opinion by attributing to its influence the course of government policy.[29]

Nevertheless, Canning, though not a Whig, represented an important example of the political creed expounded in the Scottish universities; of a sense of movement in society and that good government would result from heeding that movement. Canningism did not invest public opinion with the authority to act as an enlightened guide but Palmerston's education found in Canningism a certain embodiment of philosophic principles learned as a student. This held true if only as a counter-point to the scepticism displayed by the Duke of Wellington over the role of public opinion in such matters but on these grounds at least, then, there was reason enough for the Canningites to disassociate themselves from the Tory ranks and effect a marriage of convenience with the Whigs, although even here there was not complete accommodation of Palmerston's increasingly mature views on foreign policy.

Significantly, though, Palmerston had learned from Stewart not only an intellectual appreciation of the importance of the public opinion in politics, but also how to speak the Whig language. There was in the Canningite attachment to the force of public opinion and the Whig orthodoxy to which Palmerston had been exposed at Edinburgh a rhetorical over-lap and this was not unimportant in the development of an alliance between the Whigs and Canningites in the late 1820s. Palmerston's commitment to a popular foreign policy was driven by a desire to secure the continued dominance of Parliament and the traditional governing elite by acceding to the moral imperative of giving voice to the 'national' opinion and to allow those beyond the pale of the constitution to enjoy a vicarious interest in national politics. Simultaneously, however, this would ensure public opinion was contained within appropriate channels.

The Whig world was, as Leslie Mitchell observes, 'as much a social organism as it was a political party' and references to family ties, both real and rhetorical, were common.[30] Palmerston was not directly descended from any of the great Whig families, although by association and later by marriage to Emily Cowper (née Lamb) he did establish sound Whiggish credentials and, more importantly, through his wife, as hostess of one of the major Whig salons of the period, Panshanger, Palmerston came to occupy a central role in Whig circles of the period.[31] Whigs themselves were not an homogeneous political party which perhaps made accommodation of Palmerston more acceptable, yet much of Palmerston's success in integrating himself within this milieu was due to his penchant for foreign affairs above all other issues.

Traditionally Whigs and especially the Foxites among them (now led by Fox's nephew, Lord Holland) were suspicious of monarchical influence and authority, and George III's reign had done little to assuage such concerns, and thus parliamentary government, no longer simply the eighteenth-century system of checks and balances, was held up as the means of resisting a malign monarchical power and enforcing the principle of representative government. Democratic government, however, was envisaged in a very limited sense and in speaking of 'government' the Foxites meant for rather than of the people; and in speaking of the 'people' (whom Fox taught 'were the legitimate sovereign in every community'[32]), they alluded to propertied members of the population and not the masses.[33]

The Reform Bill of 1832, then, was a Foxite measure in that it sought to extend the representation of property owners, and thereby extended the virtual representation of the people. While the Government now perceived itself as more accurately and legitimately representing the people, however, the people commensurately expected more in return. For not only did the Act redistribute the franchise, but also as a natural corollary of this, increased ministerial accountability at both a local and national level.[34] Representation was still for many virtual, but government authority was now much more clearly grounded in popular acquiescence rather than in royal power. It was the necessary accommodation of social and economic change, an acknowledgement of movement.

Palmerston himself consented to the measure, although he disapproved of the manner of its execution, for while he distrusted the integrity of many portions of the population, he had already learned the value of popular support. Over his foreign policy, however, while he found not all Whigs and members of the governments of Grey and Melbourne approved of his conduct, mutual interest held them together since party was a necessary function of the protective responsibility of government. As Angus Hawkins has argued, the Whigs believed if Parliament was to remain autonomous, and not become the instrument of either monarchy or the people, then 'political associations' were required. Only in this way could the preoccupations of Westminster be properly defined as the 'demarcation of respectable politics', keeping down dangerous populism and preserving at the head of this an aristocratic leadership committed to civil and religious liberty.[35] Thus party unity became a bulwark against a dangerous fracturing of politics into extremes, as Holland observed to his son in 1824, 'if you have any publick object for yourself or others you will, you ought, nay you infallibly must, under whatever name you disguise it, persue [sic] it by party means'.[36] For the Whigs, an increasingly popular and 'national' minister such as Palmerston represented a force for cohesion within the party and between the Government and people.

Throughout the 1830s, until his death in 1840, Holland, believing himself entitled to a prominent role in foreign affairs yet excluded formally from such a role on the grounds of general distrust of his political integrity,[37] continued to interest himself in foreign policy and indeed in the early 1830s, Holland House 'for a moment became the Foreign Office'.[38] A personal connection with Talleyrand of France and Holland's Foxite Francophilism served, in Mitchell's phrase, to provoke 'guerrilla warfare' between Holland House and Palmerston's Foreign Office, and threatened to undermine the new Grey government. Despite the close political connection between Grey and Holland, the two standing at the centre of what Disraeli spoke of as 'pure Whiggery', Palmerston retained Grey's support, although Grey certainly believed that he exercised a significant degree of control over Palmerston and did continue to consult Holland (and Lansdowne) in a sort of inner Cabinet. Under Melbourne's administration of the second half of the 1830s, however, Palmerston enjoyed a much freer hand. The Holland House set continued to interfere, but, significantly, Melbourne himself grew increasingly weary of this salon's vociferous meddling: 'the talking at Holland House is inconceivable' he complained to Lord John Russell in September 1840.[39] While Melbourne's style was to allow his ministers some degree of independence in their own departments, he had notoriously little interest in foreign affairs and the Foreign Office became largely Palmerston's personal domain during these years.[40]

Palmerston's foreign policy was tolerated in many ways because it evoked images and impressions which the ministries to which he belonged wished to exploit. A foreign policy directed explicitly in the interests of liberal causes and patriotic interests and with the general approbation of the people (or at least the perception of it) gave the governments of the 1830s and 1840s enhanced claims to be seen as the guardians of the national interest.[41] Palmerston had joined the Whigs in 1830 largely because he needed, along with his fellow Canningites, a party base which the Wellingtonian Tories were unlikely to provide and the Whigs appeared to share a common interest in extending the base of political strength. It was essentially a pragmatic response and did not indicate a move into the Whig family.

A sense of national honour and service, or at least a pre-occupation with, in Palmerston's case especially, issues of a national significance, tended to a view of politics as serving a national interest and in many ways above party divisions. Palmerston and Melbourne (no great advocate of partisan politics[42]) have been described as passive liberals, sharing other liberals' aversions, but not their dogmas; representing in short, lowest-common-denominator liberalism.[43] For some parliamentarians, diplomats and junior public figures, indeed, 'Palmerstonism' itself became an important defining motif.[44] Palmerston was associated with no particular domestic cause yet he stood clearly for a particular foreign policy, aggressive, liberal and patriotic which could unite Whigs, Liberals and even Conservatives.[45] Palmerstonian rhetoric, as Parry observes, was directed towards rousing opinion against abuses of power and in defence of local liberties. More than this through participation in groups such as the Alfred Club in the first decade of the nineteenth century Palmerston had developed a powerful sense of national destiny based on a sort of expansionist nationalist Protestantism, an enthusiasm as the Tory Robert Southey put it, for 'making the world English'. As Parry observes, this enthusiasm was founded in no small degree on a belief in a 'divine confidence in British religious and commercial values', not least in the aftermath of the seemingly providential British victory in the Napoleonic wars.[46] Such faith in a divinely ordained role for Britain is an important element in understanding the appeal of Palmerstonian foreign policy, especially when that policy was directed in the interests of morally just causes, such as the suppression of slavery, for example. By the time that Palmerston reached the peak of his career, these sentiments had developed into something not only more distinctly Palmerstonian, but also more popular.

As this book demonstrates, Palmerston's constituency extended beyond the traditional boundaries of political support and in many ways this was the product of his broad-based foreign policy. Able at different times and to different degrees to present his foreign policy as liberal, popular, patriotic, strong and godly, such by the 1850s was his reputation in the field of foreign affairs, that Palmerston was able, through his work at the Foreign Office, and indeed, later, at the Home Office, to do much to justify his image as 'the most English Minister' and even if he was not, in 1855, *l'inévitable*, he did at least enjoy a legitimate claim to be considered for the premiership. Palmerston was fortunate that he had been able to avoid entangling himself in contentious domestic political wrangles; and while his foreign policy might not always have been uncontroversial, he succeeded generally in presenting his policy as that best able to achieve results complementary to the national interest. Over Don Pacifico, for example, few sympathised with Pacifico himself, yet almost everyone applauded the evocation of the '*civis Romanus sum*' principle. Palmerston enjoyed the indulgence of Russell's fragile ministry of 1846–52 (until December 1851) largely because his foreign policy supplied much of the adhesive that held the administration together.

However, by the early 1850s, Palmerston's own personal position was much stronger. He had the opportunity now, as Mandler points out, to whip up domestic authoritarianism and patriotism against the Whigs.[47] Never truly a Whig cousin, Palmerston had struggled throughout the previous decade to establish an ascendancy over the 'natural' leader of the Whigs, Russell. With the emergence of a definite liberal identity in the 1830s and 1840s, Palmerston was able to forge a more liberal strand within the Government and ultimately to lay some of the early foundations of a Liberal party. Clearly Palmerston was not the sole architect of such a scheme, indeed to suggest that there was in any sense a deliberate search for a Liberal party at this time is misleading, but his foreign policy embodied (or was perceived to embody) important liberal principles and his contribution to the emergence of a Liberal party should not be seen to originate in the Willis' Rooms meeting in 1859.[48] As Parry claims, the Liberal party stood for British interests (as opposed to the English bias of the Conservatives), for open politics, political economy and religious diversity (though this serves to illustrate well the ambiguity of Russell ascribing to Palmerston the mantle of most English minister). Above all, it stood for national government ahead of class government.[49]

Palmerston, argues Parry, 'established his credentials with the mass of the provincial Liberal party from 1847', through his advocacy of intervention in support of liberal causes abroad, which he demonstrated particularly in 1848 and again in 1854 (however contrived the logic of that might have been in the latter case).[50] While Parry is concerned to stress the centrality of religious issues in political life, he concedes that taxation and, at least as far as this book is concerned, more importantly, foreign policy questions were also, when 'inflamed', the only issues 'able to link the world with which the politically interested public was concerned to the high political world'.[51] Arguably, however, the politically interested public was more broadly defined for questions of foreign policy than for taxation questions, while foreign policy itself was frequently bound up with, or invoked considerations of, religion. In terms of defining the 'nation', and more particularly the ever-broadening political nation, foreign affairs offer a most important means of assessment.

According to John Vincent, Palmerston paid attention to middle-class interests when he based his politics on 'crude belligerence abroad and class fear at home', while the lower classes, whom he distrusted as being 'under the control of a small clique of socialist agitators', received attention from Palmerston only from a sense of (party) duty.[52] Steele, with some justification, has challenged this view, regarding Palmerston as a 'demagogue' (agreeing with Cobden's description), and seeing in his premierships the revelation of a 'genius for adaptation'.[53] While Steele rightly signals the importance of a broadly conceived public opinion, however, he pays little attention to the manner in which it was manipulated, and to the reasons for this manipulation, and offers only a very brief explanation of the transformation of Palmerston from 'Whig' Foreign Secretary into the first Liberal Prime Minister.

Steele sees Palmerston's inexorable rise to the premiership originating in the late 1820s, and culminating in the months leading immediately to the formation of his first government as Palmerston rode the tide of popular support into office.[54] Indeed, his account of the years 1855–65 seems to take for granted that Palmerston enjoyed popular backing, yet there is no attempt to look for the foundations of this support nor, more importantly, is there any real effort made to investigate the ways in which Palmerston carefully cultivated the image of a popular minister. He certainly did not find popular approval bestowed upon him unsolicited; it had to be courted and if it was Russell (and not Palmerston) who was thought to be 'influenced by personal ambition rather than concern for the country', as Steele argues, it was not to suggest, as Steele does, that in the final analysis Palmerston did not share a similar desire for personal advancement.

Palmerston in 1852 had not been a suitable choice for Prime Minister yet within only three years was installed in that office. This owed a great deal to his ability to manipulate extra-parliamentary forces (and the fact that in this regard his contemporaries were less adept) and bring them to bear on Westminster politics in what was still essentially a pre-democratic age. The great advantage to Palmerston deriving from his popularity was not so much that he instituted a new style of government which relied for its inspiration on the determination of a broadly defined public opinion, but that he was able to present himself as capable of keeping that opinion in hand. There is something to be said for Parry's argument that Palmerston used popular approval to 'consolidate respect for him in parliament',[55] but Parry's view, if taken without qualification, is too cynical. Palmerston did recognise the value of popular involvement in foreign policy (however superficial) and while the chief benefit was that this allowed him to steal a march on less popular rivals, he did develop the Canningite belief in the force of public opinion. Steele presses his case too far, however, in seeing Palmerston as offering a *conscious* introduction to a new era of democratic politics. Palmerston had no desire to prepare the ground for a more democratic system of government: he simply saw the advantage both to himself and the country of investing his foreign policy with a sense of popular, national, support.

Clearly there are problems associated with the period 1846–55 that demand attention. Palmerston, the Tory, or Canningite, having effected a marriage of convenience with the Whigs, emerged during this period as the chief rival to Russell to lead that group. While Russell and other Whigs may have acknowledged the importance of public opinion, they failed to appreciate the importance of courting it and the techniques by which to work with that opinion. Palmerston was allowed a much freer reign than would have been expected for a minister who was not only not a true Whig but also, within high political circles, was widely distrusted. His political longevity was frequently ascribed to his 'popularity' but this short-hand explanation was not, and has not, been properly explained. This book seeks to study Palmerston's political career and the political environment of the later 1840s and early 1850s in order to provide a fuller account of politics in this mid-century 'age of equipoise' and analyse the implications of Palmerston's popularity.

The blurring of constitutional boundaries allowed Palmerston to dominate the cabinets of both Russell and Aberdeen with regard to foreign policy and to use this as the forging ground for his ultimate accession to the premiership. He was, indeed, able to outmanoeuvre many of his colleagues over key foreign policy issues, but a sense of inevitability about his appointment to the premiership in 1855 is still lacking. He said himself, as is well known, that he was, by this point, *l'inévitable*, and some contemporaries agreed, but the Queen was certainly unhappy about having to accept him, Lord Derby only reluctantly turned down his own commission, and Russell, until his own abandonment of the Government in January 1855 damaged his credibility, was not convinced that Palmerston had successfully stolen a march on him.

Palmerston's rise to the premiership, then, is easily demonstrated but the high politics of that ascendancy does not tell the whole story. The impetus for his 'inevitable' triumph rested in part on a sense of his popularity (however fragile at times) beyond Westminster. However, Palmerston's extra-parliamentary reputation was not based on a spontaneous demonstration of popular approbation. Palmerston, who saw more clearly than Canning could have done the implications of an appeal to public opinion, set out to control that opinion.

To the increasingly important middle classes, Palmerston appealed through the newspapers and periodicals. He did not regard the press as having any role in informing his conduct, whatever grandiose claims journalists made for the power of the fourth estate. Newspapers existed, for Palmerston, largely as an effective medium for communication with the people and he carefully cultivated sympathetic titles as a counter-balance to more hostile journals and through the pages of these papers placed before the country what he wanted it to know.[56] Such manipulation was particularly significant during the Aberdeen government as Palmerston sought to undermine the Aberdonian policy on the Eastern question without attracting to his own name unfavourable attention if or when the ship of state ran aground.

Palmerston's political skill, however, was to court a much broader constituency. Exploiting a reputation forged in an area of 'national' concern, Palmerston was able to present himself as the guardian of the country's interest more effectively, in that ultimately it was rhetorically more simplistic, than could his main rivals. 'Liberal', 'English', 'Protestant'; however much these labels did or did not attach to his domestic politics, they were widely apprehended to define his foreign policy and they possessed a strong emotive capacity at a time when a sense of national identity and a concept of the nation were being constructed very much by reference to other countries, that is, in terms of what Britain was not as much as what Britain was. Palmerston went out and told the country he was the national minister and then returned to Westminster with echoes of this sentiment to augment his armoury. Few other politicians had grasped the value or mastered the techniques of this form of demagoguery. Palmerston could therefore ride criticism of his policies as he played up to an increasingly vociferous public opinion. This ultimately carried a good deal of political weight, especially when parliamentary opponents were unable to muster sufficient strength to overcome Palmerston at Westminster.

This book, then, sets out to explain mid-nineteenth-century British politics on a number of levels. Palmerston emerges as an effective political operator and while this reveals a good deal about the nature and operation of the Victorian constitution, it also opens up and links a number of other important questions and issues. Public opinion and popular politics are seen not merely as interesting side-shows but, even in this pre-democratic age, as integral to the conduct of politics at the centre, particularly when there appeared a statesman capable of understanding the dynamics of extra-parliamentary politics. The middle classes are accorded a significant role but, in line with much recent work,[57] this book also seeks to explain the nature and uses of political influence among the unenfranchised. This influence, though ill-defined, possessed a curiously impelling force which a skilful politician such as Palmerston was able to harness and present to his colleagues as he wanted it to be interpreted.

Discussion of the high politics of the years 1846–55 reveals a great deal of what was happening in terms of the politics of foreign policy but, and particularly with regard to Palmerston, does not adequately explain why. Through the newspapers, which served as a means of communicating with the nation and as a barometer of the mood of a particular portion of it as well as an important battle-ground for political disputes by proxy, political issues were brought down to the level of those not only within but also without the traditionally conceived political nation. However, Palmerston, bereft of an obvious, or effective, party support, frequently alienated within the close political circles often defined by familial connection (despite Lady Palmerston's best efforts as a political hostess) needed support from a quarter largely untapped by his contemporaries. Without fully understanding and certainly without fully empathising with the 'people', Palmerston exploited a popular credibility and sense of national solidarity (however artificial it might have been) to underpin his position. He found a country widely disposed to adopt him. Finding little effective opposition voiced out of doors, Palmerston's main threat, beyond that within the Government itself, came from the opposition benches. However, disunity, inconsistency, and eccentricity weakened such critiques and left Palmerston popular, ineffectively opposed and capable of punching above his weight in government.

Notes

1   P. Guedalla, *Palmerston* (London, 1937 edn), p. 405.
2   E. D. Steele, *Palmerston and Liberalism, 1855–1865* (Cambridge, 1991), p. 367.
3   See, for example, H. C. F. Bell, *Lord Palmerston*, 2 vols (London, 1936); Guedalla, *Palmerston*; J. Ridley, *Lord Palmerston* (London, 1970); M. E. Chamberlain, *Lord Palmerston* (Cardiff, 1987); D. Southgate, *'The Most English Minister …': The Policies and Politics of Palmerston* (London, 1966); C. Webster, *The Foreign Policy of Palmerston, 1830–1841*, 2 vols (London, 1969).
4   K. Bourne, *Palmerston: The Early Years, 1784–1841* (London, 1982).
5   Steele, *Palmerston and Liberalism*. Cf. J. R. Vincent, *The Formation of the British Liberal Party, 1857–68* (London, 1966). Specifically concerned with Palmerston's premierships (though primarily with the formulation of foreign policy 1861–64), is D. F. Krein, *The Last Palmerston Government: Foreign Policy, Domestic Politics, and the Genesis of 'Splendid Isolation'* (Ames, Iowa, 1978). See also A. Hawkins, *Parliament, Party and the Art of Politics in Britain, 1855–59* (Basingstoke, 1987).
6   K. Martin, *The Triumph of Lord Palmerston: A Study of Public Opinion in England before the Crimean War* (London, 1963 edn).
7   See Chamberlain, *Palmerston*, pp. 59–61.
8   Bell, *Palmerston*, I, p. 322.
9   J. Parry, *The Rise and Fall of Liberal Government in Victorian Britain* (New Haven and London, 1993), p. 194.
10 P. Smith, review of Steele, *Palmerston and Liberalism*, in *English Historical Review*, 108 (1993), p. 145.
11 Steele, *Palmerston and Liberalism*, passim.
12 Southampton University Library, Broadlands Papers, GMC/106, R. Andrews to Palmerston, 26 Jan. 1852.
13 See below, esp. ch. 2.
14 Bourne, *Palmerston*, pp. 28–9.
15 See D. Winch, 'The System of the North: Dugald Stewart and his Pupils', in Collini, S., Winch, D. and Burrow, J., *That Noble Science of Politics: A Study in Nineteenth-Century Intellectual History* (Cambridge, 1983), pp. 34–5.
16 Bourne, *Palmerston*, p. 29.
17 D. Stewart, *Lectures on Political Economy*, ed. Sir William Hamilton, 2 vols (Edinburgh, 1855), II, p. 359.
18 Quoted Winch, 'The System of the North', p. 36.
19 Stewart, *Lectures on Political Economy*, II, p. 374.
20 Winch, 'The System of the North', p. 43.
21 J. Burrow, 'Sense and Circumstances: Bagehot and the Nature of Political Understanding', in Collini, Winch and Burrow, *That Noble Science of Politics*, p. 173.
22 Bourne, *Palmerston*, pp. 85–115.
23 H. L. Bulwer, *The Life of Henry John Temple, Viscount Palmerston*, 3 vols (London, 1870–74), I, p. 150.

24   Chamberlain, *Palmerston*, p. 28.

25   Bourne, *Palmerston*, p. 230.

26   Parry, *The Rise and Fall of Liberal Government*, p. 39.

27   Canning had used the phrase in defence of his Spanish policy in 1826. See *Hansard's Parliamentary Debates*, 2nd ser., XVI, 397 (13 Dec. 1826).

28   *Hansard*, 2nd ser., XXI, 1668 (1 June 1829).

29   Parry, *The Rise and Fall of Liberal Government*, pp. 43–4, 48–9.

30   L. Mitchell, *Lord Melbourne, 1779–1848* (Oxford, 1997), p. 3.

31   *Ibid.*, pp. 9–10.

32   Quoted P. Mandler, *Aristocratic Government in the Age of Reform: Whigs and Liberals, 1830–1852* (Oxford, 1990), p. 19.

33   L. Mitchell, *Holland House* (London, 1980), pp. 64–5.

34   See Parry, *The Rise and Fall of Liberal Government*, pp. 113, 116.

35   A. Hawkins, '"Parliamentary Government" and Victorian Political Parties, *c.* 1830–c. 1880', English Historical Review, CIV (July 1989), pp. 642, 647.

36   Quoted Mitchell, *Holland House*, p. 68.

37   See *ibid.*, pp. 11–38, 146–72, 269–301.

38   *Ibid.*, p. 278.

39   Mitchell, *Melbourne*, p. 156, Melbourne to Russell, 19 Sept. 1840.

40   *Ibid.*, p. 162.

41   Parry, *The Rise and Fall of Liberal Government*, p. 153.

42   Mandler, *Aristocratic Government*, p. 105; Mitchell, *Melbourne*, p. 117

43   Mandler, *Aristocratic Government*, p. 107.

44   Vincent, *Formation of the Liberal Party*, p. 8; G. W. Cox, *The Efficient Secret. The Cabinet and the Development of Political Parties in Victorian England* (Cambridge, 1987), p. 156.

45   Mandler, *Aristocratic Government*, pp. 109–10.

46   Parry, *The Rise and Fall of Liberal Government*, pp. 16, 34–5.

47   Mandler, *Aristocratic Government*, pp. 273.

48   See, for example, M. E. Chamberlain, 'Who founded the Liberal Party?', *Inaugural lecture delivered at the University College of Swansea, 26 November 1990* (Swansea, 1991) and Parry, *The Rise and Fall of Liberal Government* on this theme.

49   Parry, *The Rise and Fall of Liberal Government*, p. 4.

50   J. Parry, *Democracy and Religion: Gladstone and the Liberal Party, 1867–1875* (Cambridge, 1986), p. 25.

51   *Ibid.*, p. 53.

52   Vincent, *Formation of the Liberal Party*, pp. 141–9, esp. 146–8.

53   Steele, *Palmerston and Liberalism*, pp. 15, 367.

54   *Ibid.*, pp. 16, 21–2.

55   Parry, *The Rise and Fall of Liberal Government*, p. 192.

56   D. Brown, 'Compelling but not Controlling?: Palmerston and the Press, 1846–1855', *History*, 86 (2001), 41–61.

57   See, for example, J. Vernon, *Politics and the People: A Study in English Political Culture, c. 1815–1867* (Cambridge, 1993) and M. C. Finn, *After Chartism: Class and Nation in English Radical Politics, 1848–1874* (Cambridge, 1993).

2

Palmerston, the political nation
and the structure of politics at mid-century

Palmerston's own view of society, which emphasised national
prestige and patriotic honour above all else, makes the relationship
of his views to the realities of his day a complex problem and this
chapter on the structure of politics thus provides a point of reference
for the more specific discussion of Palmerstonian politics which
follows. There was, at this time, an absence of clear agreement on
the framework of constitutional practice, particularly in the arena
of foreign policy. Among other things, the Crown's constitutional
role was an inexact one and the differing interpretations of that
role offered primarily by Melbourne and Prince Albert lay at the
heart of many of Palmerston's struggles. When she came to the
throne in 1837, Queen Victoria had been in need of instruction in
the specific etiquette of diplomacy, and in the arts of government
generally. The task of educating the young Queen fell largely to
Lord Melbourne, the incumbent Prime Minister at the time of her
accession. He schooled the Queen in what he conceived to be Whig
political theory and was able therefore to exercise considerable
influence over the political role of the Court. While the Queen
became during these early years of her reign both politically and
personally reliant on Melbourne, the closeness of this relationship
combined with political scandals in the later 1830s over Lady Flora
Hastings and the Bedchamber Crisis eventually brought the integrity of the Court into question, and made the Queen herself deeply
unpopular.[1] When Prince Albert married the Queen in 1840 the
image of the monarchy was already tarnished and while the Queen's
marriage represented a caesura in her relations with Melbourne, it
simultaneously introduced an important new element into British
political life, and more specifically, to the political outlook of the

Queen, which was to have important ramifications for the future of the British monarchy.

Albert's position as consort to the Queen was constitutionally ambiguous, yet his own background – educated in political theory in Coburg and later in Bonn as a student of the 'Historical Law School', an increasingly fashionable branch of scholarship investigating the historical roots of representative institutions – made his union with the Queen in 1840, at an important transitional period for the monarchy in Britain, of vital importance to the course of British politics. Very early on, Victoria's uncle, King Leopold, urged that Albert 'ought in business as in everything to be necessary to the Queen', and that there 'should be no concealment from him on any subject',[2] envisaging him as some sort of personal secretary. Lord Aberdeen, writing to the Queen at a later date, when Albert's standing in the country was at a low ebb, viewed the Prince's 'somewhat anomalous' position in similar terms, describing it as an 'inestimable blessing' that the Queen should have 'so able, so zealous and so disinterested an adviser'.[3] Albert, however, from the outset had been concerned about the extent to which the monarchy had become embroiled in party questions under Melbourne's influence, and within a year of his marriage to Victoria was encouraging the Queen to recover rights he believed had been sacrificed to whiggish interests, urging that she 'should by degrees regain possession of the privileges which through youth and inexperience she had been induced to yield up ... The Prince said he could never feel satisfied till he saw her in the same position as when she ascended the throne'.[4] As Melbourne's ministry foundered in 1841, the Prince was able to establish himself as more than just the Queen's private secretary, and became effectively her chief political adviser, guiding her through the troubled months surrounding the end of the Government.

For the next twenty years, the British monarchy was, if not totally, then at least largely, moulded by Albert and it is significant that Frank Hardie was able to discern Victoria's own voice in politics only once the Prince was dead.[5] In Sir Robert Peel, from 1841, Albert found a Prime Minister who, unlike Melbourne, was less a rival for the ear of the Queen and more an advocate for the kind of government that Albert himself admired.[6] Albert had no desire to fashion the British monarch into an apolitical functionary of the

state, in fact quite the reverse, as his explicit demonstrations of
support for Peel's attempts to repeal the Corn Laws bears testimony,[7] though he recognised that while there was an 'immense
moral responsibility' to 'watch and control' the Government this
did not signify a right to influence the selection of ministers themselves.[8] But especially in the field of foreign affairs he clearly believed
that the Court had an important role to fulfil.

Albert was, like the Queen herself, related to many heads of
state and enjoyed an intimacy with them that could be of potential
benefit, in diplomatic terms, to the interests of the nation. However,
ministerial interests, or interpretations of events, and those of the
Court were not always identical, and even during Aberdeen's tenure
of the Foreign Office (1841–46) there was evidence of indiscretions
in Court correspondence undermining the integrity of government
policy.[9] Though Albert's connections, particularly with central
European states, were an asset to British governments, he had not
yet learned enough about the British system of government, or was
perhaps pressing revisions too rapidly, to avoid occasional clashes
with ministers, and particularly so once Palmerston returned to the
Foreign Office in 1846.

Albert's influence on British politics contributed expressly to a
contemporary concern with understanding the nature of British
constitutional practice. Debates about the constitution were not
carried on solely at a high political level and a flourishing contemporary debate prevailed among the journalistic and educated classes
concerned with the wider questions of British constitutional practice.[10] Palmerston's own conduct at this time tested many
assumptions about the constitution and thereby offered an implicit
contribution to this debate.

In 1867 Walter Bagehot published *The English Constitution* in
which he claimed to challenge (though he also actually endorsed)
many of the mainstream orthodoxies of mid-Victorian constitutional
theory. Central to Bagehot's thesis was an appreciation of the
distinction between the 'dignified' and the 'efficient' parts of the
constitution, the dignified parts being those which 'excite and
preserve the reverence of the population' while the efficient parts
were 'those by which … [the constitution], in fact, works and rules'.
Thus, the 'crown is, according to the saying, the "fountain of honour";
but the Treasury is the spring of business', he reasoned.[11] Power

in the Bagehotian model resided in Parliament and while the Prime Minister could choose in what capacity ministers would serve, he could only select from among those offered by Parliament. Implicit in this view was an undermining of the monarchy and Bagehot contended that to see ministers as in any sense the Queen's servants was 'fictional'. Only once an administration had been constructed, did the balances shift and then the Cabinet – 'a *hyphen* which joins, a *buckle* which fastens, the legislative part of the state to the executive part of the state' – became the key to government.[12] Bagehot's work has often been regarded as a prescriptive rather than descriptive analysis (despite claims made in the preface to the second edition of 1872 that his aim had been to describe the working of the constitution 'as it was in the time of Lord Palmerston'[13]) and as such might be seen to have only limited relevance to the circumstances of the 1840s. Certainly, his distinction between dignified and efficient parts of the constitution is problematic – Bagehot failed to recognise the ceremonial (or dignified) aspect of the richly ornamented new Palace of Westminster, for example[14] – yet Bagehot's study is, nonetheless, reflective of what might be termed a general Whig pre-occupation with the growing importance of parliamentary government at mid-century.

While seeking to draw attention to what he perceived as the ultimate subjugation of the monarch's governing power, Bagehot was nonetheless keen to illustrate the valuable, indeed indispensable, role the Crown still had to play in the government of the country. The monarchy offered distractions, represented religious strength, continuity, national morality and all along provided a façade of stability in a period of change and upheaval.[15] The Bagehotian monarchy therefore had no legislative power, nor did it form the executive; it had ultimately only three rights: 'the right to be consulted, the right to encourage, the right to warn'.[16]

Clearly the influence of the monarch extended beyond that of an adviser and Russell himself, though a Foxite Whig, was keen to uphold and enforce the monarch's position as a figurehead and symbol of continuity. He certainly had one eye on his rivals at Westminster, for if the opposition should ever have been able to pose a serious threat to the continuance of his ministry, then the Queen would have been called on actually rather than just theoretically to choose her Prime Minister. Often, there was no choice as in 1845 and 1846 when Russell was the only candidate capable of replacing Peel, but had a new potential leader emerged during the later 1840s, the issue might not have been so clear cut. Russell's relatively weak ministry would not have fared well against a strong challenge, and against a weak one he would probably have needed the Queen's sponsorship.

In many ways therefore, Bagehot passed over an important function of the Crown in seeing the Queen's role as largely decorative. Brougham in his study of *The British Constitution* (1861) adhered to the view that the sovereign had the right to dismiss ministers at will and Baron Stockmar, the Crown's own adviser brought to Britain by Prince Albert, counselled the Queen during one of her spats with Palmerston that 'having once given her sanction to a measure, the Minister who, in the execution of such measures alters or modifies it arbitrarily commits an act of dishonesty towards the Crown which the Queen has an undoubted constitutional right to visit with the dismissal of that minister'.[17] When Melbourne had been 'dismissed' by William IV in 1834, Peel's subsequent speech in the House of Commons had acknowledged the share he must take for what had passed. 'God forbid', he said, 'that I should endeavour to transfer any responsibility which ought properly to devolve upon me to that high and sacred authority which the constitution of this country recognizes as incapable of error, and every act of which it imputes to the advice of responsible counsellors'.[18] In thus accepting responsibility for what the King had done, Peel simultaneously accepted the power of the King to dismiss his ministers, and the King's actions acquired a certain stamp of constitutionality. Yet such conduct remained contested and not accepted constitutional practice, and this perceived royal *coup d'état* had served as a warning to the Whigs who now held the seals of office that the monarch could pose a serious threat to parliamentary government.[19] G. H. L. Le May has argued that in fact the Queen never relinquished this perceived prerogative right and would have exercised it in 1851 to remove Palmerston had Russell not been obliged to pre-empt her.[20] In the event, the Queen's strength would probably not have extended that far, but constitutionally it would have been problematic ever to test such power.

Historians of mid-nineteenth-century politics have often perpetuated or affirmed a parliament-centric view of the period. Even in discussing a figure whose fortunes were so closely bound up with issues of public support, John Vincent has observed that in the early months of Palmerston's premiership when the war in the Crimea was still raging, the 'supposed political invincibility of Palmerston in 1855–56 had some reality outside Parliament, but little inside Parliament where it mattered'.[21] To some extent this judgment derives from a Bagehotian view of the Victorian constitution which does not, perhaps, withstand retrospective application to the 1840s and 1850s. 'Parliament', Bagehot wrote, 'conforms itself accurately enough, both as a chooser of executives and as a legislature, to the formed opinion of the country. Similarly … it expresses the nation's opinion in words well, when it happens that words, not laws, are wanted'.[22] This clearly did not mean that Parliament was subject to the whims of popular moods, however. Legislative assemblies such as the House of Commons served to edify the people – here Bagehot was concerned primarily, even exclusively, with the educated middle classes and not with the working classes[23] – and it was only from within Parliament that the lead might be taken in national affairs. Thus, when it came to choosing ministers, for example, while 'there is a tacit reference to probable public opinion', nevertheless, 'there is much free will in the judgement of the Commons. The House only goes where it thinks in the end the nation will follow; but it takes its chance of the nation following or not following; it assumes the initiative, and acts upon its discretion or caprice'.[24]

Recent work by Angus Hawkins develops these themes. Like Vincent, Hawkins has argued that Palmerston's rhetoric after 1855 illuminates only the political world 'outside parliament and Clubland' and in this sense such rhetoric 'is *not* an explanation of Palmerston's political ascendancy following the fall of Aberdeen's coalition' since 'it tells us very little about the reality of Palmerston's situation within Westminster'.[25] Hawkins, however, has offered a more subtle account of the role of public opinion in parliamentary politics in the nineteenth century. Looking back to the 1830s, he points to Melbourne's underpinning of his Government's claims to legitimacy with arguments of a sort of Burkean virtual representation. However qualified by arguments that the House of Commons acted as a bulwark between the Crown and the people, still to some extent Melbourne believed that legitimacy derived from the House of Commons being elected by the people.[26] This immediately raises questions about who 'the people' were. News-papers, for example, spoke confidently of the influence of the 'people' and their duty to relay the sentiments of these people through their papers as well as to educate them, but they represented only a relatively small, though influential, section of the population. Edit-orials interchanged freely the terms 'people' and 'readers', yet they were clearly not synonymous, if only because the national press, still in essence metropolitan, was far from enjoying a position of widespread currency, as circulation figures indicate,[27] and no paper was able to reach and therefore claim to represent the majority of the population.

Writing to Palmerston in 1851, James Grant, editor of the *Morning Advertiser*, measured the growing success of his paper by the nature of its readership. Grandly claiming that the paper was now 'read among *all* classes', he emphasised the increased stature of the title, saying that it 'is taken into all the Clubs and Reading Rooms'.[28] Significantly, the clubs and reading rooms, as well as public houses in which the London newspapers were made available gave many more people access to the press output. Newspapers may have been written primarily for the middle classes, but they were read also by many members of the working classes. Publicans not only subscribed to certain newspapers, but they would frequently organise for the papers to be read to their illiterate customers; other venues of social interaction, such as barber's shops, coffee houses and mechanics institutes also took a number of newspapers and a number of news items would find their way onto the street in the form of ballads. According to Donald Read such arrangements saw readership among the urban working classes escalate during this period.[29]

Grant's *Morning Advertiser* was perhaps read by 'all classes' but generally the constituency to which the metropolitan press appealed was not that comprising all social classes, but rather all classes within the political nation, and that the 'high' political nation. As *The Times* suggested in one of its leaders, public opinion was properly represented in the Imperial Parliament where dissentient voices were heard through figures such as Richard Cobden.[30] And, however widely newspapers were read, the interaction with 'public opinion' or 'the people' worked on different levels. The middle classes claimed to be represented by, or even define, public opinion, whereas the lower classes read newspapers simply to be informed. The Leeds Operative Conservative Association, for example, looked to the press for guidance, reading 'to furnish our minds by means of newspapers and other publications with correct views on political subjects, and to furnish an antidote to those publications of a dangerous tendency which are everywhere obtruded upon us'.[31] It was not surprising to find a conservative association seeking thus to be informed, but the sentiment is echoed in a motion passed by the Manchester Literary Society which was 'essentially a radical institution'. On 7 November 1848 that Society voted by a margin of 16 to 2 in favour of the motion 'Is the tendency of the [journalistic] literature of the present day in England to elevate and enlarge the public mind?',[32] clearly indicating an appreciation of the didactic qualities of the press.

Palmerston's conception of public opinion never extended beyond the opinion of the educated middle classes in whose (commercial) interests his foreign policy was regularly directed and whose opinion he could readily read and engage with through newspapers, pamphlets, and occasional letters and petitions. It is clear that it was to such sources that Palmerston paid particular attention and to which he attributed particular significance, keeping and sometimes annotating newspaper cuttings, pamphlets, letters and petitions and in the case of December 1851 actually assembling a separate file of such material relating to his dismissal.[33] He would probably have shared Bagehot's definition of public opinion as '"the opinion of the bald-headed man at the back of the omnibus" ... the opinion of the ordinary mass of educated, but still commonplace mankind'.[34] He did not ignore or disparage the support which he received from the working classes, indeed this support was often very important to his position,[35] but neither did he seek to give to their voices a dignity and political value which he thought properly belonged to middle-class (or 'public') opinion. This is made quite clear in his fear that Russell's reform proposals in 1853 would 'overpower Intelligence & Property by Ignorance & Poverty'[36] and that the working classes ('men who murder their children to get 9£ to be spent in drink'), were they enfranchised, would only 'sell their vote for whatever they can get for it'.[37]

In 1858 Lord Grey, writing in a similar vein to that which

Bagehot would later adopt, published the first edition of his study
of *Parliamentary Government*. Like Bagehot, Grey argued for the
primacy of the Cabinet, but more interesting are his observations
on the role of public opinion:

> In Parliamentary Government, as it now exists among us, the contest
> for power is still substantially a contest for the favour of the People.
> Public opinion determines, in the last resort, to what hands authority
> shall be entrusted; for though the Ministers are the servants of the
> Crown, and are appointed by the Sovereign, yet as the Sovereign
> must choose who can command the confidence of Parliament, it is
> practically the People who decide, through their Representatives, by
> whom the powers of Government shall be wielded.[38]

Not that this meant direct popular control of the executive, of course:
'There is ... a vast difference in the effect produced by giving to
the People, instead of the power of nominating their rulers by direct
election, only an indirect control, through their Representatives,
over the selection of the Ministers by whose advice the powers of
the Crown are exercised'. Thus, 'Parliament, and especially the
House of Commons,' Grey continued, 'is become, not only the
authority which virtually decides the contest for power among the
different candidates for it, but also the arena in which the contest
is mainly carried on'.[39]

If Grey, Bagehot and others are correct, although competition
for public favour directed many MPs' actions, this was not to say
that public opinion determined the course of politics. While Clarendon, as he told his friend Henry Reeve of *The Times*, might have
'had some talk with Ld John about the expediency of rousing public
opinion & *informing* the people of England that they are not the
powerless effete community wch Foreign Powers delight in thinking
them',[40] this was not to say that such public feeling should be allowed
to become dominant. The *Morning Post*, for example, identified a
prevalent desire to keep this opinion within bounds when it
announced its duty to be to 'contend against the dogma that what
popular newspapers call "public opinion" is to be the all-prevailing
power and director in matters political'.[41] According to Angus
Hawkins, 'it was not in the nature of mid-Victorian elections to
pass plebiscitary judgements on incumbent administrations. Where
national issues infiltrated constituency contests they were shaped

by local circumstances'.[42] There is with such a model of the constitution little room for a definite role for public opinion in national
politics. Palmerston's perceived ability to use public opinion to
underpin his position would then seem to be something of an
aberration.

Yet, according to an article in the *Daily News*, published in the
wake of one of Palmerston's most notable parliamentary successes,
'There are three classes in this country which direct their views to
foreign politics, and feel excited and interested in them'. First was
the aristocracy, 'ever trembling for their supremacy, and deeming
their privileges menaced by an advance of revolution', while the
'commercial and industrious class, dreading alike war and disturb-
ance', demanded little more of foreign policy than that it preserved
'general amity and tranquillity, with a satisfactory state of the funds
and of foreign exchange'. Finally were 'the people, who have no
selfish interests to consult, and who entertain no more than sentiments on that subject. Wherever they see a people oppressed, they
put up their vows for its liberation'. No 'English minister', claimed
the *Daily News*, could afford to ignore any one of the three; nor,
however, could he hope ever to satisfy the wants of all classes
simultaneously.[43] Interest was, of course, not necessarily the same
thing as influence or a direct role. It is a contention of this book,
however, that Palmerston did make that opinion of the commercial
and industrious class and of the people count.

It was relatively straightforward for Palmerston to court the
support of the newspaper reading public – primarily the educated
middle classes – in that there was, by definition, a ready and effective
medium through which to communicate with them. Even so, Palmerston had to work hard to secure sympathetic representations
in the press. Whereas Newcastle and his fellow Peelites were able
to exercise a guiding influence over the *Morning Chronicle* after
1848, for example, because ownership conferred certain rights over
editorial policy, at no point did Palmerston enjoy the privileges of
proprietorship of a newspaper and was obliged to win favour more
subtly. He could, of course, ingratiate himself with individual journalists and Palmerston did meet them socially, indeed invited them
to Lady Palmerston's soirées, and even bribed some with material
rewards and in order to accommodate reporters' deadlines, Palmerston would often re-arrange the times of the meetings, or provide

advance notice of his speeches. According to James Grant, of the *Morning Advertiser*, such efforts appear to have brought rewards since there 'never was a man who was so great a favourite personally with, not the reporters only, but with all the gentlemen filling higher positions on the press, as ... Lord Palmerston'.[44]

More importantly, however, Palmerston needed to gain the support of whole newspapers. He was able to win over various titles, although each one fulfilled a different role. Of these, three are particularly important. The *Globe*, for instance, placed itself so much at Palmerston's disposal that he was able to direct its articles to suit his own purposes, while the *Morning Chronicle*, before 1848, and the *Morning Post*, after 1849, though well disposed towards Palmerston, were never in his pocket in the same way.

Palmerston had been in close connection with the *Globe* for several years and by the late 1840s many of its articles were written at Palmerston's initiative;[45] indeed, it was widely believed, and with good reason, that Palmerston also wrote directly for the *Globe*, supplying notes on foreign affairs, articles to be reproduced verbatim and carefully coaching the editor about the tone of articles.[46] Palmerston used his influence at the *Globe* not so much to effect changes in public opinion, but rather primarily as a means of correcting falsehoods and mis-representations.[47] In many ways, the *Globe* became Palmerston's mouthpiece, and though this afforded him an invaluable means of putting his case forward, it was not necessarily the most useful political support he possessed.

While he had enjoyed a long connection with the *Morning Chronicle*, pre-dating even that with the *Globe*, Palmerston's treatment of this paper was noticeably different from that of the *Globe*. Palmerston's letters to John Easthope and Andrew Doyle at the *Chronicle* were friendly and contained much useful political intelligence, but they fell short of dictation. Information was exchanged, but as the basis for the *Chronicle's* articles and not for direct use; in a sense Palmerston was buying the editor with news. Unlike the *Globe*, the impression given by the correspondence between Palmerston and the *Chronicle* is one of a connection based on mutual good understanding and respect.[48] In contrast to his dictation to the *Globe*, when he sought to influence the *Chronicle*, Palmerston acknowledged that 'it may appear intrusive on my Part to make any suggestions on the Subject'.[49] Throughout Easthope's tenure of the editorship, the *Chronicle* remained generally well-disposed towards Palmerston yet within a month of its take-over by the Peelites in February 1848, the tone of the paper changed markedly and articles became more critical of Palmerston's diplomacy.[50]

By contrast, the *Morning Post* of the 1840s was essentially a Protectionist journal quite hostile to Palmerston.[51] After a change in ownership in 1849, however, Palmerston found the paper a much more sympathetic witness. As with the *Chronicle*, Palmerston could not command support, merely win it, and this he was obliged to do rapidly in order to counteract the loss of the *Chronicle*. The Borthwicks, Peter (the paper's editor) and Algernon (Peter's son and the *Post*'s Paris correspondent), were keen to cultivate Palmerston as a source, but at the same time, were not disposed to rely on him alone for information about foreign policy.[52] The *Post* was broadly won over to the Palmerstonian line, however, through a series of social meetings and also a frank interchange of political news between the Borthwicks and Palmerston. The *Post* maintained its Protectionist views throughout, yet managed to combine this with an enthusiasm for Palmerston and his foreign policy. While there was not a direct correlation to be made between party allegiance and foreign politics, it would have been easier for Palmerston to maintain friendly links with a Whig title such as the *Chronicle* (prior to 1848) than with a paper whose principles in a crucial area of domestic politics were at variance with those of the party to which he belonged.[53]

Less obviously could Palmerston speak to the broader population, however. In large part, his reputation with 'the people', of whatever social class, from those deprived of the vote to the commercial middle classes, rested on the construction (and appreciation) of positive images and impressions of Palmerston and Palmerstonism, propagated variously by potent rhetorical devices invoking notions of national greatness and solidarity. Caricatures of Palmerston, in *Punch*, for example, re-inforced the image of Palmerston as, above all, the patriot minister, willing (and able) to cut through myths and falsehoods and, when it came to a showdown, to take on, single-handed, the great powers of Europe.[54]

It has been suggested that the Victorian high-political view of the people, or commonalty, was akin to that held of the Roman mob, as represented in entertainments popular during this period such as Shakespeare's *Coriolanus*.[55] The allusion, indeed, is not unduly contrived and it is no coincidence that an extension of this view resulted in December 1853 with the *Press,* essentially Disraeli's newspaper, ascribing to Palmerston the mantle of Coriolanus himself.[56] Whether or not Palmerston shared Coriolanus's dislike of the people and popular politics ('I would they would forget me like the virtues/Which our divines lose by 'em') and found that only obligation caused him to solicit such support ('Why in this wolvish toge should I stand here/To beg of Hob and Dick that does appear/Their needless vouches? Custom calls me to't'), he certainly, like his supposed literary alter-ego, heeded the advice of Menenius that he would 'mar all', if he did not speak to the people 'in wholesome manner'.[57]

The worlds of high and low politics came together at elections and it was here that a politician could most clearly demonstrate his view of the value and role of the people, both members of the electorate and the disenfranchised masses whose place in the constitution was ill-defined but nevertheless important. Here symbolism had a key role to play in Victorian politics. While it was no easier for a disenfranchised citizen to secure a place in the official political nation, it was increasingly being recognised by those at the centre of political life that ceremonies and symbolic practices were important means by which to allow such people to participate in the theatre of politics. Not least, this legitimised the prevailing power balance and symbolic practices and ceremonies, according to James Vernon, were 'used to "convey and reaffirm the legitimacy of governing in thousands of unspoken ways"'.[58]

At an election the presence of the candidate could be just as important as what was said. The public, enfranchised and otherwise, would commonly turn out by way of demonstrating their gratitude for the candidate's decision to contest the seat on their behalf, while for the candidate this was an early opportunity 'to project the romantic image of themselves as the people's choice, bravely battling on their behalf'.[59] Often, indeed, such was the superficial nature of the event, that just 'a sight of a candidate seems to have been enough to create that fiction of personal familiarity which was so important'.[60] Yet, the nomination ceremony and hustings contests were vitally important aspects to an election. The approbation of the disenfranchised members of the audience, which could be demonstrated through a show of hands, was a crucial demonstration of moral support for a candidate, but these public demonstrations of political sparring were also one of the few opportunities the disenfranchised had to challenge a member of the ruling class, a means by which they could 'avenge themselves upon the official political arena and ... assert their right to be included within the story the local political community was telling itself'.[61] Palmerston himself recognised this, as he told a meeting in Glasgow when receiving the freedom of that city. 'It is, gentlemen', he said:

> the privilege of the people of a free country, thus in public meetings to express their opinion of the conduct of those whose lot it may have been, in any capacity, high or less exalted, to serve their country. In countries where the Governments are unfortunately framed upon a different model, public opinion is gagged, and expresses itself only in ways which do not often conduce to public tranquility [sic] or to the general welfare; but it is the privilege and the good fortune of constitutional countries that public men are there enabled from time to time to have as their guide the expression of public opinion; and when they are fortunate enough to obtain, as I have now the honour to obtain the approbation of their countrymen, they receive the greatest reward for their past conduct, and the most ample encouragement to pursue that course which they have thought for the benefit of the country. (Loud cheers).[62]

The political world was no longer defined and limited to Parliament and a metropolitan clique. By mid-century it was apparent to the astute observer that the parameters of this world had shifted, as W. R. Greg suggested in the *Edinburgh Review* in 1852:

> Before the Reform Bill, Parliament was the arena where, by the theory of the Constitution, and with nominally closed doors, the affairs of the nation were discussed and settled; – it was the body to which the people delegated the task of thinking and acting for them in all political concerns; – ...
>
> But now all this has changed ... Parliament is no longer the only, nor the chief arena for political debate. Public meetings and the Press are fast encroaching upon and superseding its originally exclusive functions. Every man has become a politician ... The country often takes precedence of the Legislature, both in the discussion and

> decision of public affairs. Public opinion is formed out of doors; and
> is only revised, ratified and embodied within ... The functions of
> parliament are no longer *initiary*; or in far less degree than for-
> merly ... The independent thinker originates; the Country listens,
> disputes, sifts, ripens; the Parliament revises and enacts.

Not that Greg welcomed this change. Popular selection of representatives mitigated against the appointment of the most able
parliamentarians, he argued, while the tendency to make MPs
reliant on their constituents only served to weaken Parliament:
'Constituents who regard and treat their members as "mere acoustic
tubes, through which their commands are blown to the legislative
chamber," and who endeavour to reduce them to this disreputable
level, must be content to be served by an inferior order of men'.
But as Greg conceded, while the desirability of the growing strength
of extra-parliamentary opinion may admit of doubt, 'the fact that
is so, admits of none'.[63]

The early nineteenth century had witnessed a politicisation of
the lower classes which was to have far-reaching ramifications in
the politics of the post-1832 period. As Margot Finn observes,
'although local patriotisms continued to flourish beyond the eighteenth century, their grip on even plebeian culture was increasingly
tempered by the wider claims of the nation', yet Finn herself
perpetuates an Anglo-centric view of this period by identifying these
local patriotisms within an English national identity.[64] Nevertheless,
this phenomenon, the product of cultural, technological and economic influences, tended to the emergence of a national identity in
Britain in advance of other European countries, and external affairs
and warfare were essential means by which this identity was consolidated. As Linda Colley has argued, only since the Act of Union
of 1707 which linked Scotland to England and Wales does a notion
of 'Britishness' have any resonance, and this derives largely from a
negative impetus to define 'Britain' and 'Britishness' by reference
to 'the Other'.[65] During the eighteenth century this meant that
Britain came to be defined largely in terms of what the nation's
chief enemy, France, was not: thus Protestant Britain stood as a
natural counter-point to Catholic France. France could be represented as inferior to Britain in terms of civilisation and freedom,
thereby assuaging envious feelings about French high culture and

military prowess and offering therein grounds to rally around a notion of Britishness if only to emphasise this superiority.[66]

While 'Britishness' did not supplant internal differences – the notion of a 'blended' modern British identity which had currency in the nineteenth century still speaks of a mix or amalgam comprising the original ingredients of 'Englishness' and 'Scottishness' and (although rarely meriting specific contemporary mention) 'Welsh-ness'[67] – a collective identity was to some extent superimposed over this array of internal divisions, if only gathering together the component parts of the one other crucial factor separating Britain from its rivals, that of being an island.[68] It has been suggested that Colley has overstated the importance of Protestantism as a common bond among Britons,[69] but as Colley argues, while there were indeed profound divisions within the Protestant Church, Protestantism as a supposed national characteristic went beyond theological disputes and took on more overtly secular connotations. Thus: 'the Protestant world-view was so ingrained in this culture that it influenced people's thinking irrespective of whether they went to church or not, whether they read the Bible or not, or whether, indeed, they were capable of reading anything at all'.[70] Despite the ultimate artificiality of this concept of a national identity founded on a common Protestantism, rhetorically it remained a powerful image and certainly contributed to the evolution of a 'Victorian world picture' in which 'a national pecking order for European countries', according to David Newsome, placed Germany at the top, Switzerland and the Low Countries 'in the second rank', and Latin nations at the bottom, clearly symbolic of this supposed overarching Protestant outlook, though not necessarily accurate.[71]

Inevitably, a growing sense of national identity and belonging brought within the political realm social classes officially excluded from that domain. Consequently it was important for a statesman such as Palmerston concerned with foreign affairs to consider these sections of society. The working classes, while generally displaying more interest in cheap sensationalist stories than in domestic political news did, nevertheless, want to read about foreign affairs in the newspapers. As Virginia Berridge has observed, there was 'a noticeable amount of working-class concern', inspired in no small measure by a sympathy for continental struggles of the 1830s and 1840s (especially Belgium in 1830; significantly a cause with which

Palmerston was closely identified), which it was felt were not unconnected with the history of an English liberal tradition. Thus it was reported to the Newspaper Stamp Committee in 1851 that 'foreign news is as attractive as any other matter' that appeared in the papers read among the working classes.[72] Debates conducted at the Hope and Anchor Inn, a public house in Birmingham, for example, in the years following the repeal of the stamp duty on newspapers, point to a working-class concern with foreign affairs above all other issues, energised perhaps by the greater availability of information after 1855.[73]

The impetus for this search for a national identity came from within, it rested on an idea of English history since the sixteenth century, but it was perpetuated by constant references to foreign identities and interests. Concomitant with this developing sense of nation was a growing perception among all classes of the potential for, and indeed necessity of, combined action. In the lower classes, this naturally led to a greater belief in their political influence. In 1834, for instance, a working-class socialist proclaimed: 'Those who call themselves the liberal statesmen of the present day, must go progressively with the people; but in the word PEOPLE ... they must, brethren, include us, the productive labourers, for what are the people without us?' But as the writer also observed, 'while we work not for ourselves, but for the capitalists and profit-mongers, we can hardly rank with the people'.[74]

Few mid-century politicians would have disagreed with Richard Cobden when, in advocating a broadening of the political nation, he spoke of 'the middle and industrious classes' as 'the people'.[75] In domestic politics, such a view was certainly widespread, but in the field of foreign affairs – where questions might boil down to ones of peace or war – the nation, on whose behalf a Foreign Secretary spoke, comprised all members of the population, high and low. In this sense, while still remaining beyond the pale of the constitution in any official capacity, a wide spectrum of the population was given a role in political life through the Coriolanean approach of a figure such as Palmerston.

Alongside the growing confidence of the lower classes, important shifts in intellectual life were occurring during this period. In publishing *On Heroes, Hero-Worship, and the Heroic in History* in 1841, Thomas Carlyle to some extent captured the spirit of the early to mid-nineteenth century. Among the educated classes, Romantic influences and the effects of the late-eighteenth-century Hellenic revival inspired Victorians with 'the power to see man as a hero and the heart to respond with the appropriate worship'.[76] Heroic imagery from Scott and Byron, and from the Napoleonic Wars (Nelson and Wellington) abounded in Victorian culture. Thus, enthusiasm and a disposition to acknowledge 'the superior being', infused nineteenth-century life with a tendency to hero-worship, and as Walter Houghton has suggested, this tradition was nourished and thrived in such conditions, for 'it answered, or it promised to answer, some of the deepest needs and problems of the age. In the fifty years after 1830 the worship of the hero was a major factor in English culture'.[77]

Patriotism had been used throughout English history to mark out important characteristics of the hero, and figures such as Hampden, Sydney and Cromwell all loomed large in such works.[78] A member of Palmerston's own constituency, Tiverton, indeed, made just such an association in writing to Palmerston in 1848 urging the Foreign Secretary to use his influence to secure religious liberty and self-government in Europe. 'And what cannot you now do in Italy & Spain!', he wrote, adding: 'Old Cromwell would not let such an opportunity pass and I trust your Lordship will not do less'.[79] Cromwell, however, as an essentially non-conformist 'hero', inspired only limited reverence in an age of significant religious differences – particularly among the middle classes and in the north[80] – and Palmerston, while he might thus win particular non-conformist support, had to establish his popularity in a much broader context and exploit the unifying properties of being a 'national' minister. Victorians imbued patriotism with notions of virtue and godliness; the embodiment of national greatness. According to Houghton, then, 'the nationalistic and the moralistic functions of patriotic hero worship tended to merge, and in the concreteness of experience a great soldier or statesman was an inspiration to a noble life – for the glory of England'.[81] Heroism and hero-worship, therefore, acquired above all a political significance, and something of a unifying strand in Victorian political life: 'it exorcises the antisocial forces of personal or class ambition, bred by the doctrines of liberty and equality, and in their place calls forth the uniting emotions of loyalty and reverence for one great man who is our common leader'.[82] For the anti-democrats the hero-governor would stem the tide of popular politics; for the democrat he would draw the nation together – in some respects a natural corollary of democratic government. Yet in a heterogeneous and disparate state, such a common leader had to court a wide range of popular feelings and sentiments.

Radical politics in mid-century are commonly seen to have suffered by the supposed failure of Chartism in 1848, and the decades between the late 1840s and the emergence of socialism in Britain in the 1870s are widely held to have represented a caesura in British lower and middle-class political life. Work published in the 1990s has acknowledged this impression, but sought not simply to consign the history of the middle decades of the nineteenth century to a closed file labelled 'age of equipoise'. According to Margot Finn, radicals, and particularly Chartists, focused on the national aspect of their liberalising course, relegating notions of class conflict to a secondary position. Having embraced the revolutions of 1848 in terms of a class issue, wherein the 'Chartist internationalists wilfully ignored distinctions between national and economic liberation', in the aftermath of these revolutions attention turned to the common ties between working- and middle-class interests. There were similarities to be drawn between the Chartist movement and the European upheavals from which there emerged a fear of perpetual class conflict which might be engendered in Britain. Thus was the emphasis laid upon notions of national identity, a community of interests, which would bind the country together. It was at this time, therefore, that Harriet Martineau, the well-known advocate of political economy and middle-class improver of the lower orders, and the Chartist Charles Knight, launched *Voice of the People* in which they sought to down-play the vitality of class differences: 'The "Populus" of the Romans, the "Peuple" of the French, the "People" of the English, each, in the broad and comprehensive sense of the term, means the whole community – the nation', they asserted.[83]

Against such interpretations – regarding the shift to liberalism 'not as a political development, but as a retrograde step in class-consciousness' – Miles Taylor has argued that taken from a longer perspective, the developments of the 1850s acquire a different significance. Changes in the political landscape since the Reform Act of 1832, granting radicals a much greater influence at Westminster, had eroded much of the *raison d'être* of radical politics while the changing realities of international as well as domestic politics contributed to the shaping of British liberalism during these years in advance of the Gladstonian influences of the 1860s.[84] Despite the differences in interpretation between Taylor and Finn, it is striking that both focus on the importance of nation, patriotism and notions of British politics being crafted by reference to international (primarily European) developments. Indeed, Jonathan Parry has argued that it is largely only by reference to a European context that we can fully understand the course of British politics in the nineteenth century.[85]

It was against this background – of radical politics focusing more emphatically on the significance of the nation, of the appeal of hero worship, or at least the disposition in Victorian society to such elevation of the individual, and of the perhaps fortuitous coincidence of European revolution and consequent challenge to the *status quo* – that Palmerston was able to build a rapport with the people, but more than that, with the nation, in order to strengthen his hand at Westminster. He was the natural candidate in mid- century for the title of Patriot Minister and came in many ways to embody the very essence of 'Englishness'. As Parry has convincingly argued, English constitutionalism was central to notions of that Englishness and furthermore, when 'patriotism, in all its manifestations, was the major bond between Liberals, Palmerston, "the English mastiff", was without doubt the best representative of that patriotism'.[86]

To the reform-minded and radical members of the House of Commons, Palmerston came to be seen very much as the Patriot Minister in the aftermath of the revolutions of 1848 and 1849. As Miles Taylor has demonstrated, the close of the parliamentary session of 1849 saw the radical members of the House 'in a hiatus'.[87] Financial reform and Irish relief, for instance, elicited from within the Reform party different and conflicting strategies, while the Whig ministry, and especially its supposedly most reform-minded members, Russell and Wood, was proving to be a great disappointment. Thus, partly in consequence of this fissuring of the radical movement, Taylor argues, members of the Reform party turned to Palmerston, and gave their support to his foreign policy, notably that concerning Hungary, when it went before the House in the summer of 1849. Palmerston, at least, demonstrated 'purpose' (if nothing else) and ultimately, 'his popularity arose from his patriotism – but a patriotism which had more in common with eighteenth-century constitutionalism than bombastic nationalism'.[88]

From the Palmerstonian perspective, the nation, clearly, as any perceptive political observer was aware, was becoming increasingly important to political life; in the arena of foreign affairs it was vital, and it encompassed people from all social classes. Palmerston found that, like Canning, his foreign policy carried more weight when invested with what was termed vaguely 'popular support', and by mid-century the conditions were ripe for a populist, liberal, national and purposeful policy to elicit a broad demonstration of approbation. Yet Palmerston was not to win popular acclaim with a monolithic approach: his appeal was manifold and his characterisation as the Minister of England is as much a symbol of his ability to bridge the differences inherent within the nation as about his bellicose defence of national interests overseas.

By the early nineteenth century comprehensive military defeat of France in 1815 and emancipation of Catholics in Britain in 1829 had to some extent undermined the usefulness of Protestantism as a cement in British society. While there was a certain residual Protestant feeling which Palmerston was still able to exploit, as will be seen, he needed some other rhetorical device if he was to secure popular support for his policies. Palmerston himself failed to appreciate, or rather did not see any distinctions between 'British' and 'English' and used the latter term as synonymous with the former.[89] This in itself was not necessarily inconsistent with English contemporary usage, as a ballad entitled 'The Englishman' demonstrates:

> The Briton may traverse the pole or zone,
>   And boldly claim his right;
> For he calls such a vast domain his own,
>   That the sun never sets on his might.
> Let the haughty stranger seek to know
>   The place of his home and birth.
> And the flush will spread from cheek to brow,
>   As he tells of his native earth.
> 'Tis a glorious charter deny it who can!
>   That's breathed in the words 'I'm an Englishman'.[90]

'Englishness' to Palmerston meant certain values, applicable to the whole of Britain and not England exclusively. In place of a rigid anti-Catholic prejudice, though not to its complete eradication, a national consciousness could now be forged more simply by representing Britain as more liberal, tolerant and wealthy than continental rivals. Thus Palmerston's support for the abolition of the slave trade, for example, was not just a humanitarian impulse, but also an implicit demonstration of the moral legitimacy of a *pax Britannica*. When he heard of slave-trade atrocities in Zanzibar in 1846 Palmerston did not hesitate to declare that 'the nations of Europe are destined to put an end to the African slave trade and that Great Britain is the main instrument in the hands of Providence for the accomplishment of this purpose'.[91] Palmerston's appeal to such a divine role for Britain is a telling illustration of the potency of such notions in the fashioning of a convincing national identity, and even national mission, to underpin, or validate, Palmerstonian foreign policy in the estimation of the country. Still, therefore, there was the construction of a national consciousness which was defined by reference to external factors and which could thus cut across social classes. Palmerston was writing to the local British consul about the grievances in Zanzibar, but the sense of British liberalism and freedom which lay behind Palmerston's declaration found echoes elsewhere in society. Significantly, in Dickens' *Little Dorrit*, published in the mid-1850s, the inhabitants of Bleeding Heart Yard, by common agreement, 'poor', 'hard-up', earthy and coarse, continued to regard the foreigner as inferior to an Englishman. It was, in such places, regarded as 'a sort of Divine visitation upon a foreigner that he was not an Englishman, and that all kinds of calamities happened to his country because it did things that England did not, and did not do things that England did'. Furthermore:

> They believed that foreigners were always badly off; and though they were as ill off themselves as they could desire to be, that did not diminish the force of the objection. They believed that foreigners were dragooned and bayonetted; and though they certainly got their own skulls promptly fractured if they showed any ill humour, still it was with a blunt instrument, and that didn't count. They believed that foreigners were always immoral; and though they had an occasional assize at home, and now and then a divorce case or so, that had nothing to do with it.[92]

The failure to recognise or acknowledge the inherent contradictions in their own position was something Palmerston could play upon. He need not advocate far-reaching domestic reform, since British (or English) liberties were not thus defined. Concerning itself exclusively with foreign affairs and defining itself purely by reference to nationalisms that were less liberal, free and providentially favoured, a broad-based national identity for Britain was thus fostered and consolidated.

To the commercial middle classes, Palmerston's appeal was not simply that of a minister with some degree of dynamism. By the 1850s, the radical politicians through whom they had typically expressed their interests were failing. Manchester School philosophies seemed by mid-century to be flawed and a new darling of the industrial classes was sought to replace Cobden. Palmerston again offered the required alliance. The cause of free trade, it has been argued, embodied most visibly in the Cobdenite, or Manchester School, campaign for repeal of the Corn Laws, ushered in a decline in the fortunes of the commercial classes and caused them to re-evaluate their political sympathies. It has been demonstrated, however, that the economic crisis of 1847, the effects of which were felt in the economy until 1849, was a relatively short-lived one in which downward cyclical trends in textiles and railways, alongside increased speculation in food prices and a credit crisis all exacerbated a downward spiral. Certainly an unfavourable balance of payments situation, particularly over corn imports, lay at the heart of this crisis, yet it was the instability of 1848 and the external disruption of markets that did as much to prolong the depression as any domestic commercial policy.[93] Thus while it appeared, according to V. A. C. Gatrell, that the diagnoses of the Anti-Corn Law League regarding the economy 'were indeed at fault', and Manchester's commercial classes, the bedrock constituency of the Cobdenite school, were gradually 'emancipated ... from their respect for the League's efficiency in the 1840s, and tacitly justified their political realignment in favour of the foreign policies of the Manchester School's arch-enemy Palmerston',[94] it is significant that the Manchester industrial output, particularly the dominant textile industry, relied on many markets beyond the relative safety and familiarity of the European continent. It was a dependence on these markets 'which were most vulnerable to the incursions of diplomatic, commercial and if need be naval pressure, by which Palmerstonian policy was to be characterised' that allowed Palmerstonian policy to gain an ascendancy.[95] Free trade and Cobdenite doctrines were not necessarily moribund, but Palmerston's 'gun-boat diplomacy' offered reassurance to cotton merchants with interests in far-off markets.

Integral to this is what Colley has called a 'cult of commerce', in which 'stout-hearted commercial activity and ideal patriotism were one and the same'. Patriotism was not simply something orchestrated from above, but something that was expected to generate profits for all.[96] Romantic images contributed as much as economic realities to a Palmerstonian ascendancy among the commercial classes. Cobdenite critiques, after all, remained persuasive explanations of the declining fortunes of the later 1840s, and the widespread continental sympathy for Cobdenite policies demonstrates the continued popularity of this creed in the face of Palmerstonian bluster.[97] But the textile elite of Manchester by mid-century were growing weary of questions of domestic reform and turned their attentions more frequently towards Europe. As Anthony Howe has argued, 'Palmerston's policy in Europe which brought him most criticism from his fellow aristocrats, mirrored, in some ways, the international concerns of the liberal bourgeoisie', concerns which were motivated less by conceptions of vested interests and more as a reflection of important middle-class attitudes. Support for Italy, for example, mobilised a latent Protestantism within the English middle class, while simultaneously standing as a model for the working classes in their search for political emancipation.[98]

In turn, this faith in mercantile interests impacted on the political centre. As Professor Searle confirms, under these circumstances, 'Cobdenite cosmopolitan pacifism seemed economically irrational, as well as politically unacceptable, whereas Palmerston's foreign policy had much more to offer'.[99] For Palmerston, such a shift was significant indeed. Harold Perkin has argued that it was the entrepreneurial class which held the balance of power in Victorian politics during this period: this class, he argues, 'ruled, as it were, by, remote control, through the power of its ideal over the ostensible ruling class, the landed aristocracy which continued to occupy the main positions of power down to the 1880s and beyond'.[100] It was the fulfilment of Marx's claim that the British middle class was content to entrust government to the great Whig families, to act as the *'aristocratic representatives* of the bourge-oisie'.[101] This was not mere hyperbole, for as Perkin asserts, in accepting Repeal in 1845, the aristocratic or ruling class had, in effect, accepted the middle-class view of national interest – whereby the needs of consumers and the prosperity of producers were placed before the unearned incomes of the landlords. Maybe this was, as Kitson Clark maintained, the 'Indian summer of the British aristo-cracy', but nevertheless, what emerges is a sense that it was the entrepreneurial spirit that now held considerable sway over the Government.[102] Thus, Palmerston, the advocate of free trade which, as he told an audience at Tiverton in 1851, he regarded as 'that system which is for the benefit of all classes of the community',[103] became the new hero of the Manchester School entrepreneurial class.

Palmerston's appeal, however, went deeper than his declared political faith. In attracting popular support outside Parliament from radical and working classes, he relied as much upon his reputation and charisma, as he did on support for his political beliefs. He might have been one of the aristocratic representatives of the bourgeoisie, but he was also the aristocrat with whom the greatest number of the people could identify. Palmerstonianism, according to Antony Taylor, 'acted as the main mode of mass political expression prior to the emergence of the movements for parliamentary reform in the middle 1860s',[104] which perhaps held true following the demise of Chartism. Not only was attention increasingly being paid to international affairs, while domestic politics appeared relatively quiet by comparison, but Palmerston himself demonstrated qualities with which working classes could identify. His love of boxing and reputed sexual prowess as they became enshrined in popular folklore and through the medium of the popular press, endeared him to the people at street level, Taylor argues, and 'his image as the "bucolic squire", and his inveterate gambling and womanizing earned him the affectionate sobriquet of "Lord Cupid" and reinforced his identifi-cation with the outward excesses of popular culture'.[105] In his treatment of the Haynau affair in 1850 and his determination to receive Kossuth the following year, Palmerston did much to appeal to radicals and Chartists.[106] To the working classes and radicals Palmerston embodied European liberty and defence of constitutionalism. To middle-class educated and entrepreneurial classes, he represented a particular form of patriotic heroism, a just and honourable crusader in the national interest. He was able to latch on to the classically inspired search for a hero and to supply the leadership, or focus, for the radical campaign for nation and defence of liberty. The search for a figurehead to represent interests was a pan-class phenomenon and it was something Palmerston, forging his reputation in the field of foreign affairs, was able to exploit in order to counter-balance opposition from the Crown and Cabinet which both sought, throughout this period, to rein Palmerston in.

Notes

1 See Mitchell, *Melbourne*, pp. 240–3.
2 F. Eyck, *The Prince Consort: A Political Biography* (Boston, USA, and Cambridge, 1959), p. 22, memorandum by George Anson (Albert's private secretary), Aug. 1840.
3 A. C. Benson and Viscount Esher (eds), *The Letters of Queen Victoria: A selection from Her Majesty's Correspondence Between the Years 1837 and 1861*, 3 vols (London, 1907) (hereafter *LQV*), III, p. 4, Aberdeen to Queen, 6 Jan. 1853.
4 Eyck, *Prince Consort*, p. 24, memorandum by Anson, 2 Jan. 1841.
5 F. Hardie, *The Political Influence of Queen Victoria, 1861–1901*, 2nd edn (Oxford, 1938), pp. 19–20.
6 Hawkins, '"Parliamentary Government"', p. 655.
7 See Eyck, *Prince Consort*, p. 36.
8 *Ibid.*, p. 138, memorandum by Prince Albert, 11 July 1850.
9 *Ibid.*, p. 33.
10 See Hawkins, '"Parliamentary Government"'; P. Smith, 'Editor's Introduction' to W. Bagehot, *The English Constitution* [1867], ed. P. Smith (Cambridge, 2001), pp. xiv–xv.
11 Bagehot, *English Constitution*, pp. 5, 9.
12 *Ibid.*, p. 10.
13 *Ibid.*, p. 193.
14 See R. Quinault, 'Westminster and the Victorian Constitution', *Transactions of the Royal Historical Society*, 6th ser., II (1992), 79–104; T. A. Jenkins, *Parliament, Party and Politics in Victorian Britain* (Manchester, 1996), pp. 18–19.
15 Bagehot, *English Constitution*, pp. 37–8. Cf. D. Cannadine, 'The Context, Performance and Meaning of Ritual: The British Monarchy and the "Invention of Tradition", *c.* 1820–1977', in E. Hobsbawm and T. Ranger (eds), The Invention of Tradition (Cambridge, 1992 edn), pp. 108–20.
16 Bagehot, *English Constitution*, p. 60. Bagehot's thesis finds credence in a letter from the Queen to Palmerston of 11 Nov. 1840 in which she implicitly acknowledged that her role was essentially a consultative one (Broadlands

Papers, RC/F/212/1–4); similarly, in 1848 Albert noted that, in this case about Greece, he saw his role as that of 'an impartial judge' (Broadlands Papers, RC/H/26, Prince Albert to Palmerston, 4 Jan. 1848).

17 *LQV*, II, p. 282, memorandum by Baron Stockmar, 12 March 1850.

18 *Hansard*, 3rd ser., XXVI, 216 (24 Feb. 1835).

19 See Mitchell, *Melbourne*, p. 147.

20 G. H. L. Le May, *The Victorian Constitution: Conventions, Usages and Contingencies* (London, 1979), p. 34.

21 J. R. Vincent, 'The Parliamentary Dimension of the Crimean War', *Transactions of the Royal Historical Society*, 5th ser., XXXI (1981), 37.

22 Bagehot, *English Constitution*, p. 117.

23 *Ibid.*, pp. 30, 116.

24 *Ibid.*, pp. 94–5.

25 Hawkins, *Parliament, Party and the Art of Politics*, p. 23.

26 Hawkins, '"Parliamentary Government"', 650.

27 *The Times* in 1850 for example, had an average daily circulation of 38,141; that of its five main metropolitan rivals combined was an average of 17,889 (T. Morley, '"The Arcana of that Great Machine": Politicians and *The Times* in the Late 1840s', *History*, 73 (1988), p. 38, n. 1). See also A. P. Wadsworth, 'Newspaper Circulations, 1800–1954', *Transactions of the Manchester Statistical Society* (1954–55), esp. pp. 7–11.

28 Broadlands Papers, GC/GR/98, James Grant to Palmerston, 27 Dec. 1851.

29 D. Read, *Peel and the Victorians* (Oxford, 1987), pp. 39–42. See also A. Jones, *Powers of the Press: Newspapers, Power and the Public in Nineteenth-Century England* (Aldershot, 1996), pp. 181–7.

30 *The Times*, 15 March 1851.

31 Read, *Peel and the Victorians*, p. 41, C. Richardson [of the Leeds Operative Conservative Association] to Peel, 26 March 1835.

32 Quoted Jones, *Powers of the Press*, pp. 194–5.

33 Broadlands Papers, GMC/47–128.

34 Bagehot, *English Constitution*, p. 30.

35 See, for example, the way in which Palmerston played to the crowds at election hustings in Tiverton described in F. J. Snell, *Palmerston's Borough: A Budget of Electioneering Anecdotes, Squibs and Speeches* (Tiverton, 1894).

36 Broadlands Papers, GC/LA/110, Palmerston to Lansdowne, 8 Dec. 1853.

37 Chamberlain, *Palmerston*, p. 88, Palmerston to Aberdeen, 12 Feb. 1854.

38 [3rd] Earl Grey, *Parliamentary Government Considered with Reference to A Reform of Parliament: An Essay* (London, 1858), p. 25.

39 *Ibid.*, p. 26.

40 Bodleian Library, Oxford, Clarendon Deposit, MS.Clar.dep.c.534, fols 43–6, Clarendon to Henry Reeve, 1 April 1847. Clarendon concluded: 'I told him that this altho difficult might be possible if the Govt & the Press acted together, but that the latter wd become ridiculous & perhaps mischievous if it blew up a great fire & the former had nothing *to cook* by it.'

41 *Morning Post*, 7 July 1846.

42 A. Hawkins, *British Party Politics, 1852–1886* (Basingstoke, 1998), p. 62.

43 *Daily News*, 25 June 1850.

44 J. Grant, *The Newspaper Press – its origins – progress – & present position*, 3 vols (London, 1871–72), I, pp. 205–6.

45 Broadlands Papers, PRE/A/11–12, Palmerston 'to the Globe', 22 Feb. 1849 and 9 July 1849.

46 *Ibid.*, PRE/B/137–47, letters and articles 'for the Globe', 26 Nov. 1848–30 June 1851.

47 Brown, 'Compelling but not Controlling?', pp. 56–7.

48 Broadlands Papers, GC/EA/49–56, Palmerston to Easthope, July–Dec. 1846; *ibid.*, GC/DO/65, 71, 100/1, Palmerston to Doyle, 16 February 1846, 2 August 1846, n.d.

49 *Ibid.*, GC/DO/82/1, Palmerston to Andrew Doyle, 18 March 1847.

50 See, for example, *Morning Chronicle*, 27 July 1848.

51 See, for example, *Morning Post*, 17 June 1848, 24 July 1848, 12, 18 Aug. 1848.

52 Glenesk-Bathurst Papers, MS.Dep.1990/1/1082, Algernon Borthwick to Peter Borthwick, 6 May 1850.

53 See Brown, 'Compelling but not Controlling?', for more detail on Palmerston's manipulation of the press.

54 See, for example, *Punch*, XXV (July–Dec. 1853), pp. 149, 269, XXVIII (Jan–June 1855), pp. 45, 65.

55 Chamberlain, 'Who founded the Liberal Party?', p. 5.

56 *Press*, 24 Dec. 1853.

57 Shakespeare, *Coriolanus* (Oxford, 1994 edn), 2.3.55–6, 2.3.111–13, 2.3.57–9.

58 Vernon, *Politics and the People*, p. 48. For a full discussion of what Vernon terms 'power imagined', see pp. 48–104.

59 *Ibid.*, p. 85.

60 *Ibid.*, pp. 86–7.

61 *Ibid.*, p. 91.

62 Broadlands Papers, SP/B/3/2, newspaper cutting from the *Glasgow Constitutional* reporting a speech of Lord Palmerston in the City Hall, Glasgow, Sept. 1853.

63 W. R. Greg, 'The Expected Reform Bill', *Edinburgh Review* (Jan. 1852), 214–20.

64 Finn, *After Chartism*, p. 22.

65 See L. Colley, 'Britishness and Otherness: An Argument', *Journal of British Studies*, 31: 4 (1992), 309–29 and L. Colley, *Britons: Forging the Nation, 1707–1837* (New Haven and London, 1996 edn).

66 Colley, *Britons*, pp. 3, 5–6, 19, 36.

67 See K. Robbins, *Nineteenth-Century Britain: Integration and Diversity* (Oxford, 1988), pp. 2, 5.

68 Colley, *Britons*, pp. 6, 18.

69 L. Brockliss and D. Eastwood, 'Introduction: A Union of Multiple Identities', pp. 1–8 in L. Brockliss and D. Eastwood (eds), *A Union of Multiple Identities: The British Isles, c. 1750–1850* (Manchester, 1997); D. Eastwood, L. Brockliss and M. John, 'Conclusion: From Dynastic Union to Unitary State: The European Experience', in Brockliss and Eastwood (eds), *A Union of Multiple*

Identities, pp. 193–212. These writers agree with Colley that the idea of Britain was forged during the eighteenth century largely by reference to France, but they argue that there were other factors at work (p. 3). Crucially, they highlight the importance and persistence of religious diversity. From the Act of Union of 1800 the 'religious culture of the new State was already diverse and became still more heterogeneous' (p. 1). By 1851 the religious census revealed that the country was reconciled to religious pluralism (p. 194). See also K. Robbins, *Great Britain: Ideas, Institutions and the Idea of Britishness* (Harlow, 1998) and J. Cannon, 'A Nation Unforged', *The Times Literary Supplement*, 17 April 1998, p. 10.

70   Colley, *Britons*, p. 32.

71   D. Newsome, *The Victorian World Picture: Perceptions and Introspections in an Age of Change* (London, 1997), p. 94.

72   V. S. Berridge, 'Popular Journalism and Working Class Attitudes, 1854– 1886: A Study of *Reynolds Newspaper, Lloyds Weekly Newspaper* and the *Weekly Times*' (unpublished PhD thesis, University of London, 1976), pp. 36–7, 285–6.

73   See Jones, *Powers of the Press*, p. 198: 'Numbers and categories of subjects debated at the Hope and Anchor Inn, Birmingham, January 1858 to December 1862'. The *approximate* figures (derived from Jones' histogram) are: The arts: 9; British politics: 31; Economic policy: 12; Foreign affairs: 61; Local politics: 12; Military: 5; Moral issues: 14; The press: 3; Religion: 21; Science: 4; Social policy: 47; Other: 4.

74   P. Hollis, 'Pressure from Without: An Introduction', in P. Hollis (ed.), *Pressure from Without in Early Victorian England* (London, 1974), p. 18, n. 55, 'Senex', *Pioneer*, 28 June 1834.

75   *Ibid.*, p. 18, speech of Richard Cobden, 26 Nov. 1849.

76   W. E. Houghton, *The Victorian Frame of Mind* (New Haven, 1957), pp. 306–7.

77   *Ibid.*, p. 310.

78   See P. Karsten, *Patriot Heroes in England and America. Political Symbolism and Changing Values over Three Centuries* (Madison, Wisconsin, 1978), esp. pp. 110–64.

79   Broadlands Papers, GC/BR/35, Ambrose Brewin to Palmerston, 6 March 1848.

80   See B. Worden, 'The Victorians and Oliver Cromwell', in S. Collini, R. Whatmore and B. Young (eds), *History, Religion, and Culture: British Intellectual History, 1750–1950* (Cambridge, 2000), pp. 119–22. Witness also, for example, the controversy over the omission of Cromwell when statues of past British sovereigns were installed at the new Houses of Parliament in 1845. See Karsten, *Patriot Heroes*, pp. 144–5, 156.

81   Houghton, *The Victorian Frame of Mind*, p. 325.

82   *Ibid.*, p. 330.

83   Finn, *After Chartism*, pp. 67, 79–80. *The Voice of the People: A Supplement to All Newspapers*, 22 April 1848, quoted p. 80.

84   M. Taylor, *The Decline of British Radicalism, 1847–1860* (Oxford, 1995), pp. 2–3.

85   J. Parry, 'The Impact of Napoleon III on British Politics, 1851–1880', *Transactions of the Royal Historical Society*, 6th ser., XI (2001), 147–75.

86   *Ibid.*, p. 170.

87   Taylor, *The Decline of British Radicalism*, p. 149.

88   *Ibid.*, p. 150. For discussion of the 'Reform party', see pp. 19–60.

89   Colley, *Britons*, p. 174.

90   'The Englishman', Harding Collection, Bodleian Library, Oxford, B. 11 (1080).

91   Quoted Colley, *Britons*, p. 380.

92   C. Dickens, *Little Dorrit* (1857; Oxford, 1982 edn), pp. 112–13, 119, 254–5. *Little Dorrit* was first published monthly between December 1855 and June 1857.

93   H. M. Boot, *The Commercial Crisis of 1847* (University of Hull Occasional Papers in Economic and Social History, no. 11, Hull, 1984).

94   V. A. C. Gatrell, 'The Commercial Middle Class in Manchester, *c.* 1820–1857' (unpublished PhD thesis, University of Cambridge, 1971), pp. 382–3. As Gatrell demonstrates the markets for Manchester produce plummeted in the free-trade environment from about 1846 until the early 1850s. Export prices, domestic consumption (estimated value and value per capita) all fell between 1844 and 1851, improving only in the returns for 1854–56, according to Gatrell's calculations (p. 387). Thus, he concludes, 'there was little in the state of the domestic market to enforce among home traders any real gratitude to the League'.

95   *Ibid.*, pp. 403–4.

96   Colley, Britons, pp. 61–2, 391.

97   On the popular reception of Cobden and his free trade principles on the Continent in the late 1840s, see A. Howe, *Free Trade and Liberal England, 1846–1946* (Oxford, 1997), pp. 73–86.

98   *Ibid.*, pp. 240–1.

99   G. R. Searle, *Entrepreneurial Politics in Mid-Victorian Britain* (Oxford, 1993), p. 12.

100 H. Perkin, *The Origins of Modern English Society, 1780–1880* (1969; London, 1985 edn), pp. 271–2. Searle quotes this argument approvingly, *Entrepreneurial Politics*, pp. 14–15.

101 See Searle, *Entrepreneurial Politics*, p. 15.

102 Perkin, *The Origins of Modern English Society*, p. 373; G. Kitson Clark, 'The Repeal of the Corn Laws and the Politics of the Forties', *Economic History Review*, 2nd ser., IV, No. 1 (1951), 13; Searle, *Entrepreneurial Politics*, p. 44.

103 *The Economist*, 27 Sept. 1851.

104 A. D. Taylor, 'Modes of Political Expression and Working Class Radicalism, 1848–1874: The London and Manchester Examples' (unpublished PhD thesis, University of Manchester, 1992), p. 249.

105 A. Taylor, 'Palmerston and Radicalism, 1847–1865', *Journal of British Studies* 33: 2 (April 1994), 160–1.

106 See *ibid.*, p. 162.

3

Palmerston and the palace: the struggle for control of foreign policy, 1846–50

Palmerston's third, and final, tenure of the Foreign Office between 1846 and 1851 during Lord John Russell's first government, was dominated by a struggle between the Crown, Prime Minister and Foreign Secretary. When, in 1848, Palmerston had to defend his record before the House of Commons and famously declared in answer to charges of inconsistency that Britain had no eternal allies and no perpetual enemies,[1] he was, perhaps, offering also a fitting epigram for himself. Russell's role has often been described as that of a broker between the Court and the Foreign Office, perpetually striving to maintain some semblance of harmony and stability by which his fragile administration might survive. While there is some value in seeing the Prime Minister as an intermediary between Crown and minister, there remains more to be said of this subject.

Russell and Palmerston had both served in the Whig ministries of Lords Grey and Melbourne between 1830 and 1841, in both of which Palmerston had filled the office of Foreign Secretary while Russell had served successively as Paymaster-General (until 1835), Home Secretary (until late 1839) and finally Secretary for War and Colonies. While Russell did not necessarily become, in the course of these early ministerial associations, a proselyte to the Palmerstonian frame of mind, he tended frequently to concur with Palmerston and side with him within the Cabinet on foreign affairs.[2] Not until the closing months of the Melbourne Government, however, did Russell became in any meaningful way interested in foreign politics.[3]

Initially Palmerston had been able to carry Russell with him on most aspects of foreign policy, but Russell had not been at the Colonial Office long before he started to come into much more frequent contact and friction with Palmerston, in particular over the Eastern question.[4] When in the late 1830s Mehmet Ali, Pasha of Egypt, sought to secure independence from the Ottoman Empire, France had adopted an equivocal line, hoping through tacit support of Mehmet Ali to construct a viable counter-poise to British influence in the Mediterranean. An increasingly Francophobic Palmerston, meanwhile, became more receptive to Russian overtures for Anglo-Russian cooperation, at the expense of the Anglo-French *entente*,[5] bringing him into direct conflict with the Cabinet which contained a sizeable Francophile element, not least among the Holland House Foxites. A proposed Turco-Egyptian settlement of 1840, quite possibly brokered with French support, moreover, was rejected by the Porte at the bidding of the British minister at Constantinople, Lord Ponsonby, acting on Palmerston's direction.

Russell declared that he did not regard the difference between British and French proposals as a reasonable cause of war, and told the Foreign Secretary that he 'must therefore propose at the Cabinet on Monday that some step should be taken to demonstrate our willingness to settle the question by negotiation'.[6] Following this Cabinet meeting, Russell wrote once again to Palmerston, saying he would resign thereby 'leaving to you the whole credit of the success of your policy', since, he said, it 'seems to me that I have no right to share in any claim to foresight, when my predictions are anything but sanguine'.[7] Russell was dissuaded from this course and ultimately moved closer to the Palmerstonian stand-point once Palmerston had secured the support of Russia, Austria and Prussia; it was a clear demonstration of Palmerston's ascendancy within the Government. In seeking some sort of reconciliation, Russell wrote to Palmerston early in November tacitly acknowledging Palmerston's approach to have been workable and proposing possible instructions to be issued forthwith to advance the situation.[8] On the letter containing Russell's proposals, however, Palmerston has minuted rather caustically that they were 'Not adopted by me'.[9]

Nevertheless, while Palmerston had lost much favour with the Cabinet by the end of the negotiation, Russell was once more sympathetic to the Palmerstonian line. This may well have been a pragmatic decision since Russell was acutely aware of the importance of maintaining party unity in fashioning an effective anti-Conservative alliance. When the Melbourne Government fell in 1841 Russell, cognisant of the need to keep Palmerston with him if the Whigs were to stand as a viable opposition to the Tories under Peel, wrote, 'Before we meet again, we must not only be organized, but it must be considered for what purposes we are organized. There is sufficient matter, as I think, both in the principles of free trade, and in the maintenance of the general policy we have maintained in Poland, to give us a distinct ground for party union'.[10] Not only was Palmerston's handling of foreign policy seen as a triumph of liberalism and self-determination – despite his stand over Egypt – but he was also widely recognised as an able and capable statesman. Indeed Russell could hardly afford not to appease Palmerston when even Aberdeen, Peel's Foreign Secretary, was forced to admit that Palmerston's management of the Eastern question during the 1830s had, as Palmerston gleefully reported to Melbourne, 'made him forgive me many things of former years, which he had thought he never should have forgiven'.[11]

Palmerston had established himself as an able manager of foreign policy and though his manner was offensive to many at Westminster none could deny that he was now vital to any resurrection of Whig and Liberal fortunes. As Peel brought his party towards a wreck on the rocks of the Corn Law question towards the end of 1845, attempts were made to bring into office a Whig ministry which would be headed by Russell. While a Whig Government would uphold the Peelite insistence on the need to repeal the Corn Laws, it was felt, or at least hoped, that such a ministry could pass this legislation without destroying itself. In fact it was to prove impossible for Russell to pull together the various factions with whom he sat on the opposition benches in order to supplant Peel. On the immediate political programme to be pursued, especially support for free trade and policy towards Ireland, Russell was able to secure widespread concurrence among his allies.[12] And despite his conservative reputation in domestic affairs, Palmerston was not so vehement in his objections to the repeal of the Corn Laws as was widely suspected, proclaiming himself happy to serve in a ministry committed to such measures. Charles Greville thought, somewhat cynically but not unreasonably that:

> as Palmerston's objection was grounded on the assumption that it

[the Edinburgh Letter in which Russell expressed his conversion to the principle of free trade] would *strengthen* Peel, now that Peel is out of office, and the doors of the F. O. are open to him, he will no doubt be reconciled to it; for I don't imagine he cares about corn, fixed duty, sliding scales, or anything else except so far as they may bear upon his return to that abode of his bliss.[13]

Nevertheless, while Palmerston was quite genuinely prepared to serve in a Russell Government, an influential minority, led by the third Earl Grey but including also Labouchere, George Grey and Macaulay were unwilling to accommodate him.[14] It has been suggested that Lord Grey and Sir Charles Wood had long sought to establish some sort of Conservative–Liberal coalition and were exploiting opposition to Palmerston as a means of furthering this end.[15] Palmerston was not the only member of the proposed Cabinet to whom Grey objected but he was a politically useful target.[16] Having failed to establish an alliance with Peel, despite sharing common views on financial policy, Grey and Wood joined the Russell Government in July 1846 preferring that to remaining in opposition with few immediate prospects of government. Russell's offer of the Chancellorship of the Exchequer to Wood certainly made the decision easier, but as Minto's journal reveals, the Grey faction continued to look to a future as a separate political body.[17] Opposition to Palmerston was founded on more than the personal ambition of his antagonists, however, and rested to a large extent on fears about Palmerston's inability to avoid costly foreign entanglements.

Russell stood little or no chance of forming a ministry without Palmerston which would be sturdy enough to weather the coming parliamentary storms; yet he faced similarly bleak prospects of forming a ministry with him at the Foreign Office, and Palmerston would take no other post. Palmerston wanted a heavyweight office in order to be able to check Russell and certainly had personal, political, reasons for this. But doubts were also being expressed in Whig circles at this time about Russell's aptitude; Palmerston felt he had a national responsibility to monitor Russell's conduct,[18] and even Russell's brother, the Duke of Bedford, was uneasy about the prospect of Lord John becoming Prime Minister.[19]

Palmerston therefore insisted on taking the Foreign Office and in the face of various objections to such an arrangement, Russell could not fulfil his commission. Peel might have adverted to the 'want of deference shown to the Queen' and the 'new and unconstitutional' nature of Russell's failure to follow through his promise to form a new administration;[20] but Russell could do nothing else, acknowledging that fissures among his colleagues meant that, 'I cannot form a government which can have a chance of success, even in the first measure they would have to propose'.[21] Russell felt 'a great sense of relief on public affairs', he told his wife the day after his audience with the Queen. 'The Queen, as usual, was very gracious and was angry with Lord Grey for his determination; she was, in short, convinced that I was right in wishing to retain Palmerston at the Foreign Office'.[22]

It is significant that the Queen concurred in the necessity of retaining Palmerston at the Foreign Office and this was one of the last royal endorsements of Palmerston's abilities and claims to the control of foreign policy. In the early years of her reign, the Queen confined the majority of her communications with Palmerston to simple questions about diplomatic practice and conventions.[23] The first letter from the Queen which survives in the Broadlands collection to deal with a specific question of policy is dated 11 November 1840 and in it the Queen is keen to point out that in raising points about Palmerston's drafts she 'does so with strict impartiality having had ample opportunity of hearing both sides of this intricate and highly important question'.[24] This was in effect no more of an interest than that already claimed for the monarchy by William IV.[25] The experienced and self-assured manner of Palmerston had instilled in the Queen a genuine feeling of confidence in his abilities. When she feared losing Palmerston, she wrote lamenting the loss of 'his valuable services, wh. he has performed in so admirable a manner, & which have so greatly promoted the honour & welfare of this country in its relations with Foreign Powers'.[26] And again, in 1841, when Palmerston did go out of office, she wrote expressing her wish 'for his and Lady Palmerston's welfare and happiness'.[27]

However well disposed the Queen was towards Palmerston, this did not compensate for the antagonism towards Palmerston among the disaffected Whigs and Russell was unable to form a government in December 1845 and thus Peel was obliged to resume the premiership. But, with the passing of the repeal of the Corn Laws, Peel could not hold a ministry together any longer and Russell was required to construct an administration somehow. Overtures made to Cobden and to the Peelites were unproductive and Russell himself ruled out the only other possible alliance, one with the Protectionists.[28] Thus the ministry was to be assembled from among Russell's friends, but this raised for a second time the troublesome Grey–Palmerston dilemma. However, Grey was now far more amenable, recognising the necessity of a Russell government. He could comfort himself with the knowledge that Palmerston had done much in the intervening period to repair his reputation abroad: a visit to Paris over Easter 1846, for example, had ensured that there at least, *ce terrible Lord Palmerston* had become *ce cher Lord Palmerston*,[29] however short-lived that might have been.[30] Thus, Charles Wood was able to report to Russell at the end of June that Lord Grey 'was quite prepared to waive any objection on the score of Palmerston ... and that he felt the necessity of making the machine work easily if he came in. He felt the separation from all his friends very much if he was not included'.[31] Palmerston's return to the Foreign Office was widely applauded at home. The progressive *Daily News*, for instance, saw 'the light which emanates from Downing-street in August is much more full of clearness and truth' than had been the case when Aberdeen had been Foreign Secretary.[32] Even the ultra-Tory *Standard* initially welcomed Palmerston back, praising the moral conscience of his speeches against slavery.[33] *The Times* saw some measure of 'personal sacrifices' in Palmerston's return to office,[34] but this served only to highlight the difficulties in seeing foreign affairs as a matter for party political differences.

On 6 July 1846 Russell accepted the Queen's commission and the new ministers assumed their seals of office at Osborne. Yet the divisions which had hampered Russell in December 1845 were to plague him still. Even to Prince Albert the factional nature of the new ministry was obvious:

> There is the *Grey Party*, consisting of Lord Grey, Lord Clarendon, Sir George Grey, and Mr Wood; they are against Lord Lansdowne, Lord Minto, Lord Auckland, and Sir John Hobhouse, stigmatising them as old women. Lord John leans entirely to the last-named gentlemen. There is no cordiality between Lord John and Lord Palmerston, who, if he had to make a choice, would even forget what passed in December last, and join the Grey Party in preference to

Lord John personally. The curious part of all this is that they cannot keep a secret, and speak of all their differences.[35]

Modern analyses of Whig-Liberal politics have agreed with the Prince in viewing this as a period of factions, though offering a more refined view of Whig-Liberal differences.[36] Clearly the ministry was susceptible to internal division but more than this, within Parliament, too, support for the new Government was weak. Taking the division lists for the third reading of the Corn Bill and the second reading of the Coercion Bill in *Hansard*, it has been estimated that the 'nominal supporters of the Government were in a minority and probably numbered altogether something like 270 to 280 members. The Protectionist party represented about 270 and the Peelites about 110'.[37] It was an inauspicious beginning, something which the Queen recognised. With Peel and Aberdeen at the helm, she told her uncle, the King of the Belgians, in July, she had felt safe: 'Never ... did they *ever* recommend a *person* or thing which was not for my or the Country's best, and never for the Party's advantage only; and the contrast now is very striking; there is much less respect and much less high and pure feeling', adding a week later: 'The present Government is weak, and I think Lord J. does not possess the talent of keeping his people together'.[38] These weaknesses were to have important ramifications for Palmerston and the conduct of foreign policy during the subsequent five and a half years.

During the Russell Government, Victoria sought to be more than a source of counsel over foreign policy. Inspired no doubt by Albert, the Court was to complain frequently of Palmerston's handling of foreign affairs and notes were often exchanged between the Queen and Russell and Russell and Palmerston in which Victoria's complaints about her Foreign Minister's conduct were aired. Over the practice of sending despatches to the Queen before they were sent abroad, for example, Aberdeen had declared himself willing to 'make any necessary alterations, by additional instructions, or he would humbly represent to Your Majesty the reasons which induce him to think that the interest of Your Majesty's service require [sic] an adherence to what had already been done'.[39] The Queen clearly expected a similar treatment from Palmerston when he returned to the Foreign Office under Russell. Yet when in the autumn of 1848 Palmerston wrote to Russell expressing his fears that, 'Unfortunately The Queen gives Ear too readily to Persons who are hostile to her Government, and who wish to poison her mind with Distrust of her Ministers; and in this way, she is constantly suffering under groundless uneasiness',[40] Russell agreed that all was not well with the Queen, but replied:

> That the Queen is constantly suffering under uneasiness is too true, but I own I cannot say it is always groundless. It is surely right that a person speaking in the name of Her Majesty's Government should in important affairs submit his dispatches to the Queen & obtain the opinion of her Prime Minister before he commits the Queen & her Government.
>
> This necessary preliminary you too often neglect, & the Queen naturally, as I think, dreads that upon some occasion you may give her name to sanction proceedings which she may afterwards be compelled to disavow.
>
> I confess that I feel some of the same uneasiness, but as I agree with you very constantly in opinion, my only wish is that in future you will save the Queen anxiety, & me some trouble by giving your reasons before, & not after an important dispatch is sent.[41]

Relations between the Palace and Palmerston were never warm and Albert was to become one of Palmerston's sternest critics from the outset in 1846. These relations became increasingly strained by late 1847 as Albert continued his practice of maintaining a regular correspondence with foreign sovereigns,[42] and by 1848 Russell was receiving summons to attend the Queen to hear her complaints against Palmerston. Russell stood by Palmerston in the face of royal pressure to replace him with Clarendon, yet by 1850 the Prime Minister too was tiring of Palmerstonian abrasiveness. In February 1850, for example, the Queen wrote to Palmerston complaining that a draft despatch which she had wished to be altered according to the recommendations proposed by Russell, had been sent off without modification. 'The Queen must remark upon this sort of proceeding,' she wrote, 'of which this is not the first instance & plainly tell Lord Palmerston that this must not happen again. Lord Palmerston has a perfect right to state to the Queen his reasons for disagreeing with her views & will always have found her ready to listen to his reasons, but she cannot allow a servant of the Crown,

& her Minister to act contrary to her orders & this without her knowledge'.[43] Palmerston denied the validity of these complaints,[44] but this was a clear demonstration that the Queen, influenced no doubt by Stockmar, looked for obedience from 'a servant of the crown & her Minister'.

Whatever might be judged about the role of the Crown in the conduct of everyday governmental and parliamentary business, it cannot be doubted that where foreign affairs are concerned the environment is unusual. As Evelyn Ashley observed in 1879, 'Foreign policy is that policy in which Sovereigns, who are thus brought into competition with their equals, take the most interest'. Meanwhile, Stockmar, counsellor to the royal couple, Ashley argued, 'was clearly no admirer of popular or Parliamentary control over foreign affairs, which he regarded as the special concerns of royal and imperial minds'.[45] Not only did Stockmar's view of the royal position encourage the Queen to see in foreign policy an important role for herself, but by virtue of the fact that foreign policy brought her face to face with her fellow sovereigns, Victoria's impression of her role was exaggerated by these 'equals' with whom she was now in competition. Letters from foreign royalty, founded on the assumption that Victoria's constitutional position mirrored their own, engendered in the Queen a feeling that she could really control her country's foreign affairs. It was in part on this basis, then, that Victoria saw one of her duties being to monitor all diplomatic communications and to insist that they acquired her approval before being sent off.[46]

The sheer volume of material with which a Foreign Secretary had to deal meant that it was often impractical for the Queen to see everything. With a liked and trusted Foreign Secretary, such as Aberdeen (1841–46) this had not been too problematic, and although the Queen had been troubled by the failure to submit to her all drafts of despatches, she had accepted that it was not always possible.[47] Conversely, Palmerston was not well liked and the Queen and Prince took literally Aberdeen's parting injunction 'you must try to keep him straight'.[48] By the late 1840s, Palmerston did not enjoy the confidence of the Crown as he had when he had served at the Foreign Office during the reign of William IV, nor indeed as he had when Queen Victoria had first ascended the throne.[49] The Queen now was concerned not only with what was said by her government to others, but also by whom, for, clearly, the Foreign Secretary could not meet personally everyone with whom he dealt. Victoria therefore took a keen interest in both the content of despatches and the selection and appointment of diplomats.

The appointment of diplomatic representatives was the responsibility of the Foreign Secretary and they were, in effect, instruments of his own work. Palmerston argued that candidates for postings overseas should be assessed solely on the basis of merit and not as functionaries of party interests.

> Depend upon it [he told Russell] you will find the greatest advantage to the public Service & to the Credit of your Government in Selecting Men for Foreign Missions of Importance from a Regard for their Fitness; The advantage of so acting is permanent and felt in Times of Difficulty which may arise when least foreseen. The Advantage of acting upon other Considerations is Temporary, & when Evil arises from it, even those who may have pressed it upon you at the First will be the last to stand up and justify the Selection on the Grounds which it was made.[50]

Russell acknowledged the need to appoint men of ability to Britain's overseas postings, but unlike his Foreign Secretary he was also keen to pay attention to the political tendencies of candidates. 'I quite agree with you that in making diplomatic appointments the merit and fitness of the candidates are the chief points to be considered', he replied. 'But at the same time in this representative govt. the general means of carrying on a govt. are to be likewise taken into account'.[51] Nevertheless, although no letter seems actually to suggest that Palmerston decided appointments alone, there are several examples of Russell praising the Foreign Secretary's choice of diplomatist. Constitutionally certain appointments, such as attachéships, were exclusively in the gift of the Foreign Secretary,[52] and in general it would have been too time consuming for any Prime Minister to usurp this role, and Palmerston created a diplomatic staff with which Russell was generally satisfied.

The Queen, however, did take a close interest in the selection of diplomats. If she could not choose her Foreign Minister unfettered, she would at least try to influence the choice of diplomats through whom he would have to work. On one occasion, for example, she seized 'this opportunity of mentioning two very deserving people

in whom she takes interest & whom she wishes shld not be over-
looked in any change wh. may take place – viz: Mr Clarke, the son
of Sir J. Clarke, & Mr Lonsdale. They would both be found very
useful, & we are not rich in promising Diplomatists'.[53] The Queen
agreed that merit and fitness must be the governing factors in
making appointments, as Palmerston himself had said to Russell,
but she did not believe that Palmerston always abided by his own
rules and felt compelled on one occasion to spell out the grounds
upon which selections must be made. 'The principle wh. the Queen
wld. wish to see acted upon in her diplomatic appointments in
general is, that the *good of the service* should preclude every other
consideration & that the selection of an Agent should depend more
on his personal qualifications for the particular post for which he
is to be selected, than on the mere pleasure & convenience of the
person to be employed, or of the Minister recommending him', she
wrote.[54] Palmerston, however, regarded royal interventions in this
field as a nuisance. When Prince Albert forwarded to the Foreign
Secretary through Russell some suggestions for diplomatic appointments, Palmerston scribbled on the letter: 'H.R.H. seems also to
have forgot that there is a responsible Secy of State for Foreign
Affairs which however I am not likely to forget', returning at a later
date to add, 'I did not take any steps in furtherance of this Extraordinary attempt to Interfere with the arrangts of my Department'.[55]

However contentious diplomatic appointments might have
been, ultimately it was the character of the policies those diplomats
were charged with pursuing that lay at the heart of Palmerston's
struggle with the Palace. In the early days of the ministry, the
Court's surveillance of drafts bore the appearance of advice rather
than dictation. On a draft despatch written very soon after the
establishment of the Russell government Victoria found 'that its
perusal has raised some apprehensions in her mind', which she was
anxious to put before Russell and Palmerston.[56] Palmerston
conceded in a letter concerning another draft a few days later that
he had happily amended it according to Russell's suggestions which
caused the draft to be now 'much better'. To some extent a wary
eye cast over diplomatic drafts helped guard against error, as
Palmerston admitted on one occasion, having written the draft 'late
last night & in a Hurry', he had 'relied upon your correcting what
might require it'.[57] Not only was pressure of business prone to cause

Palmerston himself to miss flaws in documents, but his staff too were susceptible to lapses. 'The obscurity, a delicate word for nonsense, observed upon by The Queen', Palmerston wrote on one occasion, 'was occasioned by a Blunder of my Clerks who had put in a "not" where it had no Business to be. I have struck out that word & made sense of the Passage'.[58] In monitoring Palmerston's correspondence there was a clear and valuable service to be performed by the Court (if only as proof-readers), but generally Palmerston viewed royal interventions as an implicit undermining of his authority in foreign affairs.

So long as royal interference went no further than raising queries about drafts where there was indeed something to question – fulfilling the Bagehotian consultative role – Palmerston had little cause to complain. But when the Queen's interest went beyond that of the style of the drafts and started to involve also the substance Palmerston raised serious objections. Palmerston's pride was certainly at stake, but so too was the integrity of the country's foreign policy. Minto became increasingly concerned about the likely ramifications of the constant royal attacks on Palmerston, believing that 'the violent prejudice which the Queen has conceived against him ... has encouraged the factions abroad & at home to combine in a vast conspiracy for his overthrow'.[59]

Once the Queen started to bring into question Palmerston's ability satisfactorily to frame a despatch, and to demand regular and indeed full accounts of proceedings, the Foreign Secretary, therefore, began to resist royal intervention ever more strenuously. In August 1846 Prince Albert had written to Palmerston to thank him for sending to the Queen a private letter received from Lord Howard de Walden. The Prince hoped such would become a standard practice 'as our chief wish and aim is, by hearing all parties, to arrive at a just, dispassionate, and correct opinion upon the various political questions. This, however, entails a strict scrutiny of what is brought before us'.[60] By 1848, however, the Queen and Prince were paying ever closer attention to Palmerston's drafts, even going so far as to compile a dossier on his diplomatic misdemeanours.[61] Spain, for example, became a source of tension between the Palace and Foreign Office at this time, Victoria arguing that the country was suffering 'under the evil consequence of that system of diplomacy, which makes the taking up of party politics in foreign

countries its principal object' which Palmerston was bent on pursuing.[62] More than seeking simply to restrain a Foreign Secretary
who behaved 'like a naughty child',[63] she wished to see a policy of
non-intervention directed towards the preservation of established
authority, reflecting a sort of Hanoverian reactionary spirit, the
chief author of which it was not difficult to identify.

Palmerston himself did little to appease the Queen and appears
to have paid little attention to his wife's admonition that 'you
contradict her notions too boldly';[64] believing that he could disarm
the Court simply by restricting the flow of information to the Palace.
Early attempts to forestall royal criticisms by dispatching documents before they had been reviewed were met with relative good
humour,[65] yet within a year of his return to the Foreign Office the
Queen's reprimands were becoming much sterner. 'The Queen has
several times asked Lord Palmerston through Lord John Russell, &
personally, to see that the Drafts to our Foreign Ministers are not
dispatched *previous* to their being submitted to the Queen; notwithstanding, this is still done, as for instance *today* with regard to the
Drafts for Lisbon', she wrote. 'The Queen therefore once more
repeats her desire that Lord Palmerston shld prevent a recurrence
of this practice'.[66] Palmerston made a poor job of preventing a
recurrence of this practice, however, and as late as December 1849,
Victoria felt compelled to write acidly: 'The Queen sends these 2
Dispatches to Lord Palmerston in order to draw his attention to the
date of their *reception* at the *Foreign Office*; viz: *Nov 26*; & they were
only sent to the Queen on *22d* of *Dec*. The Queen wishes that similar
delays in sending her the Dispatches shld not again take place'.[67]

Palmerston was not always guilty of holding up drafts for
lengthy periods and was on occasion the victim of his own poor
reputation at the Palace leading the Queen to make erroneous
assumptions about his conduct,[68] but he could be a pedant, and was
not averse to fulfilling the letter while subverting the spirit of his
constitutional obligations. Thus was Russell forced to complain in
February 1849:

> The Queen spoke to me the other day about the drafts sent to her
> for her approval – that they were sometimes sent at the bottom of
> a box, which she did not conceive required immediate attention: That
> sometimes they were sent as immediate & the messenger ordered to

wait when there was no reason for hurry; but above all that they were sent to her for approval before I had seen them, & while they were still liable to alterations suggested by me, or by the Cabinet.

She desired these irregularities to be corrected, & that in future the drafts should be sent in a separate box, & after they have been returned by me to the office, or settled by the Cabinet.[69]

The Queen was not the only one whose interventions were unwelcome, however, and Palmerston resented intrusions from any quarter equally. Russell and the rest of the Cabinet found themselves marginalised on occasion. In February 1850, for example, Russell rebuked Palmerston for prematurely sending a despatch 'on an important subject which is not in conformity with the Queen's opinion, or mine, or that of the Cabinet'. 'This is a serious deviation from the usual and right course on such subjects', he complained.[70]

Palmerston, in his own defence, regularly cited pressure of business which by the middle of the nineteenth century was indeed considerable. He told Lord Normanby in 1848, for example: 'As to your not always getting letters from me by every messenger who passes through Paris, never wonder at that nor think it extraordinary. Wonder rather when I am able to find time to write at all; I am sure you would if you saw the avalanche of despatches from every part of the world which come down upon me daily, and which must be read, and if you witnessed the number of interviews which I cannot avoid giving every day of the week'.[71] It was not necessarily obstructionism then that limited Palmerston's supply of correspondence to the Queen; as Palmerston told Russell in January 1849, he really had no option but to act alone at times:

> You are very Expeditious & regular, but She often keeps Drafts a long Time, and as Despatches cannot be sent off Every Day, like Letters by the Post, it often happens that the Delay of Two or Three Days by preventing a Despatch from going by one periodical opportunity involves a Delay of several Days further; and when Events are going on at a Hard Gallop, ones Instructions become rather stale before they reach their Destination, ... But if you & The Queen wish it I can alter the present Arrangement & order all drafts to go first to you, & not to the Queen till after you have returned them but this will reduce my Flint Gun to a Matchlock. The number of

Despatches received & sent out in 1848 was upwards of 29,000. The number in 1828 was a little above 10,000.[72]

Palmerston, aware that his own position was dangerously threatened with isolation, was also determined that Britain's external relations could not be managed effectively if all foreign business was not channelled through the Foreign Office. Hence his censure of Russell when he found the latter guilty of passing over the Foreign Office in communicating with the Admiralty: such communications were, he told the Prime Minister, embarrassing:

> First of all because they throw apparently a Responsibility upon the Secry of State for Foreign Affairs, in regard to orders as to which he has not been consulted, & of which he has been kept in Ignorance till after they have been given; & secondly because it is impossible that the First Lord of the Treasury can know what may have passed at former Periods upon similar matters, & he may therefore give Directions which he would not have given if he had been more fully informed … & Thirdly this course of proceeding renders the Records of the F. O. imperfect & misguiding for succeeding Govts inasmuch as important acts bearing upon our Foreign Relations will have been done, without the Records of the F. O. having any Trace of an Explanation as to why or wherefore such acts were ordered.[73]

The irony of this complaint appears to have been lost on Palmerston, yet he had already warned Russell of this danger, advising him that if business concerning his department was to be conducted without his knowledge, 'it is impossible that I can continue a Member of your Government. No man who has any Regard or respect for himself would serve upon such terms'.[74] He could legitimately appeal to pressure of business, to the transient and volatile nature of foreign affairs and to his uniquely advantageous position to justify his perceived want of respect towards the Crown and his colleagues, but Palmerston found he could not appease the Queen. She was genuinely concerned about the damage she believed he was doing to Britain's external relations. So strained did relations between the Palace and Palmerston become that the Queen was eventually prompted to write a letter to Russell, 'in order to *prevent any mistake* for the *future*', in which she laid down precisely what she expected of her Foreign Secretary:

She requires 1st That he will distinctly state what he proposes in a given case, in order that the Queen may know as distinctly, to what she is giving her Royal Sanction.

2ndly Having *once given* her Sanction to a measure, that it be not arbitrarily altered or modified by the Minister: Such an Act she must consider as failing in sincerity towards the Crown, & justly to be visited by the exercise of her Constitutional Right of dismissing that Minister.

She expects to be kept informed of what passes between him & the foreign ministers, before important decisions are taken based upon that intercourse – to receive the foreign dispatches in good time, & to have the drafts for her Approval sent to Her in sufficient time to make Herself acquainted with their contents before they must be sent off.[75]

Palmerston pledged himself to remedy the situation, appealing (again) to the 'great Pressure of business, & … the many Interruptions and Interviews &c to which I am liable' as the reason for the delays of which the Queen complained, and said that in order to revert to the old practice of making immediate copies of despatches as they were received as a way of resolving the problem, he would 'require an Additional Clerk or Two. You must be liberal & allow me that assistance'.[76]

The Queen concerned herself with diplomatic practice as here questions of prestige were paramount since this was where her peers seemed to have more independence and encouraged her to believe that she, too, could exercise similar power. However, when the Queen sought to influence policy, her comments were often over-ridden and the Queen's constitutional position was such that she could do nothing but accept this. Even if she were to have dismissed her ministers for failing to enact her wishes, as William IV had with Melbourne, she would have required another Peel to accept responsibility for her actions and there were no obvious candidates to form a ministry to succeed Russell's.[77] With no-one to replace Russell, the Queen could not dismiss him, and thus her views on policy were, ultimately, of limited import. But this is not to suggest that Victoria was ignored: frequently she would be able to offer wise counsel,[78] but in the final analysis, responsibility for policy rested with the Cabinet, which collectively endorsed and therefore took responsibility for the construction of that policy. This was no mere phenomenon of the Russell Government either. A few years later, when Palmerston's and Russell's roles of 1846–51 were reversed, the Queen found herself again running up against the same wall. 'What is the use', she asked Russell, 'of the Queens open & she fears at times wearisome Correspondence with her Ministers, what [is] the use of long Deliberations of the Cabinet if the very Policy can be carried out by indirect means which is set aside officially, & what Protection has the Queen against this Practise'.[79] In fact the parallels with 1846–51 are striking, and Russell in seeking to control the business of his department at the Foreign Office under Palmerston offered defences very like those employed by Palmerston during the Russell Government, even reserving the right to resign if his policy was over-ruled.[80]

The Queen's early input into discussion of foreign policy was really that of adviser, satisfying Bagehot's criteria for monarchical influence; to be consulted, to encourage and to warn. Early in the Russell administration's term the Spanish Marriages question dominated west European diplomacy. The matrimonial intrigues which brought the Duc de Montpensier to the side of Luisa, younger sister of the Queen of Spain, Isabella, were a source of consternation to Victoria and Albert. Victoria complained bitterly of the turn events had taken. 'If our dear Aberdeen was still at his post', she wrote to her uncle the King of the Belgians, 'the whole thing would not have happened; for he would *not* have forced Enriquito (which enraged Christine),[81] and secondly, Guizot would not have *escamoté* Aberdeen with the wish of triumphing over him as he has done over Palmerston, who has behaved most openly and fairly towards France, I must say, in this affair. But say what one will, it is he again who indirectly gets us into a squabble with France!' Yet, Victoria concluded, Palmerston's want of tact and sense of propriety could be easily overcome: 'Lord Palmerston', she declared, 'is quite ready to be guided by us'.[82] Since she and Russell, she believed, were generally in accord over foreign policy, her role was, then, to be that of adviser to Palmerston.[83] In July 1848, for instance, in a letter to Palmerston, Victoria could not help but notice contradictions in Britain's policy:

> She cannot conceal from him that she is ashamed of the policy we are pursuing in the Italian Controversy, in abetting wrong, & this

for the object of gaining *influence* in Italy. The Queen does not consider influence so gained as an advantage & though this influence is acquired to do good, she is afraid that the fear of losing it again will always stand in the way of this. At least in the Countries where the greatest stress has been laid on that influence, & the greatest exertions made for it, the *least good* has been done; the Queen means in Spain, Portugal and Greece. Neither is there any kind of consistency in the line we take about Italy & that we follow with regard to Schleswick; both cases are perfectly alike (with the difference perhaps that there is a question of right mixed up in that of Schleswick); whilst we upbraid *Prussia*, caution her &c., we say *nothing to Charles Albert* except that if he did not wish to take all the Emperor of Austria's Italian Dominions, we would not lay *any obstacles* in the way of his moderation.[84]

Similarly, a few months later, she remarked upon the manner in which Britain was seeking to force Austria to give up her 'lawful possessions', when the parallels with Ireland and even with Canada and Malta and other British territories seemed so obvious. British actions ought really in all instances, she suggested, to be governed by the simple principle: 'Was du nicht willst, dass dir geschieht, das thu' auch einem andern nicht'.[85]

Had the Court offered little more than advice, Palmerston would in all probability have found little of which to complain. After all, Prince Albert, through whom much business was actually transacted, especially during the 1840s when the Queen was frequently confined through pregnancies, was regarded by Palmerston as a generally well-informed and able statesman. Prince Albert himself was keen to assist Palmerston whenever he could, even after relations between the Palace and the Foreign Office had become decidedly cool. In May 1849 for instance, he sent a note to Palmerston about German affairs. 'As you say you would like to converse with me on the affairs of Germany,' he wrote, 'I shall be ready to see you to day after Ld. Ponsonby's audience'. And as evidence of a desire to promote open government and fair dealing with the Foreign Secretary, or at least to coerce rather than dictate to him in favour of 'legitimate' interests, the Prince added: 'I got a letter from my brother yesterday of which I enclose a translation (I have had made for you) just to show you an example of how difficult the

situation of these poor smaller Sovereigns is'.[86] This was not the
first private letter from his brother which the Prince so shared with
Palmerston. Yet while Palmerston had a high regard for the Prince's
knowledge, he could not escape the view that the Prince was just
a little too German for the British government at that time. Thus
while the Prince's desire for the reorganisation of Germany under
the suzerainty of Prussia would indeed be 'advantageous for the
peace and general interests of Europe', and 'conducive to the Interests of England', the Foreign Secretary argued that 'the British
Government would, I think, be stepping beyond its legitimate or
its safe ground, if it were to become the Partisan or the advocate
of any particular scheme or of the views of any particular German
Power'.[87]

Palmerston feared that Albert's influence at Court threatened
to undermine the integrity of his foreign policy. Too easily, he
believed, the Queen, not understanding German affairs, adopted the
Prince's views on them and this served only to make Palmerston's
position at the Foreign Office increasingly untenable. On one such
occasion, he complained that the Queen's 'real objections are so
much at variance with our settled Policy on this important Question
that I cannot undertake to frame a Despatch which shall remove
these objections, or be in Conformity with the German & Prussian
views of the Prince'.[88] Furthermore, Albert was establishing contacts with members of the Cabinet other than Palmerston with
whom he could discuss foreign affairs. Lansdowne enjoyed an occasional correspondence with the Prince, primarily with regard to
France, in which he discussed policy openly and exchanged diplomatic documents with the Palace.[89] More ominously from
Palmerston's perspective, Lord Grey, still apprehensive lest Palmerston's foreign policy led the country into expensive overseas
adventures and compromised trade, met with the Prince to discuss
public business and just at the time that Albert was becoming ever
more sceptical about Palmerston's policies in 1848, Grey found
himself 'much inclined to believe him [Albert] to be right' in his
disapprobation of Palmerston's course over Germany and Italy.[90]

Increasingly, the royal antagonism towards the Foreign Secretary became a more personal issue and by 1850 Minto was
complaining that the Queen's growing dislike of Palmerston
'prejudices her judgement of whatever proceeds from him to such

a degree as to be a constant source of difficulty and embarrass-
ment'.[91] Tacitly acknowledging that her own position was indeed
subordinate to that of the Cabinet with regard to policy, the Queen,
having heard little of foreign affairs recently, wrote to Palmerston
'to urge ... [him] to keep her informed of what he hears, & of the
views of the Government on the various important questions before
us'.[92] Yet still she was keen to uphold the façade of monarchical
control, a manifestation of her concern with presenting an image
of control to other sovereigns, and is to be found in June 1848
complaining of a draft about Austrian policy that 'Lord Palmerston
speaks in the beginning of the letter only of the *Cabinet* & adverts
nowhere to the proposition having been submitted to *her*'.[93]

The revolutions which swept across the continent in 1848 did
little to soothe the strained relations between Palmerston and the
Court. The Queen became increasingly disturbed about the rise and
spread of republicanism, while Palmerston, already the popular
champion of constitutionalism, now became in Guedalla's words,
'more than ever, ... a European figure. Perhaps there were no others
left. The waters of 1848 had submerged so many of his equals'.[94]
To the Court such an ascendancy boded ill for the country, as the
Queen recorded, she had told Russell how, 'I had no confidence in
him [Palmerston], and that it made me seriously anxious and
uneasy for the welfare of the country and for the peace of Europe
in general, and that I felt very uneasy from one day to another as
to what might happen'.[95] The Foreign Secretary, despite working
theoretically under the jurisdiction of his ministerial colleagues,
seemed not to be controllable by them. Conceding that royal opposition to Palmerston was founded on both policy differences and
on personal grounds,[96] the Queen admitted, in effect, that not only
was monarchical ability to control a minister brought into question,
but so too was the notion that the Cabinet could control Palmerston.

Russell, however, keen that such an exposure should not be
allowed to scuttle his ministry, clung to the impression of a united
government. He had, he stressed, 'always approved in the main of
the foreign policy of Lord Palmerston', and maintained therefore,
'I am quite ready to resign my office, but I could not make Lord
Palmerston the scapegoat for the sins which will be imputed to the
Government in the late negotiations'.[97] Whatever else might be at
issue, questions of policy were the Cabinet's preserve and, like

Palmerston, Russell knew this. The conflict with the Crown, then, obscured the real arena of political struggles: within the Cabinet.

Notes

1   *Hansard*, 3rd ser., XCVII, 121–3 (1 March 1848).
2   See, for example, Broadlands Papers, GC/RU/13, Russell to Palmerston, 27 Sept. 1835.
3   J. Prest, *Lord John Russell* (London, 1972) p. 165.
4   *Ibid.*, p. 165.
5   M. S. Anderson, *The Eastern Question, 1774–1923* (London, 1966), pp. 94–5.
6   Broadlands Papers, GC/RU/41, Russell to Palmerston, 24 Sept. 1840; *ibid.*, GC/RU/48, Russell to Melbourne, 1 Nov. 1840.
7   *Ibid.*, GC/RU/42, Russell to Palmerston, 29 Sept. 1840.
8   *Ibid.*, GC/RU/50, Russell to Palmerston, 7 Nov. 1840.
9   *Ibid.*, GC/RU/51, note in Palmerston's hand on letter from Russell to Palmerston, 7 Nov. 1840.
10   *Ibid.*, GC/RU/60/1–2, Russell to Palmerston, 4 Oct. 1841.
11   *LQV*, II, pp. 79–82, Palmerston to Melbourne, 26 Dec. 1845.
12   *LQV*, II, pp. 69–71, memorandum by Prince Albert, 20 Dec. 1845.
13   C. C. F. Greville, *The Greville Memoirs (second part): A Journal of the Reign of Queen Victoria, from 1837 to 1852*, ed. H. Reeve, 3 vols (London, 1885), II, p. 318 (12 Dec. 1845).
14   Durham University Library, Grey Papers, 3rd Earl, C3/12, 3rd Earl Grey, journal, 18 Dec. 1845.
15   F. A. Dreyer, 'The Russell Administration, 1846–52' (unpublished D.Phil thesis, University of St Andrews, 1962), p. 31. Dreyer claims to be able to trace this scheme of Grey's back to 1841 when Melbourne's government fell.
16   Broadlands Papers, SHA/PD/4, Shaftesbury diary, 22 Dec. 1845.
17   National Library of Scotland, Minto Papers, MS 11996, second Earl of Minto, journal, 2 Feb. 1850.
18   'Oh, he's a very foolish fellow, but we shall go on very well now', Palmerston is reported to have said to Shaftesbury, at this time: see A. Wyatt-Tilby, *Lord John Russell* (London, 1930), p. 106.
19   Prest, *Lord John Russell*, p. 219.
20   *LQV*, II, pp. 72–3, memorandum by Prince Albert, 20 Dec. 1845.
21   Broadlands Papers, GC/RU/99, Russell to Palmerston, 19 Dec. 1845.
22   Russell to Lady John Russell, 20 Dec. 1845, S. Walpole, *The Life of Lord John Russell*, 2 vols (London, 1889), I, p. 416.
23   See Broadlands Papers, RC/F/1–14 (letters from the Queen to Palmerston, 1837).
24   *Ibid.*, RC/F/212/1–4, Queen to Palmerston, 11 Nov. 1840. Brian Connell discerns in this letter the beginning of Prince Albert's influence over the Queen in such questions, B. Connell (ed.), *Regina v. Palmerston: The*

Correspondence between Queen Victoria and Her Foreign and Prime Minister, *1837–1865* (London, 1962), p. 27.

25 H. J. Hanham (ed.), *The Nineteenth Century Constitution* (Cambridge, 1969), p. 54, Sir H. Taylor to Earl Grey, 19 April 1832.

26 Broadlands Papers, RC/F/103, Queen to Palmerston, 9 May 1839.

27 *Ibid.*, RC/F/259, Queen to Palmerston, 30 Aug. 1841.

28 See Walpole, *Russell,* I, pp. 423–6.

29 E. Ashley, *The Life and Correspondence of Henry John Temple, Viscount Palmerston,* 2 vols (London, 1879), I, p. 499. See also the *Standard,* 8 July 1846, which reported that Palmerston's visit had 'improved the eeling which existed in regard to his intentions and policy'. Sir John Easthope, editor of the *Morning Chronicle,* appears to have played an important role in paving the way for Palmerston's favourable reception: see Broadlands Papers, GC/EA/45, Palmerston to Easthope, 2 May 1846; Sir John Easthope Papers, Duke University Special Collections Library, Easthope to Guizot, 1846 and Guizot to Easthope, 14 July 1846 (reply to Easthope's letter).

30 Cobden, touring Europe at this time, met Louis Philippe, King of France, in August and noted in his diary: 'He [Louis Philippe] was not very complimentary to Lord Palmerston, applying to him a French maxim which may be turned into the English phrase "if you bray a fool in a mortar he will remain a fool still"' (M. Taylor (ed.), *The European Diaries of Richard Cobden, 1846–1849* (Aldershot, 1994), p. 44 (6 Aug. 1846)).

31 Walpole, *Russell,* I, pp. 427–8, C. Wood to Russell, (?) 1 July 1846.

32 *Daily News,* 10 Aug. 1846.

33 *Standard,* 11 July 1846.

34 *The Times,* 7 July 1846.

35 *LQV,* II, pp. 101–3, memorandum by Prince Albert, 6 July 1846.

36 See, for example, Mandler, *Aristocratic Government,* pp. 13–120.

37 Dreyer 'The Russell Administration', p. 80; for more detail on voting patterns and party allegiance see pp. 80–2.

38 *LQV,* II, pp. 103–5, Queen to the King of the Belgians, 7, 14 July 1846. The Queen's faith in Aberdeen and Peel was not shared by Palmerston, however, who criticised Aberdeen for having damaged British interests by 'making himself under secretary to Guizot' (Russell Papers, Public Record Office, London, 30/22/5F, fols 96–7, Palmerston to Russell, 8 Dec. 1846). See also *ibid.*, PRO 30/22/5D, fols 114–15, Palmerston to Russell, 6 Oct. 1846.

39 M. Charlot, *Victoria: The Young Queen* (Oxford, 1991), p. 302, Aberdeen to Queen, Jan. 1844.

40 Russell Papers, PRO 30/22/7D, fols 115–17, Palmerston to Russell, 25 Sept. 1848.

41 Broadlands Papers, GC/RU/225/1–2, Russell to Palmerston, 1 Oct. 1848.

42 Eyck, *Prince Consort,* pp. 58–9.

43 Broadlands Papers, RC/F/438, Queen to Palmerston, 17 Feb. 1850.

44 Russell Papers, PRO 30/22/8C, fol. 358, Palmerston to Russell, 18 Feb. 1850. Palmerston argued that he had altered the draft according to an agreed version and that: 'I think however that you will see from what I have stated

that you have according to a Colloquial Phrase "picked me up before I was down"'.

45   Ashley, *Palmerston*, II, pp. 194–5.

46   Southgate, '*The Most English Minister* ...', pp. 192–3.

47   Chamberlain, *Palmerston*, p. 70.

48   Southgate, '*The Most English Minister* ...', p. 181.

49   William IV made relatively little trouble about foreign policy, perhaps because he placed great faith in the abilities of Palmerston. 'I believe I am the only one of the Ministers whom the King likes personally', the Foreign Secretary wrote to his brother, William Temple, in 1836. Quoted Webster, *The Foreign Policy of Palmerston*, I, p. 26.

50   Russell Papers, PRO 30/22/5B, fols 190–3, Palmerston to Russell, 14 July 1846.

51   Broadlands Papers, GC/RU/101, Russell to Palmerston, 15 July 1846.

52   See S. T. Bindoff, 'The Unreformed Diplomatic Service, 1812–1860', *Transactions of the Royal Historical Society*, 4th ser., XVIII (1935), pp. 160–5.

53   Broadlands Papers, RC/F/345, Queen to Palmerston, 5 Feb. 1848.

54   *Ibid.*, RC/F/477/1–2, Queen to Palmerston, 31 Jan. 1851.

55   *Ibid.*, GC/RU/214, Russell to Palmerston, 10 Aug. 1848.

56   *Ibid.*, RC/F/268, Queen to Palmerston, 17 Aug. 1846.

57   *Ibid.*, GC/RU/985, Palmerston to Russell, 23 Aug. 1846.

58   Russell Papers, PRO 30/22/6A, fols 56–8, Palmerston to Russell, 6 Jan. 1847.

59   Minto Papers, MS. 11996, Minto, journal, 22 May 1850.

60   *LQV*, II, p. 113, Prince Albert to Palmerston, 9 Aug. 1846.

61   Connell (ed.), *Regina v. Palmerston*, p. 78.

62   *Ibid.*, p. 80, Queen to Russell, 17 June 1848.

63   *Ibid.*, p. 80, Queen to Russell, 18 June 1848.

64   E. Longford, *Victoria, R.I.* (London, 1967 edn), p. 260, Lady Palmerston to Palmerston, 1848.

65   *LQV*, II, p. 132, Queen to Palmerston, 28 Nov. 1846.

66   Broadlands Papers, RC/F/316, Queen to Palmerston, 17 April 1847.

67   *Ibid.*, RC/F/432, Queen to Palmerston, 25 Dec. 1849.

68   British Library (hereafter B. L.), Lansdowne Papers, Lans. 3/42, fol. 30, Palmerston to Lansdowne, 27 March 1850.

69   Broadlands Papers, GC/RU/253, Russell to Palmerston, 3 Feb. 1849.

70   *Ibid.*, GC/RU/319, Russell to Palmerston, 18 Feb. 1850.

71   Ashley, *Palmerston*, II, p. 78, Palmerston to Normanby, 31 March 1848.

72   Russell Papers, PRO 30/22/7F, fols 343–5, Palmerston to Russell, 18 Jan. 1849.

73   Broadlands Papers, GC/RU/1058, Palmerston to Russell, 8 Nov. 1849.

74   *Ibid.*, GC/RU/241/enc. 1, Palmerston to Russell, 5 Jan. 1849 (copy).

75   Russell Papers, PRO 30/22/9E, fols 78–9, Queen to Russell, 12 Aug. 1850 (copy).

76   *Ibid.*, PRO 30/22/9E, fols 80–1, Palmerston to Russell, 13 Aug. 1850.

77   Palmerston wrote to his brother on 1 September 1850, in the aftermath of

Peel's death: 'Perhaps Sidney Herbert, or Aberdeen, or Gladstone may set up for leader of the Conservative Free Traders, or the Free Trade Conservatives; and perhaps Stanley may invite a junction with him by some compromise about putting off Protection. I have been told by a person who had it from Stanley himself, that during the time when a change of Government was expected, Aberdeen said to Stanley that in that case he, Aberdeen, would be commissioned by the Queen to form a Government! This would have been a curious dish to set before a Queen! On the whole, I rather am inclined to think that the Government is made stronger by the events of last session, and that we may look forward to getting successfully through the session of next year' (quoted Ashley, *Palmerston*, II, pp. 164–5).

78   Cf. Disraeli's regard for royal experience in the 1870s, arguably intended to flatter but nevertheless emphasising the importance of the Queen's experience above any other perceived royal qualities: 'It may be unconstitutional for a Minister to seek advice from his Sovereign, instead of proffering it; but … Your Majesty cannot but be aware how highly Mr Disraeli appreciates your Majesty's judgement and almost unrivalled experience in public life'. Disraeli to Queen, 17 April 1874, quoted Hardie, *The Political Influence of Queen Victoria*, pp. 37–8.

79   Broadlands Papers, RC/G/34, Queen to Russell, 5 Sept. 1859 (copy).

80   H. Hearder, 'Queen Victoria and Foreign Policy. Royal Intervention in the Italian Question, 1859–60', in K. Bourne and D. C. Watt (eds), *Studies in International History* (London, 1967), pp. 185–6.

81   Enrique (Enriquito), Duke of Seville, had been Palmerston's choice for suitor to Isabella, largely because of his connections with the English Liberal Party, Connell (ed.), *Regina v. Palmerston*, pp. 35–7. Christine was the Queen Mother.

82   *LQV*, II, pp. 121–3, Queen to the King of the Belgians, 14 Sept. 1846.

83   See, for example, *LQV*, II, pp. 214–15, Queen to Russell, 18 June 1848.

84   Broadlands Papers, RC/F/371/1–2, Queen to Palmerston, 1 July 1848.

85   *LQV*, II, pp. 237–8, Queen to King of the Belgians, 10 Oct. 1848.

86   Broadlands Papers, RC/H/38, Prince Albert to Palmerston, 9 May 1849.

87   *Ibid.*, RC/HH/4/1, Palmerston to Prince Albert, 19 June 1849 (copy).

88   Russell Papers, PRO 30/22/9, fols 9–10, Palmerston to Russell, 4 Sept. 1851.

89   Lansdowne Papers, Lans. 3/46, Albert to Lansdowne, 26 Nov. 1849, 29 Nov. 1850.

90   Grey Papers, 3rd Earl, C3/14, Grey, journal, 16 Aug. 1848.

91   Minto Papers, MS. 11997, Minto, journal, 26 June 1850.

92   Broadlands Papers, RC/F/350, Queen to Palmerston, 17 April 1848.

93   *Ibid.*, RC/F/362, Queen to Palmerston, 4 June 1848.

94   Guedalla, *Palmerston*, p. 253.

95   *LQV*, II, pp. 231–3, memorandum by the Queen, 19 Sept. 1848.

96   *Ibid.*, II, pp. 279–82, memorandum by Prince Albert, 3 Mar. 1850.

97   *Ibid.*, II, pp. 250–1, Russell to the Queen, 22 Jan. 1849; *ibid.*, II, p. 288, Russell to Prince Albert, 18 May 1850.

4

Palmerston and the politics of foreign policy, 1846–50

Given that the Cabinet was, according to Bagehot at least, the central focus of the legislature, it remained important, theoretically at least, that there should appear to be concurrence among its members in the line of policy to be pursued about any particular issue. Indeed, it was Palmerston who had established the principle of collective responsibility when, in 1838, he had defended the government's colonial policies on the grounds that all members of the ministry, and not just the Secretary of State, were responsible for government actions.[1] Towards the end of his career, Palmerston re-iterated the point in a letter to Gladstone, arguing that a minister 'divests himself of that perfect Freedom of individual action which belongs to a private and independent Member of Parliament', when joining a government.[2] When, in the early months of Russell's administration, Austria annexed the free state of Cracow and effectively signalled the extinction of this last remnant of an independent Poland, causing a breach of the Treaty of Vienna as well as affronting western liberal opinion,[3] the Prime Minister thought that 'so grave a proceeding, while the Cabinet is ready to assemble, ought to be placed before them'. Even though he was determined to support Palmerston's proposed course and expected little opposition, he would not allow such an important question to pass without consulting the Cabinet.[4]

Essentially Palmerston, and to a slightly lesser degree Russell, had to be the spring of business concerning foreign affairs if only because he was, and never tired of telling people, the one best qualified to pronounce on such questions. 'On matters where he fully believed that he was master of the subject his conclusions were very decided and positively unchangeable,' remembered the Earl of

Shaftesbury, who had good claims to know Palmerston's mind.[5] Palmerston was unwilling to subordinate himself to the Cabinet, not least because he believed there were 'very few public men in England who follow up foreign affairs sufficiently to foresee the consequences of events which have not happened'.[6] It was essential that Palmerston enjoyed the confidence of his colleagues and initially it appeared, outwardly at least, that he did. 'I have the greatest reliance on his sagacious perception of the true interests of his Country and I have the truest satisfaction in constant cooperation with him upon all our foreign relations', Russell told Count Jarnac, the French envoy, in October 1846, in a rejoinder to French insinuations that Palmerston was 'actuated by personal Feeling' in his conduct of foreign policy.[7]

Palmerston's foreign policy did not unite a Cabinet prone to division, however. From the outset, as we have seen, Lord Grey had had his reservations about Palmerston, and his fears were echoed in a pamphlet by a 'Free Trader' published in December 1845:

> You may think to control tendencies – but not intentions ... You may expect new things from caprice, but not from determined will ... You may check what you know, but you may be fatally committed by acts concealed and purposes unavowed. Such *has* been before, the case between us and this colleague – between him and Parliament ... [He] is not to be trusted. Be it from arrogance – be it from inveterate, unacknowledged, yet not deliberately culpable predilections if you will:– still, the fact remains, he has undershafts and galleries in which he labours at his solitary tasks ... which are only disclosed to us when some mine is to be sprung, when the match is already lighted, and we have nothing to do but retire behind the screens he provides ... [He] *cannot* be controlled, and ... we have oft-times been puppets in his hands ... Lord Palmerston cannot act secretly, and at the same time enjoy the benefits of frankness and candour.[8]

With the control of foreign policy in his hands, Palmerston's conduct raised fears among his colleagues which went beyond the domestic political implications of his actions. As Sir Charles Wood, who was concerned about Palmerston's Francophobic obsession with British defences, observed, while the difference between the two of them was 'of a very small amount, & arises a good deal from

my being *paymaster'*, he could not help but remark that he was 'sure
that the character we have to acquire & maintain, as a Government,
is that of being prudent steady people, & thus re-assuring the great
bulk of the world who have been taught to look upon us as likely
to set everything in a blaze, at home & abroad. We have quite
enough upon our hands at present'.[9] Concern spread also to sections
of the press, where, on the Tory side, for example, the *Standard*
grew ever more critical of the 'officious coxcombry' of 'an aged fop'
and by November was calling for Palmerston's removal.[10]

That national defence should have been such a live issue in the
late 1840s was not surprising, according to Wood for, as he told
Hobhouse, 'all the foolish alarm about [a French] invasion was
caused by Palmerston's correspondence & perpetual broils'.[11]
Palmerston might have aroused fears within the Cabinet, but concern about the state of national defence was a problem bequeathed
to the Russell Cabinet by Peel's Government and Palmerston's
pre-occupation with a potential French invasion originated in the
earlier 1840s. A conversation between Russell and the King of the
French in 1845, suggestive of a threat to Britain in its current
defenceless state, had highlighted the issue and convinced Palmerston of the need for action.[12] Although Palmerston was the only
consistent and pro-active advocate of greater defence provisions,
the issue was not without resonance for other ministers and the
opposition within the Government to expansion in the arrangements for national defence was based on questions of economic and
political (domestic rather than foreign) considerations, especially as
the issue became tied up with questions of a national militia.[13] Even
members of the Government who sympathised with Palmerston's
concern, such as Minto, eventually began to feel 'beaten & disheart-
ened, seeing the low views that prevailed in all great questions of
external policy' among the majority of the Cabinet.[14]

Palmerston's foreign policy became increasingly disagreeable
to many of his colleagues. As he emerged as the European figure
of 1848, it was not only the royal couple whose concerns about the
Foreign Secretary became more pronounced. 'His dispatches are ...
couched in a language that ought never to be addressed to an
independent state', wrote Hobhouse, the President of the Board of
Control, at the beginning of that year, 'and I think that his diplomatists – Bulwer and Normanby and Lyons mix themselves up a

good deal too much with the internal politics of the country to which they are sent'.[15]

Sir Henry Lytton Bulwer, the British Minister at Madrid, had been implicated in designs to re-introduce Leopold of Saxe-Coburg's name to the list of possible suitors to Queen Isabella, allegedly with Palmerston's approval, and his conduct caused particular consternation at home. In the autumn of 1847 Clarendon had confided to Lansdowne that he felt that although Bulwer 'writes very able dispatches & honestly thinks himself the pivot upon wch all things turn I fear he is usé & now not much made [?more] apt for business than the King is for matrimony'.[16] The Cabinet's doubts about Bulwer were not assuaged as Palmerston continued to withhold from them details of what was transacted between the Foreign Office and Bulwer. When Bulwer was expelled from Spain on account of his meddling in the internal affairs of that country, Palmerston successfully kept his colleagues in the dark and as Hobhouse recorded in his diary, 'we knew nothing of the Bulwer correspondence until it was over – nor did the Cabinet know that Bulwer's conduct had received the approbation of the Government until we saw the fact in the papers laid before Parliament'.[17] It may have been, as Palmerston maintained on one occasion, that it 'is of course for the Secy of State to judge what Papers in his office shall be laid before Parliament to Explain the Grounds on which the Government may have acted',[18] but it was dangerous for him to act without Cabinet support in this manner.

Only Russell's ineffectiveness preserved his position. He was not able to exercise a dominating influence over Palmerston, begging Lansdowne in March 1848 to interfere in the matter, 'before I say all I think' in an implicit acknowledgement of the political hold Palmerston had over the ministry.[19] As Lord Grey observed, this represented a 'very lamentable weakness' on Russell's part. 'Had P[almerston] played such a prank in my father's administrat'n', he continued, 'he wd have been dismissed without ceremony, nor can I conceive any prime minister submitting to such conduct without requiring it to be so punished'.[20] Grey believed that finally Palmerston would have to go. The Bulwer incident was merely the latest of many 'offences' and now Grey 'thought that it must have led either to Palmerston's retirement or the break up of the Govt. – the former wd. have given me infinite satisfact'n'.[21] But Palmerston had, by this point, further consolidated his popular, liberal reputation with the country, taking advantage of set-piece parliamentary and extra-parliamentary contests to underline his continued political vitality.

At the general election of 1847, he was given an important opportunity to test his popularity with the people of Tiverton in the face of the challenge from George Julian Harney. At first Palmerston was not unduly troubled: 'I have been so little with my Constituents of late', he told Russell, 'that I am advised to make a personal Canvass although I have no opponent but a certain Mr Harney a Chartist who announces his Intention of proving on the Hustings that I am not, and that he is, a fit Person to represent Tiverton. Such a Contest is more likely to be amusing than dangerous'.[22]

Harney ventured down to Tiverton with no more object than to 'get at' Palmerston. He arrived three days before the nomination was due, and attempted to whip up the electors with Chartist speeches and general charges against Palmerston. By the third and final speech, he had succeeded, it seemed, in winning the popular support of the people: 'The town was now in a very lively state; some thousands were at the meeting, and the enthusiasm of the Chartists rose to the highest pitch when Mr Harney concluded a lengthy and impassioned appeal … – "Tonight we sleep upon our arms; to-morrow we march to battle and victory!"'[23] The 'effect was electrical; one mighty roar of applause showed the delight and determination of the people', observed a partisan pamphlet afterwards.[24] Harney had addressed questions of education, the State Church, Ireland and the New Poor Law, but the main theme of his orations up to this point had been Palmerston's discreditable conduct. At the hustings, Harney promised, 'I will prove him to be devoid of true patriotism, a breaker of pledges, and a foe to the liberties of the people, whose dearest rights he will trample in the dust', promises that were met with 'tremendous cheering'.[25] It was not the policies which Palmerston represented that Harney sought to attack, but the image of Palmerston as a popular hero.

Harney ranged over the whole of Palmerston's ministerial career and endeavoured first to damn him by association with the governments headed by Spencer Perceval ('a constitutional tyrant'), Canning ('a clever jester, a talented buffoon, the able and brilliant flunkey of the aristocracy'), Wellington (the ally 'of despotism'), Melbourne (leader of 'the profligate Whig Government'), before entering into a careful and minute criticism of Palmerston's foreign policy since 1830.[26] Contrary to custom, Palmerston had waived his right to speak before Harney, preferring to make his defence in answer to charges actually made rather than assaults anticipated, though Harney's supporters had initially opposed this and Harney was allowed a second speech in which, having attacked Palmerston, he could discuss those reforms he deemed 'necessary for the welfare of the country'.[27] Both candidates appeared to appreciate that the theatrical nature of the platform addresses, where all speeches tended to be received with cheering, favoured the most recent speaker.

Palmerston 'was received with mingled cheers and groans' when he stood to answer Harney.[28] Harney's speech, Palmerston declared, was in many respects unobjectionable, but there were certain grounds upon which he took exception. Firstly, he sought to remedy a mis-representation, that 'I displayed a want of due feeling and sympathy for the misfortunes of the lower classes' in the House of Commons. Harney, he claimed, 'knows that what he has stated is not true (cries of "Oh, oh," and "Hear, hear")', given the approaching close of the parliamentary session when the subject was raised. Against Harney's other charges, Palmerston defended himself, and 'twitted' Harney 'with being a Tory in disguise'. He denied that his Irish estates yielded increased incomes, despite his attempts to improve them; he asserted that he was 'a decided advocate of reform', but that he wished to see it introduced 'by agitation of mind, and not by the agitation of physical force'; he acknowledged his political debt to Canning, but stressed the 'honour to his country' of Canning's conduct; he declared that he drew no distinction between Ireland and England nor Irish and English and fully supported attempts to relieve the distress caused by the famine; and he identified himself as a champion of factory, health and educational reform.[29] But he focused for the rest of his speech on foreign policy, his acknowledged specialism:

> Now, when I say that he knows nothing of the matters he has been talking of, all I mean is, that he appears to me to have got by rote a certain number of empty declamatory phrases (great laughter and

interruption), a jargon and jingle of words – (Renewed laughter and loud cheers) – which have no reference to facts, which have no bearing upon anything that has happened, and that his statements are founded on a total misconception of the history of the last twelve or fourteen years. Mr Harney is of opinion that the great object and the grand result of my foreign policy has been the establishment of tyranny and despotism all over the world – (A voice, 'So it has,' and laughter) – and the suppression of the liberties of the people.

This Palmerston found amusing, since, as he continued, 'I have been accused all over Europe of being the great instigator of revolution – (Laughter) – the friend and champion of all popular insurrections, the enemy of all constituted authorities', and this opinion, he said, was founded on 'matters which are not really matters of opinion'. Like his opponent, Palmerston retired from the front of the husting at the end of his speech, 'amid loud and prolonged cheering'.[30]

Harney might have won a show-of-hands poll on the day with a majority support of two-thirds of the audience, but until put to the test of an official ballot, which Harney declined to contest on the grounds that the existing franchise excluded 'the majority of adult male inhabitants of the borough',[31] the victory was somewhat illusory. Perhaps the show of hands demonstrated a ground swell of support among the disenfranchised, but it was from this same body that Palmerston also received loud and prolonged cheers. Harney may have seemed plausible as 'the friend of the people' which his proposer Rowcliffe had promised, but Palmerston, too, could offer similar rhetorical assurances, and crucially, he could also offer more convincing leadership. He was the gentleman leader, not *of* the people, but certainly *for* them. Harney's charges of illiberal and unpatriotic conduct did not stick, and even though doubts may have been expressed in certain middle-class, educated circles about Palmerston's sincerity,[32] he continued to flatter his audiences and exploit the need for strong-willed leadership, to be, as Carlyle would have had it, a great man.

Meanwhile, in Parliament, Chartists and Radicals found their charges against Palmerston were little better represented. David Urquhart, a disaffected former diplomat and polemicist on foreign affairs, had entered Parliament at the election of 1847 where he hoped he would be better able to condemn Palmerston as a Russian agent.[33] Outside Parliament Chartists had lent Urquhart measured support, doubting the veracity of Urquhart's charges of Palmerstonian treason and Russianism,[34] but this extra-parliamentary pressure seemed to be having comparatively little impact, and Urquhart sought a parliamentary role for himself, securing the seat for Stafford in the general election of 1847 standing as a Tory, but winning his seat with some Chartist support and later showing himself sympathetic to certain non-protectionist principles. Urquhart actually shared many radical concerns over questions of national expenditure (particularly the increasing army and navy estimates since 1835) and a commitment to free trade, which, along with his supposed Russophobia, underpinned much of his criticism of Whig foreign policy,[35] but principally he sought to attack Palmerston. Once in Parliament, he found in Thomas Anstey a recent but committed addition to the Urquhartite movement.[36] Anstey, a barrister and a Catholic, was, during this Parliament, MP for Youghal and while described as a Liberal, his political career appears somewhat erratic and inconsistent. Having acted alongside Urquhart in the later 1840s, Anstey was easily won over to Palmerston a decade later by means of a little Palmerstonian flattery.[37] Anstey's Urquhartism of the late 1840s speaks of little more than a temporary commitment, one which, nevertheless, promised at the time to be a useful source of Urquhartite strength which was still pre-eminently extra-parliamentary. In February 1848 Urquhart persuaded Anstey to introduce a motion in the House of Commons for the production of papers relating to British foreign policy since 1830 as a preliminary to an impeachment of Palmerston.[38]

On 1 March Palmerston came before the House to defend his record and delivered a speech which deflected the assault made by Anstey (but with which there was certainly much wider sympathy) and which has gone down as a defining exposition of Palmerstonian politics. Anstey's motion comprised forty points attacking Palmerston, but as the Foreign Secretary observed at the outset, he had 'skipped about from transaction to transaction, and jumbled the various matters adverted to in his notice in such a manner, that the topics of his speech might be likened to the confused mass of luggage brought to the Custom-house by some of the continental steamboats, when no man knows where he is to find his own'.[39] Nevertheless, Palmerston proceeded to address, as best he could, the charges point by point.[40] In defence of a certain degree of secrecy in diplomatic business, he argued that the competence of the Foreign Secretary would be undermined if all of his transactions were made public (although if the House wished to appoint a secret committee to go through the 2,775 volumes of documents, he wished 'them joy of their task'). He claimed that Anstey's arguments about the Treaty of Adrianople were ill-informed and charges against the Treaty of Unkiar Skelessi failed to appreciate the considerations by which it was necessary to balance steadfast defence of minute details against a desire to go to war. Palmerston acknowledged Urquhart's own role in helping to frame the Treaty of Commerce of 1838, but pointed out that this did not give Urquhart a direct say in the conduct of foreign policy and any belief that he had been wronged by the Foreign Secretary demonstrated a misunderstanding on the part of the Urquhartites of the constitutional position of a Secretary to an Embassy.[41] On the Treaty of 1840 and other questions, Palmerston was adamant that enough information had already been laid before Parliament and while happy to contest points, he felt confident that his conduct would be borne out by the balance of information available. Many of the charges were in some way designed to prove Palmerston's duplicitous connection with the Russian court. This general charge Palmerston refuted directly:

> what then becomes of the charge which the hon. and learned member makes against me of being such a determined instrument in the hands of Russia? He says from 1830 to 1839, during the nine years in which I was in the office I have now the honour to hold, there had been such mutual distrust between the English and the Russian Governments that it was necessary Baron Brunnow should be sent as Ambassador to represent the real views of the Emperor, in order to remove that distrust. I am satisfied with that statement, which is likely to be true.[42]

Palmerston defended his conduct and handling of various affairs against such charges and argued that his policy had been either misunderstood by Anstey, or had acquired validity through popular approval. Whenever there had been a genuine infringement of British interests or failure to fulfil treaty obligations (as it was perceived was the case with regard to Polish struggles against Russia), Palmerston maintained that this did not justify war. He concluded with the famous peroration that Britain had no eternal allies and no perpetual enemies, only interests that were eternal and perpetual, and in a catch-all defence of his career to date he concluded: 'And if I might be allowed to express in one sentence the principle which I think ought to guide an English Minister, I would adopt the expression of Canning, and say that with every British Minister the interests of England ought to be the shibboleth of his policy'.[43]

Palmerston effectively crushed this Urquhartite assault with his grandiloquence and confident manner.[44] It was also both the first and last significant attempt by the Urquhartites to effect a parliamentary defeat of Palmerston by direct means. They had found little support for their cause in the newspapers and within Parliament, and both Anstey and Urquhart found their stock much diminished. Jenks has written of how any further parliamentary efforts of Urquhart's were ridiculed, when they were listened to at all, for whenever he attempted to speak there was often either a 'general exodus' or 'obvious impatience, occasionally amounting to uproar'.[45]

Palmerston therefore by the late 1840s could argue that his foreign policy suited the mood of the nation and with popular backing his position at the Foreign Office appeared a strong one. Thus the Peelite Sir James Graham noted when Russell sought to strengthen the Government by bringing him into the Cabinet in January 1849, there were two main objections to joining the ministry. One was finance, the second the Foreign Secretary: 'Palmerston', he wrote to Peel, 'has had too much and too long his own way to yield either to the influence of his colleagues or to the control of public opinion'.[46] Such fears were not motivated simply by a determination to prevent Palmerston gaining too much in personal stature, but also by parliamentary considerations.

Although by 1850 it seemed that almost every aspect of the ministry's business was under attack,[47] up to this point, much of the Government's strength had derived from the fact that its opponents, still reeling from the rupture caused by Peel in 1846, could not present a viable alternative to the Government. Opposition members had good reason to desire the preservation of the Government, as Minto discovered when he shared a train ride with a group of 'ultra-tories' in late 1848. They had been 'amusingly complimentary to Lord J. Russell & anxious for his continuance in power; this being the expression of their fear and hatred of Peel their old idol', he noted in his journal afterwards, adding that 'we were all very good friends notwithstanding my Whiggism'.[48] Indeed, Palmerston's foreign policy tended to find a favourable reception across the floor of the House of Commons, not least because of Disraeli's connection with the Foreign Secretary. In December 1845, Disraeli had acted as Palmerston's go-between in Paris, exploiting his contacts with the King of the French, whom he persuaded that 'all may be well' with Palmerston at the Foreign Office after all. Disraeli also indicated a sympathetic desire to assist Palmerston in the presentation of his foreign policy in the House of Commons.[49] Indeed, two years after the formation of the Russell Government, Disraeli conceded that: 'As for Palmerston, I have not only not opposed him, but, to the occasional dissatisfaction of my comrades, have even interfered to prevent parliamentary criticism, or any concerted move, against him'.[50] The extent to which he was 'Palmerston's factotum' says Vincent, cannot be ascertained, but nevertheless it was remarkable that a Tory politician was working secretly for a Whig leader.[51] In the later 1840s, indeed, Vincent has suggested that Disraeli sought a diplomatic posting from Palmerston in return for the services rendered in Paris, and again in 1855 that Palmerston proposed Disraeli for the Istanbul embassy, although Vincent offers no evidence to corroborate this latter 'secret connection'.[52]

If nothing else, Palmerston and Disraeli shared a certain common heritage in their reverence for George Canning. As he demonstrated in his biography of Lord George Bentinck, a Canningite Tory of former days, Disraeli had learned the importance of extra-parliamentary support, repeating Bentinck's judgement that once the 'people out of doors [are] with you', then 'all the rest follows'.[53] More explicitly, Disraeli had laid claim to a share of the Canningite legacy in 1845 when he told the Commons that the name of Canning was 'never to be mentioned, I am sure, in the House of Commons without emotion. We all admire his genius; we all, at least most of us, deplore his untimely end; and we all sympathize with him in his fierce struggle with supreme prejudice and sublime mediocrity, – with inveterate foes, and with – "candid friends"'.[54] Disraeli's Canningite sympathies may have weakened his position within the party, as Edward Henry Stanley, later the 15th Earl of Derby, suggested when he observed in May 1850 that Disraeli, 'wanted, like Canning, to combine Liberal ideas with Tory connections: but Canning had failed. There is certainly a very prevalent impression that Disraeli has no well-defined opinions of his own: but is content to adopt, and defend, any which may be popular with the Conservative party at the time'.[55] Disraeli had long maintained that in politics 'I come forward on independent grounds, & am resolved to coalesce with no one',[56] but it was not possible for him to remain entirely indifferent to party connection.[57] Hence the impression that he took up only what was popular with the Conservative party at any given moment.

Not only did Disraeli share an admiration for an old political leader with Palmerston; he also looked to Palmerston himself with a good deal of approval. He had warmly applauded Palmerston's speech on the Corn Laws in March 1846,[58] and once Palmerston had returned to the Foreign Office, Disraeli was gratified to learn from Jarnac, the French ambassador, 'that foreign affairs are all right' and that 'every thing went right betn. Palmerston & France, except the Sonderbund affair & that they were in almost hourly expectation of his acceding to the solicitation of all the other great powers under the Treaty of Vienna, for a mediation'.[59]

Disraeli still, after all, regarded Palmerston as 'a man for whom I have the greatest regard, & a statesman for whom I have always entertained the greatest admiration'.[60] Palmerston's political conduct, though it may have possessed no didactic force in the Disraelian mind, at least mirrored to a large extent Disraeli's own conception of the political nation. While Disraeli claimed never to have welcomed letters from his Buckinghamshire constituents,[61] this was more an example of his style than a statement of fact. The moral (such as it was) of Disraeli's novels *Coningsby* (1844) and *Tancred* (1847), says Paul Smith, is that 'social and political reconstitution, the building of community out of conglomeration, depended on the power, not of the politician to manipulate elites, but of the genius to mobilise masses'.[62] Novel writing for Disraeli, argues Smith, in the 1840s particularly, 'was his means of by-passing a Conservative party and a House of Commons too slow to recognize his pre-eminence and appealing directly to a public opinion conceived as more powerful than an effete aristocratic elite'. In the

Vindication of the English Constitution (1835) and *Coningsby*, Disraeli demonstrated his belief that legitimate political authority derived from extra-parliamentary opinion and found its expression in the newspaper press.[63] These opinions he had arrived at quite independently of any example offered by Palmerston.

So far as he did lead opposition to Palmerston's foreign policy, then, Disraeli was forced into such a position largely by virtue of the adversarial nature of politics. Even when Disraeli did attack the foreign policy of the Government, he sought to absolve Palmerston personally. Vincent suggests that Disraeli fashioned much of his political agenda before 1865 in a sort of inverse relationship to Palmerston: Palmerston represented national interests and therefore Disraeli had to look to questions of social cohesion. In the 1850s and 1860s, Vincent contends, 'Disraeli was reduced to seeking any position that was not occupied by Palmerston',[64] although this rule does not apply universally: over Ireland and (before 1866) Reform, for example, Vincent's argument is unconvincing. Robert Blake's argument that Disraeli was 'the first statesman systematically to uphold the doctrine that it is the duty of the Opposition to oppose' seems most pertinent.[65]

By the summer of 1848 Disraeli was much under the influence of Prince Metternich and the two met frequently to discuss political affairs.[66] This connection, according to Disraeli's official biographers, served to inform the two speeches Disraeli delivered during the summer of 1848 in which he offered an alternative to the Government's foreign policy.[67] In June, taking as his subject the dismissal of his friend Bulwer from Madrid – 'a gross outrage has been inflicted upon this country' – Disraeli set about attacking the system of a liberal foreign policy. 'My objection to liberalism is this – that it is the introduction into the practical business of life of the highest kind – namely, politics – of philosophical ideas instead of political principles', he said. Palmerston, he acknowledged, was 'the great prophet of liberalism in foreign affairs', and indeed was 'the most able expounder' of the strain of liberalism embodied in the Quadruple Alliance of 1834 'which has been the characteristic of the foreign policy of England now for too many years'. However, significantly, Disraeli blamed the Liberal ministries and not Palmerston himself for this 'sentimental' approach to politics. He further exonerated Palmerston of blame for the course of foreign relations highlighting the damaging effects of the Foreign Secretary's lack of Cabinet support, something particularly unsettling to the French government he claimed. 'I am exceedingly loth to assent to any vote which singles out the noble Lord [Palmerston] as a Member of the Government who has followed a policy so pernicious to this country', argued Disraeli. 'We ought to strike at the system, and not at the individual'.[68]

The following month, Disraeli 'crossed lances with Palmerston' in a speech which dealt with British relations with Rome, Naples, Sardinia and Austria.[69] He feared that 'the sentimental principle' which guided the country's foreign policy was 'to develop the principle of nationality', but this appeared to Disraeli to raise immediate contradictions regarding the plan for independence for Lombardy but not Venetia. 'If this House does not take the earliest opportunity to discourage the sentimental principle in settling the affairs of nations', he argued, 'I am convinced that we shall be involved in difficulties which it is impossible to contemplate; for I believe that such a policy, if it be fully developed, will really resolve Europe into its original elements, and will not leave any social or political system in existence in the form which it now assumes'. It behoved the Foreign Secretary, Disraeli concluded, to demonstrate a determination to uphold 'the principles of national law'.[70] Palmerston, Disraeli clearly felt, was unpleasantly constrained by the over-arching principles of the government to which he belonged which were serving to confuse and weaken the country's foreign policy. A year later Disraeli, however, seemed to be losing faith in the Foreign Secretary, telling Metternich that the perusal of papers relating to Italy had 'somewhat lowered my opinion of Palmerston. He has been fortunate, but he has not deserved to be *felix*'.[71]

Ultimately Palmerston weathered Conservative attacks and, whether deserved or not, was *felix*. To a large extent this was due to a certain sympathy on Disraeli's part, but was also grounded in much more pragmatic political considerations. Throughout the life of the Government, Russell's ministry appeared weak and there was a constant search for a replacement. Among the Protectionists there was a disposition in the late 1840s to seek a reunion with the Peelites, but this would have required Palmerston to be replaced at the Foreign Office with Aberdeen, assuming Palmerston would not defect from his Whig colleagues. Aberdeen, however, was not

likely to accede to such a scheme even if other Peelites were and
this in itself offered an insuperable obstacle to notions of a new
Conservative administration. As Edward Stanley noted in May
1849, 'Lord Aberdeen's final alienation from us makes it useless to
displace Palmerston'.[72] By 1850, with Peel's death, however, one of
the greatest obstacles to unity among those sitting on the opposition
benches had been removed. This was particularly significant given
that Palmerston was being accused in some quarters of being no
longer up to his task, especially in the light of his 'failed' Italian
policy. Palmerston's position seemed ever more vulnerable and
though something which he would never have conceded, and succeeded in disguising quite well, nevertheless illustrated that he
needed the Cabinet on his side. Even Grey admitted in a letter to
Russell, any policy sanctioned by the Cabinet would of necessity be
consistently defended by that Cabinet. 'But', he added,

> when the fact is, that the subject never was brought before the
> Cabinet, when I & most of the members of it first saw the objec-
> tionable despatches in the newspapers, & when it is notorious that
> if the questn. had been submitted to us, we shd most of us (I believe
> including yourself) have entirely disapproved of the adoptn. of such
> a tone towards an independent Govt, the case is entirely altered, &
> I can recognize no obligatn. to support a policy which none of our
> opponents can condemn more than I do.[73]

For practical reasons and because the Cabinet had to endorse policy
in this way, there emerged something of an inner Cabinet on foreign
affairs, not in itself a novelty in nineteenth-century governments,
comprising primarily Palmerston, Russell and Lansdowne. Lansdowne was the Government's spokesman in the Lords on foreign
policy and thus would be expected to be intimately acquainted with
the details of Foreign Office business, but he was not expected, by
Russell at least, simply to peddle the Palmerstonian line. On a point
about a draft written by Palmerston in June 1848, Russell declared
that he was 'willing to be guided by Lansdowne's opinion & shall
send this note to him'.[74] Lansdowne himself assumed the function
of adviser happily, recognising Palmerston's field of expertise and
responsibility, but answered Russell's injunctions, for example, to
'write anything that occurs to me with the papers enclosed in this
box', and offered Palmerston advice without issuing orders.[75] In

return, Lansdowne expected similar fair dealing from Palmerston, which was not always forthcoming. 'Palmerston is very obliging in sending me a good deal of private information which he receives', wrote Lansdowne, 'but very seldom the private instructions which he sends'.[76]

Palmerston however, had little patience with Cabinet interference in the details of his policy. Once the general principles had been established he expected a large degree of independence and established very early on in the life of the Government that if he could not count on that, then his position would have to be reconsidered.[77] Nevertheless, given that Lansdowne had to defend the Government's policy in the upper House, Palmerston's stubbornness was a great nuisance.

Other ministers, such as Clarendon, Sir Charles Wood, Minto, Grey and Labouchere, did make observations about policy but they were apparently infrequent and inconsistent. The voicing of unease about specific questions, or the tone of the occasional draft, did not constitute profound and influential counsel, or even intimacy with the conduct of foreign affairs. Perhaps more than ever before, foreign politics was becoming a field of special expertise which demanded a serious commitment, not a trifling interest. Russell for one acknowledged this, telling Palmerston on one occasion when German affairs were pressing that: 'You who are constantly treating in these matters are alone able to judge what is the real meaning'.[78] Even Earl Grey, arguably one of Palmerston's sternest critics, found little time to write to Palmerston to discuss foreign policy, confining his correspondence to a relatively innocuous commentary on colonial affairs.[79] Charles Wood and Clarendon both sought to offer advice, but stopped short of trying to exercise control, acknowledging that they had neither the time nor the grounding in foreign affairs for such a task. Few other Cabinet members apparently concerned themselves with foreign policy outside the Cabinet meetings at all.

Within the Cabinet, however, debates over foreign policy were often the scene of bitter encounters. Significantly though, such conflicts were generally dictated more by partisan interests among the Cabinet's factions than by disagreements about the policy itself. Minto identified a 'Grey faction' within the Cabinet on foreign questions, comprising Lord Grey, Sir George Grey and Sir Charles Wood, but also including Sir Francis Baring, Lord Carlisle (who

had been, until 1848, Lord Morpeth) and possibly Henry Labouchere
which offered a regular line of opposition to Palmerston's foreign
policy and which stood as a counter-point to the pro-Palmerston
lobby of Russell, Lansdowne, Lord Campbell and Minto himself.[80]
Earl Grey became something of a *de facto* leader of this body of
dissent and frequently urged Russell to 'interfere more regularly'
in Palmerston's handling of foreign affairs.[81] Ideally, Grey would
have welcomed Palmerston's removal from office completely and in
1849 when the supply of arms to Sicily exposed Palmerston to
censure, it seemed to Grey and his allies that an opportunity to
effect such a result had arisen. In late 1848 Palmerston had effectively sanctioned the supply of arms to rebels in Sicily by a British
arms manufacturer by approving the return to the manufacturer,
whose own reserves were low, of a surplus supply which had already
been delivered to the British War Office that could then be sent to
Sicily. The story broke in *The Times* in January 1849 and was taken
by European conservatives as evidence that Palmerston was encouraging and even instigating revolution in Europe.[82]

In collaboration with Sir George Grey and Wood, Grey urged
upon the Prime Minister the desirability of dismissing the Foreign
Secretary, though Grey himself refrained from pressing the call too
firmly himself because of 'what happened in Dec/45'.[83] In a Cabinet
meeting to discuss the issue, however, such hopes were soon dashed,
much to Grey's disappointment: 'There was then some vague discuss'n in wh I was to the last degree disgusted by the apparent
insensibility of the Cabinet to the gravity of the case & to the
disgraceful figure the Govt will make in pleading "inadvertence" as
the excuse for such a proceeding. I endeavoured to treat the matter
somewhat more seriously & to show how bad a posit'n we shd be
placed in but nobody backed me'.[84]

Despite considerable Cabinet reservations about the course the
Foreign Secretary was pursuing, it seemed that there was little to
be done to alter that course and even Grey was forced, reluctantly,
to acquiesce in the policy rather than take responsibility for an
action which would almost certainly end in the break up of the
Government.[85] Meanwhile, Palmerston, perhaps guilty, as Minto
once observed, of trusting too much to fortune,[86] turned an attack
into a source of strength. 'The foolish and ignorant manner in wh
he has been attacked has almost set on its legs a policy for which

I fear the case is not really so good as it has appeared', complained Grey in defeat.[87]

Russell was in many ways susceptible to strong members of the Government taking policy hostage. Minto, while recognising Russell's sympathy for the Sicilian cause, had expressed concern in October 1848, fearing that the Prime Minister might be forced 'to yield to the opinions of some whose resignation must break up his government'.[88] This supposed threat from the Grey party eventually came to nothing, but Palmerston was able to exercise a similar influence over Russell. More than most other areas of business, foreign policy remained an area in which it was possible for a strong minister to dominate the Prime Minister, although the fragile foundations of this government were also exposed over other contentious issues such as Ireland. Only on the thorny issue of electoral reform did Russell appear inflexible: 'Lord John will not consent to abandon his intention, there is no doubt that the rest will give way to his determination', observed Minto in late 1850.[89] To some extent, by 1850, the political atmosphere was different, but foreign policy remained a unique area of business.

Nevertheless, accounts of Cabinet meetings sent to the Queen displayed no sign of discord and presented all decisions as collective ones.[90] In discussion of foreign questions, only on the question of Palmerston's proposed reception of Kossuth in December 1851 did Russell inform the members of the Cabinet that he 'would not ask for any collective resolution', but he did stress in his report to the Queen that there had been general agreement that Palmerston should not receive him.[91] Palmerston, when deputising for Russell, used these official communications with the Queen as an opportunity to expound the principles of his policy at length, but here too there is little evidence of the Cabinet discord that did occur.[92] The Queen, however, clearly suspicious about this degree of supposed accord, and perhaps disappointed that Palmerston was not being more severely checked by his colleagues, asked on one occasion to see the Cabinet minutes discussing the Sicilian guns question. Minto thought this 'strange ignorance on her part, as she ought to have known that there are no minutes of matters treated of in the Cabinet', but it also left the field open to intrigue and he expected 'some mischief' to occur during the forthcoming visit to Windsor of George Grey and Charles Wood.[93]

Thus it was on two broad counts that Palmerston needed the backing of the Cabinet; both constitutionally and in order indeed to underwrite his own political survival. As Russell put it to Palmerston as the latter drew close to his last days at the Foreign Office:

> Seeing the persevering enmity which the foreign policy of the Government excites, & the displeasure with which it is viewed in high quarters, I think it behoves you to guard most carefully against misapprehensions as well as misrepresentations. I think you owe this to me, & to your other colleagues who have stood by you in defence of the course which has been pursued in regard to our foreign relations. I think you owe it to the country, which in these difficult times ought not to be exposed in case of a rupture, to encounter unnecessary odium from the governments that be. I trust therefore without swerving an inch from our policy, you will avoid as much as possible, giving cause for irritation and hostility.[94]

Furthermore, there was a genuine sense in which the Cabinet could fulfil a useful advisory and consultative role. As Palmerston admitted, some questions stretched his capabilities to their limit and beyond. Italy in 1848, for instance, he described as 'a chaotic Labyrinth through which I can not see my way'.[95] More than this, some members of the Cabinet could bring to the Foreign Secretary's attention important information and sidelights on events which were to be gained from no other source. Clarendon, in particular, was valuable in this respect. From the Board of Trade he wrote to Palmerston with news from his clandestine 'Paris informant', probably the Paris correspondent of *The Times*, M. Reilly,[96] who was able to supply Clarendon with inside information about the French Government. Clarendon willingly shared this information 'not because it is of much consequence but because you may think it worth while to watch the unscrupulous lies that the late entente cordiale may tell'.[97] Certainly Palmerston can only have received gratefully the news that a foreign prince visiting London had told the King of the French, Louis Philippe, 'qu'il prie le gou[vernem]ent français de ne pas faire de concession à L[ord] P[almerston] parceque nous pouvons par lui correspondre avec la Reine et le Prince Albert'.[98]

Still, whatever the benefits, there were, for Palmerston, limits. However politically costly, he would not sacrifice what he believed were *his* duties and responsibilities. So long as he was at the Foreign

Office, he would do the job of Foreign Secretary, and not until he was replaced would he relinquish this role. His attitude towards the Cabinet and its role in foreign policy did not mellow with age. As Clarendon recalled to Sir George Cornewall Lewis, when Clarendon had served as Foreign Secretary in Palmerston's first ministry: 'I remember once [Palmerston] agreeing with me that Vera Cruz ought to be blockaded, and desiring me to write accordingly to the Admiralty. I said – "Surely not without bringing it before the Cabinet?" – "Oh ah: the Cabinet," was his answer, "very well; call one then, if you think it necessary"'.[99]

Since this cavalier approach antagonised some members of the Government just as it did the Queen and Prince, Russell's role as arbitrator was vital, to keep 'his incendiary Foreign Secretary in order'.[100] Sir Charles Wood recognised this at a very early stage and hoped Russell would satisfy this need. He warned that a state of hostile feeling had been produced over relations with France and concluded: 'I press upon you to look to these things yourself. I see no other remedy. The Cabinet cannot interfere, for the mischief is done before we hear of anything. It is no easy matter, I am well aware, even for you … Forgive me venturing to intrude all this advice, but I am not a little alarmed'.[101] The Queen equally placed much faith in Russell's ability to rein in Palmerston. He had, she believed, 'the power of exercising that control over Lord Palmerston, the careful exercise of which he owes to the Queen, his colleagues, and the country, if he will take the necessary pains to remain firm'.[102]

Russell recognised his position as umpire within the Government, not only between the Court and Foreign Office, but also between Palmerston and his other colleagues, and felt confident that, in the final analysis, his decision was binding.[103] To some extent Russell did succeed in keeping Palmerston in check, indeed the Foreign Secretary was, according to Minto, 'more hampered than I shd like to be in the conduct of his department by Lord John's controul',[104] but there were political exigencies which demanded this. By 1850, however, with Peel dead and opposition members increasingly able to offer an alternative ministry, and with internal Cabinet divisions bespeaking ever more fracture and defection rather than consideration of broader interests,[105] Palmerston's position became proportionately stronger. Though a situation that would not last, for the time being, there were fewer interests for which he might reasonably be sacrificed and more reasons for retaining him for his own sake. Palmerston's popularising of foreign policy struck a chord at all levels of society and he found various and diverse confirmations of the positive effects of such images with regard to his own popularity and standing. In June 1848 'A Constituent', who had been an elector for the University of Cambridge when Palmerston had represented that particular seat, wrote to the Foreign Secretary noting that he found that 'in every part of Europe, that you were the Representative of my inviolability and dignity as an Englishman' (an interesting prologue to Palmerston's *civis Romanus sum* speech of two years later). Significantly, the anonymous correspondent, assuring Palmerston of his political impartiality and desirous of apprising the Foreign Secretary of reliable intelligence, proceeded to make the following observations:

> First as to yourself. The English People trouble themselves very little about foreign politics. This arises partly from the low estimation in which they hold all Foreigners; but principally from the neglected state of general Education. The masses know so little of the geographical division of Europe, that the great majority of them might reverse the position of the Alps and the Pyrenees, or annex Spain to Italy or Germany. So they wisely avoid discussions of these subjects. Yet they fully recognize in you the Protector of constitutional Freedom on the Continent; and they consider England's honour and interests safe in your hands.[106]

It might have been true, as this writer asserted, that some of the English People were critical of certain aspects of Palmerston's Spanish policy, but essentially Palmerston had won more than just support for his political conduct, he had gone some way towards fashioning himself as 'England's Protector'. Other letters from members of the public echoed this impression. In May 1850 'A Commercial Traveller' wrote from Portsmouth seeking to reassure Palmerston as the Greek question brought foreign policy to the fore and the Don Pacifico debate loomed:

> I think it only right that you should know the feeling of the people generally of this country toward you at such a time as this & more particularly when the leading paper of the day is so mis-representing

every thing connected with the Foreign Policy of the Country. Sensible Englishmen are proud My lord to think they have so experienced & excellent a statesman filling the office you now do – you may depend you have their entire confidence. I visit many Towns & converse with numbers & I can safely say My Lord your Foreign Policy is approved by the very great majority & we all trust (as we feel sure) you will for many many years continue to serve the Country in your present official situation. *The Times* paper perhaps in the pay of the Despots does not represent the opinions of the people of this country on Foreign questions.[107]

A newspaper editor, James Birch of the *World*, was also keen to redress the false impression given in certain quarters, notably *The Times*, of the state of Palmerston's standing in the country at large:

It is impossible now to penetrate into any circle – high or low – to travel by land or water – whether you enter the aristocratic Club – or the humble free and easy or *sans souce* [sic] of the artisan – the mart of commerce – or the threepenny omnibus – without hearing the policy of Lord Palmerston discussed – and as much as it is discussed – warmly applauded. Your Lordship I do believe is now one of the most popular Ministers that ever swayed the destiny of affairs in England.[108]

Such, then, was the reported state of feeling when Palmerston was called to account by the House of Commons after a defeat for the Government in the Lords over his handling of the affairs of Greece and of Don Pacifico in particular.

Notes

1   Jenkins, *Parliament, Party and Politics in Victorian Britain*, p. 39.
2   Palmerston to Gladstone, 16 June 1864, in P. Guedalla (ed.), *Gladstone and Palmerston: Being the Correspondence of Lord Palmerston with Mr. Gladstone, 1851–1865* (London, 1928), p. 288.
3   See M. E. Chamberlain, *'Pax Britannica'?: British Foreign Policy 1789–1914* (Harlow, 1988), pp. 92–3.
4   Broadlands Papers, GC/RU/123, Russell to Palmerston, 13 Nov. 1846.
5   Southgate, *'The Most English Minister ...'*, p. 243, Shaftesbury to Evelyn Ashley, 6 Jan. 1876. Shaftesbury was Palmerston's step-son-in-law.
6   *Ibid.*, p. 243, Palmerston to Granville, 5 June 1838.

7   Russell Papers, PRO 30/22/5D, fols 302–5, Russell to Jarnac, 26 Oct. 1846; *Ibid.*, PRO 30/22/5D, fols 289–90, Palmerston to Russell, 25 Oct. 1846.

8   *Lord Grey and Lord Palmerston. A Letter Addressed to the Right Honourable T. B. Macaulay, M.P. on the occasion of his Letter to Mr M'Farlane, from a Free Trader* (London, 1846), pp. 18–19.

9   Broadlands Papers, GC/WO/20, C. Wood to Palmerston, 26 Dec. 1846.

10   *Standard*, 3, 13, 18 Nov. 1846.

11   B.L., Add. Mss. 43751, Broughton Diaries, 28 Jan. 1848.

12   Broadlands Papers, SHA/PD/3, Shaftesbury Diaries, 31 March 1845.

13   M. S. Partridge, 'The Russell Cabinet and National Defence, 1846–1852', *History*, 72 (1987), 231–50.

14   Minto Papers, MS. 11996, Minto, journal, 9 Feb. 1850.

15   B.L., Add. Mss. 43751, Broughton Diaries, 28 Jan. 1848.

16   Lansdowne Papers, Lans. 3/31, fol. 18, Clarendon to Lansdowne, 26 Oct. 1847.

17   B.L., Add. Mss. 43752, Broughton Diaries, 3 June 1848.

18   Russell Papers, PRO 30/22/9A, fols 226–7, Palmerston to Russell, 25 Jan. 1851.

19   Lansdowne Papers, Lans. 3/43, fol. 42, Russell to Lansdowne, 2 March 1848.

20   Grey Papers, 3rd Earl, C3/14, Grey, journal, 5 May 1848.

21   *Ibid.*, C3/14, Grey, journal, 7 May 1848.

22   Russell Papers, PRO 30/22/6D, fols 199–200, Palmerston to Russell, 25 July 1847.

23   Snell, *Palmerston's Borough*, p. 84.

24   *The Trial and Condemnation of Lord Viscount Palmerston, at Tiverton, July 30, 1847, containing a verbatim report of the speech of G. Julian Harney, the People's Member for Tiverton* (London, 1847), p. 3.

25   Snell, *Palmerston's Borough*, p. 78.

26   *Trial and Condemnation of Lord Viscount Palmerston*, pp. 4–11; Snell, *Palmerston's Borough*, pp. 79–80, 85–6.

27   *Trial and Condemnation of Lord Viscount Palmerston*, p. 3.

28   *Ibid.*, p. 11.

29   *Speech of Lord Viscount Palmerston, Secretary of State for Foreign Affairs, to the Electors of Tiverton, on the 31st July 1847* 2nd edn (London, 1847), pp. 3–16; *Trial and Condemnation of Lord Viscount Palmerston*, p. 11.

30   Snell, *Palmerston's Borough*, pp. 22–3, 38.

31   *Trial and Condemnation of Lord Viscount Palmerston*, p. 12. Harney did, however, pledge in an open letter to 'The Electors and Non-Electors of Tiverton' of 10 Aug. 1847 to go to the poll 'whenever another election shall take place' (Broadlands Papers, BR 195 pt. 2).

32   Snooks (pseud.), *A letter to Lord Palmerston, on the 'Condition of England Question,' elicited by his speech to the electors of Tiverton* (London, 1847), pp. 25–6.

33   For background on Urquhart see: M. H. Jenks, 'The Activities and Influence of David Urquhart, 1833–56, with Special Reference to the Affairs of the Near East' (unpublished PhD thesis, University of London, 1964);

R. T. Shannon, 'David Urquhart and the Foreign Affairs Committees', in
P. Hollis (ed.), *Pressure from Without in Early Victorian England*, pp. 239–61;
M. Taylor, 'The Old Radicalism and the New: David Urquhart and the
Politics of Opposition, 1832–1867', in E. F. Biagini and A. J. Reid (eds),
*Currents of Radicalism: Popular Radicalism. Organised Labour and Party Politics
in Britain, 1850–1914* (Cambridge, 1991), pp. 23–43; C. Webster, 'Urquhart,
Ponsonby and Palmerston', *English Historical Review*, 62 (1947), 327–51;
A. J. P. Taylor, *The Trouble Makers: Dissent and Foreign Policy, 1792–1939*
(Harmondsworth, 1985 edn), pp. 40–67.

34 See, for example, Harney's speech at Tiverton in 1847 in which he observed
that with regard to Urquhart's accusations of Palmerston's Russianism, 'I
never believed anything of the sort' (*Trial and Condemnation of Lord Viscount
Palmerston*, p. 8).

35 Taylor, 'The Old Radicalism and the New', pp. 30–1.

36 See Jenks, 'The Activities and Influence of David Urquhart', pp. 262–3.

37 Ridley, *Palmerston*, pp. 334, 524–5.

38 *Hansard*, 3rd ser., XCVI, 291–311, 1132–242 (8, 23 Feb. 1848).

39 *Hansard*, 3rd ser., XCVII, 67 (1 March 1848).

40 *Hansard*, 3rd ser., XCVII, 66–123 (1 March 1848).

41 This was ironic given that, as Asa Briggs has noted, in his Foreign Affairs
Committees, Urquhart directed that among the subjects for study were 'the
Constitution of England: what it is', the Privy Council, 'the necessity of
Impeachment', 'why the law is the safeguard of our liberties' and, most
significantly, 'Ambassadors and their Use'. See A. Briggs, 'David Urquhart
and the West Riding Foreign Affairs Committees', *Bradford Antiquary*, 39
(1958), p. 204.

42 *Hansard*, 3rd ser., XCVII, 80 (1 March 1848).

43 *Hansard*, 3rd ser., XCVII, 123 (1 March 1848).

44 Cf. the *Standard* of 2 March 1848 which concluded that Palmerston's defence
had 'left the case pretty much where it was before'.

45 Jenks, 'The Activities and Influence of David Urquhart, 1833–56', pp. 269–
72.

46 Dreyer 'The Russell Administration', p. 148, Graham to Peel, 16 Jan. 1849.

47 *Ibid.*, pp. 171–2.

48 Minto Papers, MS. 11995, Minto, journal, 4 Dec. 1848.

49 *Benjamin Disraeli Letters*, vols III–V (1838–41; 1842–47; 1848–51),
M. G. Wiebe, J. B. Conacher, J. Matthews and M. S. Millar (eds) (Toronto,
1987; 1989; 1993); vol. VI (1852–56), M. G. Wiebe, M. S. Millar and
A. P. Robson (eds) (Toronto, 1997) (hereafter *Disraeli Letters*), IV, 1453,
Disraeli to Palmerston, 14 Dec. 1845.

50 *Ibid.*, V, 1664, Disraeli to Ponsonby, 9 July 1848.

51 J. Vincent, *Disraeli* (Oxford, 1990), p. 4.

52 *Ibid.*, p. 32. 'Tory leaders are not often agents for Liberal Foreign Secretaries', says Vincent, 'which is maybe why the evidence has again disappeared.
But there was certainly a secret connection'.

53 B. Disraeli, *Lord George Bentinck: A Political Biography* (London, 1905 edn), p. 376.

54 *Hansard*, 3rd ser., LXXVIII, 155–6 (28 Feb. 1845).

55 J. R. Vincent (ed.), *Disraeli, Derby and the Conservative Party: Journals and Memoirs of Edward Henry, Lord Stanley, 1849–1869* (Hassocks, 1978), p. 29 (25 July 1850).

56 *Disraeli Letters*, IV, 1568, Disraeli to [Sir William Henry Fremantle?], 14 June 1847.

57 Nevertheless, as Robert Stewart observes, Disraeli's lack of obvious commitment to the party was noticed and when the question of leadership in the Commons arose in the late 1840s Disraeli could count on the support of only about one third of the Conservative party (R. Stewart, *The Politics of Protection: Lord Derby and the Protectionist Party, 1841–1852* (Cambridge, 1971), pp. 136–8).

58 Broadlands Papers, GC/DI/136, Disraeli to Palmerston, 28 March 1846.

59 *Disraeli Letters*, IV, 1607, 1608, Disraeli to Lord John Manners, 16 Nov. 1847, 25 Nov. 1847.

60 Broadlands Papers, GC/DI/137, Disraeli to Palmerston, 22 Nov. 1852. This letter is dated 'Nov. 1852' but is an immediate reply to a letter from Palmerston of 22 Nov. 1852 (*Ibid.*, GC/DI/142).

61 For example, he told Lady Janetta Manners on one occasion that, 'during that time I scarcely ever received a letter from a constituent, certainly never answered one' (P. Smith, *Disraeli: A Brief Life* (Cambridge, 1996), p. 85, Lady Janetta Manners to Salisbury, 10 June 1880).

62 Smith, *Disraeli*, p. 89.

63 P. Smith, 'Disraeli's Politics', in C. B. Richmond and P. Smith (eds), *The Self-Fashioning of Disraeli, 1818–1851* (Cambridge, 1998), p. 167.

64 Vincent, *Disraeli*, p. 116.

65 R. Blake, *Disraeli* (New York, 1987 edn), p. 355. Indeed, in a speech to the people of Manchester in April 1872, Disraeli asserted that: 'I believe that, without party, parliamentary government is impossible' (quoted Hawkins, '"Parliamentary Government"', p. 638). Hawkins asserts that this claim was 'in 1872 ironic and ambiguous, as the concepts of both party and "parliamentary government" were, at that moment, undergoing change' (p. 666).

66 *Disraeli Letters*, V, 1654 and n. 3, Disraeli to Sarah Disraeli, 30 May 1848: Disraeli had been introduced to Metternich by Lord Londonderry on 17 May 1848 from which point they regularly met and corresponded. See also W. F. Monypenny and G. E. Buckle, *The Life of Benjamin Disraeli, Earl of Beaconsfield*, 2 vols (London, rev. edn, 1929), I, pp. 996–8.

67 Monypenny and Buckle, *Disraeli*, I, pp. 998–1002.

68 *Hansard*, 3rd ser., XCIX, 388, 396–400 (5 June 1848).

69 *Disraeli Letters*, V, 1690, Disraeli to Lady Londonderry, 19 Aug. 1848.

70 *Hansard*, 3rd ser., CI, 147–63 (16 Aug. 1848).

71 *Disraeli Letters*, V, 1874, Disraeli to Metternich, 2 Sept. 1849.

72 Vincent (ed.), *Disraeli, Derby and the Conservative Party: Journals and Memoirs of Edward Henry, Lord Stanley, 1849–1869*, p. 8 (19 May 1849).

73 Russell Papers, PRO 30/22/7C, fols 101–5, Grey (3rd Earl) to Russell, 28 May 1848.

74 Broadlands Papers, GC/RU/202, Russell to Palmerston, 5 June 1848.

75 *Ibid.*, GC/LA/66, Lansdowne to Palmerston, 30 [?] March 1848.

76 Russell Papers, PRO 30/22/7C, Lansdowne to Russell, n.d., [*c.* May/June 1848?].

77 See, for example, Broadlands Papers, GC/RU/1006, Palmerston to Russell, 14 Nov. 1846.

78 *Ibid.*, GC/RU/339, Russell to Palmerston, 11 May 1850.

79 See *ibid.*, GC/GR/2381–408.

80 Minto Papers, MS. 11995, Minto, journal, 25 Oct. 1848, 7 Dec. 1848, 21 April 1849.

81 Grey Papers, 3rd Earl, C3/14, Grey, journal, 15 Jan. 1849.

82 See Ridley, *Palmerston*, p. 354.

83 Grey Papers, 3rd Earl, C3/14, Grey, journal, 16 and 18 Jan. 1849.

84 *Ibid.*, C3/14, Grey, journal, 23 Jan. 1849.

85 *Ibid.*, 3rd Earl, C3/14, Grey, journal, 25 Jan. 1849.

86 Minto Papers, MS. 11995, Minto, journal, 5 Dec. 1848.

87 Grey Papers, 3rd Earl, C3/14, Grey, journal, 1 Feb. 1849.

88 Minto Papers, MS. 11995, Minto, journal, 27 Oct. 1848.

89 *Ibid.*, MS. 11997, Minto, journal, 12 Nov. 1850.

90 For example, Russell to Queen, 19 Dec. 1846, 13, 16 Feb., 21 May 1847, 22 Feb., 8 Dec. 1848, 2 Oct., 27, 28 Nov. 1849, 24 May 1850, 4 Dec. 1851, *Cabinet Reports by Prime Ministers to the Crown: A reproduction of the series of manuscript letters preserved at Windsor Castle* (Hassocks, 1978, microfilm).

91 *Ibid.*, Russell to Queen, 3 Nov. 1851.

92 For example, *ibid.*, Palmerston to Queen, 30 March 1847, 23 Oct. 1850.

93 Minto Papers, MS. 11995, Minto, journal, 23 Jan. 1849.

94 Broadlands Papers, GC/RU/441, Russell to Palmerston, 29 Nov. 1851.

95 Russell Papers, PRO 30/22/7D, fols 149–55, Palmerston to Russell, 6 Oct. 1848.

96 B. L. Aberdeen Papers, Add. Mss.43188, Clarendon to Aberdeen, 26 July 1853. In this letter Clarendon identifies Reilly as his source, but concedes that Reilly's information had been 'sometimes true & sometimes absurd'. Aberdeen was not prepared to trust Reilly's intelligence regarding the views of Russia on the Eastern question which Clarendon had just received in July 1853 (Aberdeen Papers, Add. Mss. 43188, Aberdeen to Clarendon, 27 July 1853).

97 Broadlands Papers, GC/GL/462, Clarendon to Palmerston, 4 Oct. 1846.

98 This was from a copied letter from Louis Philippe to Guizot, 28 Sept. 1847, which Clarendon had received from his Parisian source and which Clarendon had felt was 'extremely disagreeable but wh it is very necessary you shd be aware of' (Broadlands Papers, GC/CL/477, and GC/CL/477/enc. 2, Clarendon to Palmerston, 8 Oct. 1847).

99 Quoted D. A. Smith, 'Cabinet and Constitution in the Age of Peel and Palmerston' (unpublished PhD dissertation, Yale University, 1966), p. 203.

100   *Standard*, 26 Sept. 1846.

101   Wood to Russell, 18 Sept. 1846, G. P. Gooch (ed.), *The Later Correspondence of Lord John Russell, 1840–1878*, 2 vols (London, 1925), I, p. 121.

102   *LQV*, II, pp. 324–5, Queen to Russell, 19 Oct. 1850.

103   See, for example, Broadlands Papers, GC/RU/416, Russell to Palmerston, 14 June 1851.

104   Minto Papers, MS. 11995, Minto, journal, 20 March 1849. Similarly, on 4 April 1839, Minto observed that it was the Treasury and Charles Wood 'who has assumed the controul of our foreign policy to which Palmerston submits more patiently than I shd do' (*Ibid.*).

105   'It is however most painful to see many of our colleagues [Lord Grey, Labouchere, Baring, Wood and George Grey] on every question looking only to Parliamentary convenience and tactics, without regard to national honour or interests', wrote Minto at this time (Minto Papers, MS. 11996, Minto, journal, 2 Feb. 1850).

106   Broadlands Papers, MPC/1523 , 'A Constituent' to Palmerston, June 1848.

107   *Ibid.*, MPC/1538 , 'A Commercial Traveller' to Palmerston, 22 May 1850.

108   *Ibid.*, MPC/1539, James Birch to Palmerston, 13 June 1850.

5

No eternal allies: from Don Pacifico
to December 1851

The year 1850 was a difficult one for Palmerston. After the contre-
temps of February in which the Queen had again voiced her
reservations about Palmerston to Russell, plans were hatched to
remove him. In May Russell told Palmerston that, if the Government survived, 'without imputing blame to you', as the country
'was encountered by more hostile feelings in her course than was
natural, or necessary', then he had told the Queen that he 'thought
if you were to take some other department, we might continue the
same line of foreign policy, without giving the same offence'.[1]

Had not the Don Pacifico affair and his *'civis Romanus sum'*
speech rescued Palmerston's ailing fortunes he would probably have
found himself out of office in the summer of 1850. Prince Albert,
for example, while he still recognised Palmerston's abilities, continued to doubt his integrity. Though 'an able politician', he said,
Palmerston remained 'a man of expediency, of easy temper, no very
high standard of honour and not a grain of moral feeling. He is
consequently quite unscrupulous as to any line of policy that he is
to follow, or any means he is to use as long as they lead to his
ends'. Furthermore, he 'is self-willed and impatient of any control
of his own [department]', arising from 'personal conceit'. His
approach, the Prince observed, amounted to 'bullying', and while
he 'has generally great luck', he concluded, 'success failing, he steers
without a compass and makes one almost doubt his sagacity'.[2]

The debate over the Don Pacifico affair in the summer of
1850 marks an important turning point in Palmerston's career.
Undoubtedly it was this 'victory' that underwrote his position at
the Foreign Office for the next eighteen months. Don Pacifico was
a Portuguese Jew who had lost personal property in anti-Semitic

riots in Athens in 1847. Pacifico laid claim to British citizenship by virtue of having been born in Gibraltar and appealed to Palmerston for assistance in pressing for what were widely regarded to be exaggerated claims for compensation against the Greek Government. Palmerston, glad of an opportunity to face down the Greek government, ordered a blockade of Athens by the British navy, much to the disgust of many politicians at home.

In June 1850 Lord Stanley introduced a motion in the House of Lords censuring the Government's handling of claims against the Greek Government, claims which, he maintained, were of a dubious and exaggerated nature and the pursuit of which could, and indeed had, damaged British relations with other great powers.[3] Palmerston, he said, was a private friend, but this was no cause for leniency: 'I am bound here to speak, not of the man, but of the Minister; and thus feeling and regarding him as a man, I must, in this case, express my deep regret at the conduct which, as a Minister, he has felt it his duty to pursue, and call upon your Lordships to recollect that this is no case in which personal feelings ought to be indulged'.[4] In reply, Lansdowne, leader of the Government in the Lords, rose to rebut the charges. Palmerston, Lansdowne declared, enjoyed the general support of the House of Commons, an assembly, he asserted, in which 'the mercantile and manufacturing interests of the country and of the world are adequately represented', and in which 'there is a party which has adopted for its standard and watchword the preservation of peace', and in which 'there has not, up to this moment, been one single intimation of an intention to bring these transactions into question'.[5] The principle which underpinned the Government's policy, namely the right of subjects to demand protection abroad, Lansdowne maintained, was not without precedent and not only had Britain adopted such a policy, but so too, in the past, had France and the United States. If the current employment of the principle had 'clouded' Britain's relations with any other power, that was temporary and not a cause of grave concern.[6]

At the end of the debate, in which the motion was carried by a majority of 37 against the Government, it is not surprising to find Lansdowne's name in the list of Non-Contents; it is perhaps a little more interesting to find also Earl Grey's name there.[7] At a Cabinet meeting held to discuss the Government's response to this defeat, Grey opposed an attempt to secure a counter vote in the Commons and advocated simply a declaration that British subjects abroad would continue to receive support from the British government, clearly acknowledging the force of the Lords' censure. He allowed himself to be carried by the rest of the Cabinet on the need to uphold the principle of collective responsibility, however, and rather than pressing for a ministerial resignation, he accepted the party line that there should be no resignation and that the Government should seek a counter vote in the lower House, even though this determination, he recorded in his diary, 'I have since seen reason to regard as a great error'.[8]

Parliamentary opposition in the House of Lords was certainly not inconsequential. However, while the Government might occasionally suffer defeats there, careful party management and the development of more sophisticated whipping procedures[9] meant that much of what was transacted in the upper House was somewhat theatrical. Indeed, ever since the passing of the 1832 Reform Act, the upper House had ceased to dominate the legislative process.[10] Even when the Lords did successfully censure the Government, as over the Don Pacifico affair, a successful counter vote in the House of Commons was sufficient to overcome the effects of such a set-back. Thus in many ways the House of Commons was the key arena for parliamentary debates over foreign policy during this period, if only because more of its members were directly involved or interested in such questions.

In the House of Commons the Government sought to deprive the Lords' resolution of any effect. When the Radical MP, John Arthur Roebuck, laid before the House a motion commending Palmerston's conduct, Russell felt obliged to make the question effectively one of confidence in the ministry and the Lords' verdict was over-turned by a vote of 310 to 264. In his own contribution to the debate in the Commons, Palmerston appealed to British patriotic feeling in declaring triumphantly that as in the days of the Roman empire when a citizen could claim protection by virtue of Roman citizenship (*'civis Romanus sum'*), so too could a citizen of the British empire expect the same support.

In the Commons, Disraeli found it difficult to condemn Palmerston's brinkmanship. Stanley, having led the censure in the House of Lords, feared that Disraeli was not to be relied upon to make a

clear and firm attack against Palmerston when the debate moved
to the Commons:

> Forgive me [he wrote on June 22] if I impress upon you the great
> importance, on many accounts, of hitting hard and not sparing.
> Anything short of *guerre à l'outrance* would have the effect of reviving,
> in suspicious minds, old misconceptions, and expose you to miscon-
> struction on the part of those who may look with envy at your
> present high position. Pray excuse me for touching on such a topic,
> which I can have but one motive for doing.[11]

As Londonderry told Disraeli, 'The Protectionists rather (I hear)
suspect your intimacy with Pal. & that you will not strike home
when the moment occurs'.[12] Disraeli did not rise to speak until the
fourth and final night of the debate (in fact he was the last person
to make a speech at all), and immediately he made it clear that it
was a sense of political obligation that induced him to say anything
at all: 'I cannot but feel that I should be wanting in, not only in
self respect but in duty to those Gentlemen with whom I have the
honour and satisfaction to act in political connexion, were I to give
a silent vote on this occasion'.[13] Rejecting claims that it was a breach
of constitutional duty that he had not moved the vote of censure
following the vote in the Lords but had allowed an independent
member (Roebuck) to introduce a motion in support of the Government, he seemed as much concerned with defending his own record
as a supposed leader of the Opposition as with attacking Palmerston
and the Government's foreign policy.[14] Significantly, however,
Disraeli proceeded to acknowledge the sagacity of Aberdeen and
though he claimed to have 'no political connexion' with that statesman, he did note that 'during the four years to which the observation
of the noble Lord applies, I can recall no one statement of Lord
Aberdeen as to our foreign affairs that was not fully justified by
preceding facts; and, I might add, no judgement which subsequent
events have not fully warranted'.[15] Disraeli concurred in the attack
on the Greek policy in that he doubted the wisdom of the *civis
Romanus sum* principle, but largely because he believed in the law
of nations and the course of legal redress rather than aggressive
military measures to demand justice. He had no doubt that legal
means could and would provide the required redress: in the case of
a wrong being committed by another government (constitutional

or despotic), 'the law of nations steps in to assist the municipal law that is deficient, and ... the remedy of the suffering foreigner is secured by treaty'.[16] Though he doubted Pacifico's claims, Disraeli drew back from censuring Palmerston directly. 'The Secretary of State', he said,

> has complained that the attack on his policy has been made, both abroad and at home, a personal attack. I can assure the noble Lord he shall have no cause to make this complaint of me. I have, before this, taken the opportunity of expressing my disapprobation of a mode which has only of recent date entered onto our discussion, and that is of visiting on the head of a department the consequences of a policy for which the whole Cabinet is responsible.[17]

If the Government believed in upholding constitutional liberty, why did its conduct not tend to the reinforcement of that belief? Disraeli found many examples of governmental betrayal of this doctrine and concluded that while an admirable motive for governmental activity, 'surely it would be monstrous for Parliament to vote confidence in a Government merely on account of its sentiments, and not on account of a policy which had aimed at and obtained results of great general importance'.[18] Moving, finally, to oppose the motion in the spirit of the Lords' censure, Disraeli concluded with the hope, and indeed expectation, that the result of this examination of the country's foreign policy would 'virtually announce to Europe and to another hemisphere, that the Parliament of England is resolved that, in future, her policy shall be conducted with a due regard to the rights of nations'.[19]

Disraeli had stopped short of attacking Palmerston outright, and in this had weakened the best line of attack the Opposition possessed. It might have been, as he claimed some years later, that a sense of unpreparedness on the Opposition benches to take over the reins of government had influenced him,[20] but this was not all. He had also recognised the hold Palmerston had over the popular imagination and had not wanted to challenge that directly. He was concerned that Palmerston's approach might set a dangerous precedent for other powers to weigh in with military force to seek redress of grievance, but he also acknowledged that Palmerston embodied that 'nationalism of the middle classes and the artisans' and thus the only real ground of attack was, as Paul Smith notes, to press for this assertiveness in foreign policy 'at the keenest price, not pushed so far as to involve expensive collisions with substantial enemies or good customers'.[21]

Yet the weakness of the opposition attack was not entirely of Disraeli's making. Stanley had not wanted Disraeli to repeat the censure passed by the Lords in the Commons recognising that it would have been foolish to attack the most popular man in the country. His aim, rather, had been to use the debate to force the Peelites into opposition to the Whigs and thereby enhance the prospects of a Protectionist reunion with the Peelites.[22] But it seemed more likely that the Peelites would themselves divide, Gladstone and Graham turning against Palmerston, while Peel supported him.[23] As hopes for such a Conservative union receded, it appeared again important to induce Palmerston to cross the floor and there were therefore good reasons for resisting the temptation to drag him down over Don Pacifico. By February 1851 Disraeli was arguing that a union between Palmerston and Lord Stanley offered the best chance of achieving a Conservative parliamentary ascendancy, as Edward Stanley recorded:

> Again and again he recurred to the idea of a coalition between my Father and Palmerston: said Aberdeen had played us false: that we ought not to trust him: we had been more than once his catspaws. 'Palmerston was a man who bore no malice, who liked office, whose tendencies were Conservative, and who would find no difficulty in throwing over former colleagues, especially as he and Russell were not on the most cordial terms[']. He felt confident that he, D., could arrange with him in 24 hours, if permitted.[24]

Nevertheless, Disraeli's name was the one most often associated with the Foreign Office in Conservative circles over the coming months. In each of the failed attempts to construct a Conservative ministry in February and December 1851 and also in February 1852, Disraeli was mentioned in some capacity with that department.[25] Disraeli himself appears not to have been particularly active in seeking such an appointment, perhaps not wanting to live in Palmerston's shadow at that moment.

Potentially more effective, however, was the Cobdenite opposition. Based on a principled system, these 'trouble makers' were fighting less for a political interest than (what they perceived at least) as a national one: prosperity, trade and peace. As Disraeli himself observed, Cobden was well-equipped for his task:

> He had great tact, & always conciliated his audience. He was a very amiable man, & extremely well informed. No man entered the house of Commons with a greater prejudice against him among the Country gentlemen, yet in time he quite overcame it. He was naturally well-bred, because he was considerate for the feelings of others, wh is the true course of good breeding. He was modest without being humble, never elated by his great success.[26]

Richard Cobden had risen from being an unknown 'Manchester business man' to become 'one of the most influential politicians in England' by the mid-1840s and furthermore, argues A. J. P. Taylor, while Cobden rejected the crude connection, there were many who saw in the gradual acceptance of Cobdenite principles the triumph of middle-class liberalism, or more specifically, of the cottonocracy, in mid-Victorian politics.[27]

Cobdenism was founded on the principle of peace and judicious interference abroad, but denigrated the manoeuvrings of governments and secret diplomatic negotiations. Through a policy genuinely directed in the interests of free trade, Cobden believed, peace and prosperity would follow. He felt, he told his colleague John Bright, 'how impossible it is to ensure the peace of the world, and guarantee us against all the burdens which our present warlike attitude entails upon us by any means excepting a free commercial intercourse between all nations'.[28] Palmerston's tenure at the Foreign Office did little to inspire Cobden with confidence, however. 'I thought free trade would have been the prelude to a wiser foreign policy', he told George Wilson, the former Chairman of the Anti-Corn Law League, 'that common sense would have been admitted to a seat at Downing Street – But we seem to be playing the fool in our foreign policy worse than ever'. More than this, he complained: 'I wish the English people knew how little good their 800 millions of debt had done for foreign nations, and how little the people of the Continent feel indebted to us for our sacrifices'.[29]

It was clear that the prevailing Palmerstonian policy was not conducive, according to the Cobdenite model, to a profitable and harmonious foreign policy. The essence of Cobdenism is captured in part of Cobden's speech on the Don Pacifico affair. 'The progress of freedom depends more upon the maintenance of peace, the spread of commerce, and the diffusion of education, than upon the labours of cabinets and foreign offices', he said.[30] Unlike Urquhartite assaults or Disraelian challenges, Cobdenism represented a more rounded and consistent form of opposition to Palmerston and the Whig government and therefore possessed greater potential for success. Over Don Pacifico the so-called rational radicals were offered their first substantial opportunity to test their principles against the prevailing Palmerstonian standard.

A. J. P. Taylor described this as possibly 'the greatest debate on the principles of foreign policy in our parliamentary records', for not only was Palmerston called to account for his conduct of foreign affairs since 1830, but the radicals used this as a platform for exploring questions of morality in foreign policy.[31] In many ways this was both an advantage and an error, for while a clear and logical opposition to the official foreign policy of the country now found its expression, the chance to use this opportunity to undermine the credibility of the ministry's chief proponent of that policy was missed.

Cobden spoke on the last night of the debate. He opened with a discussion of the essential points of the Don Pacifico case but grounded his censure of the Government's policy not in terms of the validity of the cause, but the method of its execution. 'I will not go into the merits of them [the grievances against the Greek government];' he said, 'say the Greeks were wrong, or we were wrong, just as you please; but admit they were wrong, and what I want to know is, whether the wrong was not one that might have been readily settled by other means than by sending fifteen ships of war into the Bay of Salamis?'[32] Gunboat diplomacy of this sort, contended Cobden, rather than exaggerating the potential of a nation's power actually achieved the opposite effect. Such a course placed a country such as Britain in a disadvantageous position relative to, for example, a power like Russia and thus open to abuse:

> And why are you obliged to submit to it? Because you are committing
> an injustice, and conscious you do so; for otherwise, so far from this
> country being in a condition to be menaced by Russia, such are the
> advantages you possess in your great wealth, and your maritime
> commerce, in the knowledge and use of mechanical science, and in

the advanced state of the arts over Russia, that if you behaved with dignity to small States, she would not venture even to look at you disparagingly, far less to use such language towards you.[33]

A more efficient mode of settling diplomatic disputes, Cobden maintained, was through the process of arbitration and restraint from direct intervention wherever possible.[34] Cobden's dissent from Roebuck's motion, then, ultimately was founded on his refusal to sanction a continuous trend of interventionist foreign policy during the last two decades. Palmerston, he acknowledged, was presented frequently as the champion of liberalism and constitutionalism abroad, but, Cobden stressed, 'I cannot fall into this delusion'; Palmerston, he continued, was a man 'of an active turn of mind – that he likes these protocols and conventions – and that the smaller the subject the better it suits his taste'.[35] Yet despite offering a reasoned radical alternative to Palmerstonian foreign policy, Cobden took with him into the division lobbies very few colleagues, and even then they were some of his staunchest allies such as John Bright and William Molesworth.

Taylor argues that Palmerston's victory in the debate 'was more in the nature of a caution not to do it again than a triumphant acquittal',[36] yet a victory it was nonetheless. Cobdenism, or the Manchester School interest, had, in some respects, overplayed its hand. The *Manchester Guardian*, in a leading article published a few days after the conclusion of the debate, was highly critical of John Bright for opposing the Government as he had done and rather than voting against a supposed long-standing principle of interventionism, argued that he should have moved an amendment directed specifically at the issue under discussion (in fact Bright had made no direct contribution to the debate).

> A principle or a rule of action must merely be deduced, [ran the article] either from the express declaration of the party to whom it is ascribed, or from something like an invariable practice on his part. Now, where is the practice, on the part of Lord PALMERSTON, from which any such rule can be deduced? If we grant that he interfered somewhat unnecessarily, as we believe he did, with Spain, we conceive that does not altogether establish a principle or a rule of action. And, if not, pray where are the other instances of interference in other people's affairs? [37]

Rather than demonstrating a genuine commitment to their pro-
fessed cause, the paper argued, Bright and his associates were merely
exploiting an opportunity to undermine the Russell Government
in the hope that a different, more attractive ministry, might be thus
brought in. Bright himself even tacitly admitted in private that
party considerations were as significant as those of principle when
he noted in his journal in response to hostile assessments of his
conduct such as that in the *Manchester Guardian*, that he was
determined not to be 'a mere joint of a Whig tail'.[38]

Yet the *Manchester Guardian* was no real friend of the movement
led by figures such as Cobden and Bright which emanated from the
same commercial city – John Bright specifically identified his opponents as the '*Guardian* party'[39] – and its criticism of the
Manchester School's stand in Parliament over Don Pacifico signifies
something other than a dissatisfaction with the parliamentary exposition of attitudes relating to the *Guardian*'s constituency. For,
in effect, the *Guardian* and Cobdenism represented different interests, or, more accurately, differed in their perception of those
interests. As A. J. P. Taylor suggests, the Cobdenites were 'not the
business men, but the business-like, a matter of mentality, not of
class'.[40] Entrepreneurship, which demands flair and nerve, was
attracted to Palmerstonian politics which offered a spirit of chance
and daring, whereas Cobdenism was, in a sense, almost too rational,
representing commercial interests in the abstract. The *Guardian*
represented the Manchester business-man while the Cobdenites
stood for Manchester's economic interests theoretically apprehended and understood. Cobdenism in this regard had not been
defeated in the Don Pacifico debate, although the class-interest it
was (in this sense erroneously) believed to represent had not been
well served by Cobden himself. The mercantile classes, already
growing disenchanted with the shortcomings of Cobdenite policies
and sensing that financial reform was all but exhausted, looked ever
more favourably on the promise of Palmerstonian force to defend
commercial interests and thus found in the Don Pacifico debate an
early vindication of their defection.[41] As the *Guardian* observed:

> The merchants of this neighbourhood are largely embarked in foreign
> commerce, and have numerous establishments scattered over the
> world, in countries under every variety of government, and in every

stage of civilisation. We imagine they will not hear with much satisfaction that, in the deliberate opinion of the British house of lords, they are entitled to, and must expect to receive, no other protection, in their persons or their property, than that which they can obtain from a due enforcement of whatever law may happen to exist for the time in the country in which their establishments are.[42]

Palmerston's speech demonstrated, if nothing else, the *Guardian* maintained, that there were two discernible principles of British foreign policy: political freedom and freedom of trade. 'In this point of view', ran a leading article four days after the close of the debate, 'we consider that the rights of individual and of nations, are the same; and though either may erroneously exercise those rights, there can be no more doubt of their existence in the one case, than in the other'.[43] Palmerston promised thus to protect commercial interests, which was more than could be said for the mercantile classes' erstwhile figureheads, Cobden, and, to a lesser extent, Bright. The *Guardian* was highly critical of the opposition from Cobden and Bright to Roebuck's motion upon which the Don Pacifico debate was founded, suggesting that the failure of the motion and the implicit censure of Palmerstonian foreign policy 'would have blighted their most cherished policy at home, and endangered the progress of all they profess to hold dear in the condition of European states'.[44] The *Guardian*'s readers appeared to agree and letters to that paper confirmed the popular approval of Palmerston's course, at the same time expressing dissatisfaction with the position taken up by Cobden and Bright.[45] The effects of this demonstration of typical Palmerstonian determination were still felt in the early years of Palmerston's own premiership: his stature into the late 1850s among the Manchester business community, Gatrell asserts, 'rested in large measure on the fact that he had guaranteed that protection [i.e. of their interests] without equivocation'.[46] Thus can Cobdenism be argued to have prospered, such as it did, in spite of this particular result: the supposed pacifism of British policy and its attitude to international affairs which was represented by the Great Exhibition of 1851, maintains Taylor, 'seemed to mark the victory of Cobden's outlook',[47] coinciding as it did with a Conservative (and in particular Disraelian) retreat from protectionism.

As Palmerston noted, however, the Don Pacifico debate had effectively repaired his domestic position:

> Towards the End of the Session Ld John again brought the subject [of removal from the Foreign Office] forward & proposed to me a change of office. I replied that after what had passed in the House of Commons on Roebuck's Motion and after the general and decided approbation of my Policy & Conduct which had been Expressed from one End of the Country to the other by all the Liberal Party it was quite impossible for me to consent to any such arrangement. To do so would be to pass Condemnation on myself after I had received a public approval, and to say that I thought the Hs of Lords which had blamed me was in the Right, and the House of Commons which had approved me was in the wrong. I said that ... if it was any Convenience to the Government I was ready now as I had been after the Vote in the Lords, to relieve my Colleagues of all Difficulty by retiring altogether, but that if I remained in the Govt I could not give up the Foreign Office.
>
> Ld John said that he wished me to remain a Member of the Govt, and he afterwards said that The Queen had consented thereto.[48]

In the wake of the Don Pacifico debate Prince Albert penned a note to Russell in which he conceded that: 'When overruled by the Cabinet, or convinced that it would from political reasons be more prudent to waive her objections, she [the Queen] knew her constitutional position too well not to give her full support to whatever was done on the part of the Government'.[49] The Don Pacifico affair, while it revealed much about British attitudes to nationality and British national interest, also exposed a great deal about domestic politics, for the Pacifico debate in the House of Commons was not so much concerned with the issues and problems raised by the affair, as with Palmerston's conduct of this policy. Palmerston had successfully represented the attack on his foreign policy as an attack upon himself personally. In his lengthy contribution to the debate, he had made full use of his unlimited access to Foreign Office files, and argued persuasively that to have engaged in any policy different from that which he had pursued would have been un-English.[50] The reaction was overwhelmingly favourable to Palmerston and even his erstwhile rivals had to concede that Palmerston's stock now stood higher than ever before: Earl Grey himself testified to

Palmerston's newly acquired popularity telling Greville that there could be no doubt that the debate had left Palmerston 'the most popular man in the country'.[51] Palmerston certainly saw his success over the Don Pacifico question as a triumph for public opinion. His invocation of '*civis Romanus sum*' had brought the question down to the basic interests of every member of the public and out of the exclusive realm of high political debate. As the *Globe* observed, 'Lord PALMERSTON, the House of Commons, and the Nation, are henceforth at one', and the question now before the country:

> awoke a sentiment through the length and breadth of England, to which we have been strangers since the days of Free-trade and the Reform-bill. The nation was outraged at the assumption that its contented apathy should be identified either with acquiescence in the Absolutist reaction, or indifference to the spread of German and Italian Constitutionalism. The great seats of manufacturing industry became aware that they were fighting for their own cause in supporting a Minister whose protecting arm was over every one of his countrymen, at the Court of the most arbitrary despot, or amid the mobs of the most unbridled democracy; and last night the House of Commons worthily answered the call of its constituents, by a vote which has silenced and shattered all the elaborate intrigues of these foreign exiles and their English confederates.[52]

As *The Economist* argued, it was undoubtedly true that Don Pacifico's claims were exaggerated, but it was important and 'proper' that Palmerston should campaign for redress of grievances for a British subject who was the victim of a 'popular prejudice'.[53] It was also, according to the *Globe*, something of a national referendum on Palmerston. The debate, that paper argued, confirmed 'the national affection and respect' which Palmerston had earned, but stressed also the extent to which it had demonstrated that he was the country's ablest foreign minister, not only on account of his popularity abroad, but also in uniting 'the classes which carried Free-trade', who had 'unmistakeably [sic] shown that they are determined to hold fast by their love of liberal institutions in foreign as well as in domestic politics'.[54] It applauded the strong-arm approach of Palmerston as a welcome counterpoint to the '*remplissage* for blue books' of what it derided as 'menacing Aberdonian notes'.[55] The progressive *Daily News*, moreover, saw the contest as essentially one between the liberal tradition of Palmerston's foreign policy and the reactionary spirit of the House of Lords,[56] and saw in the Commons' vindication of the Government's position an unequivocal endorsement of Palmerston's policy directed towards the 'maintenance of English interests and liberal influence abroad'.[57]

There was another aspect to the debate, however. The *Morning Post*, a paper sympathetic to Palmerston's foreign policy, touched upon it in a leading article which praised Palmerston's handling of the affair. The real object of the opposition assault on Palmerston, it contended, was the restoration to office of leading Peelites in alliance with as many Protectionists as could be persuaded to join them. This manoeuvre, however, the *Post* regarded as a most unfortunate piece of intrigue: not only did it offend the *Post*'s Protectionist sympathies as a strategy likely to damage rather than enhance the chances of the installation of a Protectionist ministry in Britain, but it demonstrated undue cynicism on the part of the protagonists in their use of this issue for other ends. It was beyond the *Post*'s comprehension that the principles which had guided Palmerston's handling of Don Pacifico's claims could legitimately be questioned.[58]

On the other side of the political debate, the moral rectitude of Palmerston's course was not so readily recognised. The Times had taken the inflated nature of Don Pacifico's claims as reason enough to undermine his case, and in May expressed doubts as to the willingness of the country to follow Palmerston – he had, after all, shown 'so little confidence' in it himself it claimed – particularly if it led (as it surely could) to war.[59] To speak in June of Palmerston as having a paramount claim to be regarded as the 'English Minister' who had 'represented with unrivalled spirit and success the interests and the opinions of this country' struck *The Times* as ridiculous. He was, above all, a statesman of the utmost inconsistency, 'for although there is no constituted authority in Europe with which Lord PALMERSTON has not quarrelled, there is no insurrection that he has not betrayed'.[60]

The debate in June 1850 seemed to the Peelite *Morning Chronicle* too broad to serve any useful purpose. While Palmerston's answers had been unsatisfactory, the subject had become obscured anyway: 'the Government, or their advocates', it wrote, 'have preferred to change the issue, and to enlarge it to a compass which compels their adversaries to prove a great deal, at the risk of now seeming to prove nothing'.[61] The only conclusion was that the Whigs were seeking to fudge the issue and win a vote over Palmerston's foreign policy in order to bolster the ministry and keep Russell in office.[62] The *Standard* went further. It had initially doubted that Palmerston's foreign policy, if put to the country, would have been so warmly approved as it had been in the House of Commons, indeed, Palmerston's speech, it said, had been 'no doubt sufficiently larded with clap-trap phrases' and it adhered to the original Protectionist view of the affair.[63] But a little over a month-and-a-half later, the *Standard* was obliged to admit that it had mistaken the real issue: the Peelites, it maintained, had been interested simply in returning Aberdeen to the Foreign Office: 'This object was so plainly discerned by some of the best and wisest members of the Country party, that they either voted with the ministers or withheld their votes. We take shame to ourselves that we did not see through the trick which has been made perfectly clear by the conduct of the *ex-Foreign Secretary* and his confidential little circle upon the Irish Franchise Bill'.[64]

In the face of Palmerston's victory, though won with a majority of only 46, yet still treated as decisive, his antagonists contented themselves with issuing a warning to the 'triumphant' Whigs. It fell to the rest of the Cabinet to rein in Palmerston at the Foreign Office; to assure 'discretion and prudence' in the management of foreign affairs, which qualities the *Chronicle* felt had been 'deplorably deficient' under Palmerston and, *The Times* urged, in the correspondence of that department 'to renounce its unbecoming acerbity of tone'.[65] But Palmerston's opponents had made a faulty attack trying to turn what was effectively presented as a moral question into one of party political intrigue. Palmerston had won a popular victory, by charming the so-called middle classes with his patriotic rhetoric. As Greville noted,

> [Lord Grey] said that it was remarkable that this discussion [the Commons debate], which was intended to damage Palmerston had left him the most popular man in the country; that of this there could be no doubt. Bright had said that his vote had given great offence at Manchester, and that Cobden's vote and speech would probably cost him the West Riding at the next election; that amongst

> all the middle classes Palmerston was immensely popular ... But he
> has achieved such a success, and has made himself so great in the
> Cabinet, and so popular in the country, and made the Government
> itself so strong, that if he turns over a new leaf, takes a lesson from
> all that has happened, and renounces his offensive manners and
> changes his mode of proceeding abroad, he may consider his tenure
> of office perfectly secure.[66]

With an ever broader popular base of support and a reputation
forged in a field – foreign affairs – which stood to some extent
above party intrigue, Palmerston's policies were not to be used to
contest party disputes.

Riding the wave of popular enthusiasm, Palmerston, whom the
editor of the *Sun* in a letter to a Colonel Freeston described as 'one
of the manliest intellects in England; one of the noblest statesmen
in all Europe, perhaps the wisest and certainly the most accom-
plished diplomatist who ever directed the foreign affairs of our
Country', did indeed appear to carry with him 'the hearty sympathies
of the people'.[67] Thus it was that the Foreign Secretary did not find
allies wanting. Declarations of support came from all over the
country, offering on occasion practical assistance. One such came
from James Aspinall who wrote from Bawtry in Yorkshire enclosing
a copy of the *Albion*, a Liverpool newspaper which had printed a
very hostile account of the Lords' censure of Palmerston's foreign
policy, criticising Stanley's laboured and insulting speech, and
observing further that 'of the Earl of Aberdeen's twaddling mediocrity in this debate it would be a waste of words to speak', and
concluding that the end result was that 'Lord Palmerston stands
higher than ever in the estimation of his countrymen'. 'I believe
that I can induce many of the liberal papers in this district to adopt
the same tone', promised Aspinall.[68] On the day of Palmerston's
contribution to the Don Pacifico debate in the Commons, he found
his arrival at the House warmly cheered and when finally he had
delivered his speech applause once more rang out, this time from
the public gallery and later outside once again.[69]

To some, it is true, Palmerston had made a poor job of defending
himself. In a letter to Palmerston published as a pamphlet, 'a Greek
Gentleman', who had hitherto been disposed to regard Palmerston
as 'the Ulysses of the Foreign Office – versatile, plausible, ingenious,

and acute', now found these qualities wanting: 'It was a wonderful performance', he acknowledged, 'and had an astonishing effect. You touched the sublime of clap-trap, and roused an accompanying enthusiasm'. Palmerston's employment of the principle of citizenship the writer found questionable and he charged the Foreign Secretary with possessing a very thin understanding of the true state of affairs in Greece. To other abuses committed by the Greek Government Palmerston had paid little attention and now, in the case of Don Pacifico, such was Palmerston's lack of acquaintance 'with the details of the reasons for which you have gone to the extent of endangering the peace of Europe, that *there is no such case whatsoever* in the list of claims'.[70] While this pamphleteer might have grasped the essence of the debate, he had missed its point. Few observers were particularly concerned with the rights or wrongs of Don Pacifico's case or the legitimacy of his claims. It was, being a debate about whether or not the Lords had the authority to effect the dismissal of a minister or indeed a government, a constitutional question, but by extension it had become a debate about Palmerston's continued tenure of the Foreign Office. And, Palmerston strove to present the attack on his foreign policy as a conspiracy against him personally.[71]

In the aftermath of the debate, Palmerston's victory was applauded widely throughout the country. Local newspapers such as the *Renfrewshire Reformer and Glasgow Saturday Post* made sure that Palmerston was acquainted with their approval of his conduct by sending him cuttings, while the *Sligo Champion*, an Irish Tory paper, reiterated the perception of Palmerston as the patriot hero by describing him as 'a second Chatham – one equal to him in vigour of mind – in perspicacity, brilliancy and strength'.[72] From other quarters, tributes to his manly conduct and 'noble generous and patriotic course' confirmed the impression that Palmerston had done much to consolidate, even enhance, his popular image of the masculine English minister.[73] Popularly, at least so it seemed, Palmerston had convinced large numbers of the British people that he was their ablest minister. His appeal went beyond the political appeal of national interest and won admiration from other quarters too, as Edwin Budell, author of a handbook, *The British Tariff, 1850–51*, observed in a letter to the Foreign Secretary:

> Your Lordship has indeed heard the triumphant cheers of the senate
> and of the club, but not less grateful would it have been to your
> Lordship to have heard, as day by day I have heard, from men of
> various shades of political opinion, and of all grades of mercantile
> pursuits, the most emphatic expressions of admiration and delight,
> in reference to Your Lordship's memorable speech – which contained
> an exposition of policy that made many Converts, by its eloquent
> force & conclusive argument.[74]

Palmerston had shown himself to be unswerving in the pursuit of
British interests and had managed to tie that in with a demonstration
of sympathy towards liberalism across Europe. He won the approval
of people across the social and political spectrum.

Thus, when in the autumn of 1851 Palmerston 'availed himself
of the leisure of the recess to pay his constituents a visit', he carefully
canvassed their support for measures which would win popular
liberal support. He opened his speech by referring to subjects
regarding some of which his sympathy was surely questionable, and
over which his responsibility was negligible, but which were undoubtedly intended to add to his reputation. 'This country', he told
his listeners,

> not long ago, had to contend with great difficulties at home, and we
> have had to witness terrible convulsions abroad. Those domestic
> difficulties, by the blessing of Providence, have, to a certain degree,
> passed away – the convulsions abroad have, for the present, ceased.
> (Cheers.) And not only this, but that dreadful scourge, the scourge
> of famine, which ravaged so large a portion of the sister isle, has, if
> not entirely disappeared, been substantially diminished.

He was not above flattering his listeners, reporting to them that
he had great pleasure in telling foreigners who expressed an interest
in the subject that the 'admirable order which our population
preserves', was owing 'in the first place to the great good sense,
the goodness of heart, and the noble qualities which belong to the
British nation', and that these noble qualities, finding expression in
public opinion, exercised a positive influence over political life. But
he reserved questions of foreign policy for his closest attention. In
this department, Palmerston could emphasise the qualities which
underpinned his popular appeal, and he contrasted the illiberal

tendencies of other, primarily southern, European countries with the liberal and constitutionalist tendencies of Britain.[75] Even the *Standard* applauded Palmerston's conduct since July 1850. 'Singular, indeed, and we believe unexampled – an administration of foreign affairs uncriticised by the people or the Parliament for 18 months, including the half of one parliamentary session and the whole of another' it observed in December 1851.[76]

In December 1851, however, Palmerston was expelled from office. Two events in the closing weeks of 1851 sealed his fate. Despite much opposition from various quarters, Palmerston intended to receive Louis Kossuth, the Hungarian nationalist leader, and was only just dissuaded from this course by his Cabinet colleagues and Russell. He dismissed suggestions that receiving Kossuth would represent a slight upon the Queen's government, arguing: 'It is not as chief Enemy of Austria that Kossuth has hitherto been looked upon, nor is it in that Capacity that he is about to be received by the British nation. He has been regarded as a Man who among others has stood up for the Rights of his Country'.[77] Palmerston was determined to have his own way, and once more resorted to a hitherto efficacious tactic when Russell wrote a stern instruction not to receive Kossuth and threatened to resign.[78] The Queen was 'deeply wounded' by Palmerston's conduct and she only desisted from pressing Russell to remove Palmerston on the grounds that this would inevitably lead to a breaking up of the Cabinet.[79] When a few weeks later Palmerston approved Louis Napoleon's *coup d'état* in France he finally pushed his colleagues too far.

As Palmerston failed to contradict reports of his alleged communication with Walewski, the French ambassador, concerning the coup, Russell's hand was forced. On 17 December he wrote 'with great reluctance' to Palmerston to ask for his resignation. The 'complaints are too frequent, & too well founded', he argued, and while professing to 'concur in the foreign policy of which you have been the adviser', he could not 'but observe that mis-understandings perpetually renewed, violations of prudence & decorum too frequently repeated have marred the effects which ought to have followed from a sound policy and able administration'.[80] Palmerston conceded defeat graciously. He wrote to offer to give up the seals of office whenever Russell might choose to appoint a time, adding that he had 'the satisfaction of thinking that the Interests, the Honor, the Character, and the Dignity of the Country have not suffered' during his term of office.[81] Russell lowered his guard and agreed wholeheartedly with Palmerston on this point.[82] Palmerston's fall had become unavoidable; he might have liked to claim that his removal from office was not universally popular within the Cabinet,[83] but Lord Truro was not the only member of the Government who felt that 'Palmerston's retirement is good'.[84] Even Lord Minto, one of Palmerston's most consistent supporters in the Government, had to tell the outgoing minister: 'In bringing my mind to the painful conviction, to which I must not expect your assent, that under all the circumstances of the case your retirement had become inevitable, I do not regard it less as a public calamity, than as a subject of private regret'.[85]

Yet Palmerston's dismissal is not so easily explained. Over Kossuth there had been agreement between Russell, Lansdowne (Lord President of the Council) and Minto (Lord Privy Seal) that while receiving Kossuth would be liable to mis-representation and it would therefore be better that he did not see him at all, he did have a right to receive him in a private capacity.[86] They certainly feared the prospect of a Palmerston-led opposition,[87] but as Lord Grey, the Colonial Secretary, conceded, the Cabinet did not appear strong or determined enough at this time to press his removal anyway.[88] In December Russell claimed that he had stood by his Foreign Secretary for as long as possible,[89] but eventually he could no longer sustain Palmerston, even though the policies he pursued were still acceptable.[90] Indeed, Russell had been at pains to reassure the French government that Palmerston's dismissal would result in no change in the policy or sentiment of the British government towards France. In an interview with Walewski, reported to Palmerston by Peter Borthwick of the *Morning Post*, Russell is said to have 'expressed himself in language *precisely similar in every respect* to that which had been originally held by your Lordship and the terms in which Walewski has conveyed the explanations of Lord John to his govt are to the full as warm as those in which he reported his first conversation with you'.[91] Yet, as both Clarendon and Lord Grey observed, it seemed surprising that Palmerston should be removed now when so many opportunities of a similar nature had presented themselves over the previous five and a half years.[92]

The Queen believed that affronts to the Court had made Palmerston's position untenable,[93] but the 'deviations from the principles laid down by the Cabinet for his conduct,' and the 'personal and arbitrary perversion of the very nature and essence of those principles',[94] of which the Queen complained were, again, not new. She also recognised that insisting on Palmerston's dismissal, as a royal demand, would not only have been 'a most disagreeable task' but also one 'not unattended with a small amount of danger, inasmuch as it would have put me too prominently forward'.[95]

Lord Grey, perhaps disingenuously, expressed surprise and regret 'that the difference was one which could not be settled without your [Palmerston's] retirement', and claimed the disagreement appeared to be a personal one between Palmerston and Russell.[96] It was, furthermore, a problem entirely of the Prime Minister's own making: 'It is quite clear that at last Ld John cd do no otherwise than take the extreme step he did', Grey told his colleague and brother-in-law Sir Charles Wood, 'but it is to my mind no less clear that he is very much indeed to blame for allowing matters to come to such a pass as to create this necessity & thus inflict what I fear will be a mortal blow to the Govt.'.[97] Allowing this to be so, it is all the more interesting to consider why Palmerston was finally sacrificed in 1851 and not at an earlier date. To suggest that Russell acted in a fit of pique – as Russell himself hinted in his published *Recollections and Suggestions* in 1875 [98] – that he was simply grabbing an opportunity to do something which he had desired for some time, is inadequate. This would still not explain why, for instance, he was able in December 1851 to execute such a plan.

Neither the Crown nor the Cabinet, while the executors of that dismissal, could offer any substantially new cause of complaint to justify the change. Indeed, contrary to Grey's private correspondence, the *Daily News*, for example, saw the friction within the Cabinet as simply a further manifestation of Grey's unwillingness to work alongside Palmerston.[99] Public opinion was still largely pro-Palmerston and dissenting voices here were scarcely sufficient to dislodge him. The press, too, largely regretted his fall and saw the potential dangers of his removal. There was, in governmental circles though, thinly disguised relief at Palmerston's removal. Clarendon, for example, though surprised, was 'glad, however it has been made

for as troublous times may be oncoming it is desireable [sic] not
to have *all* the Powers of Europe hostile to us and panting for our
humiliation'.[100] Palmerston had long been held up as a source of
tension in Britain's external relations but this was not reason enough
to dismiss him in December 1851. Palmerston had survived until
the end of 1851 because he knew how to play both a strong and a
weak hand. He had used the threat of resignation to great effect in
order to get his own way almost since the very beginning of the
Government,[101] and had been able to play off factions within the
Government to his own advantage.

Palmerston's dismissal occasioned such outrage at the *Morning
Post* that the subject was the main leader article every day from 25
December 1851 until 2 January 1852. The loss, in the 'present critical
state of European affairs', of the services of a minister whom, the
Post believed, history would accord a place 'in the very highest ranks
of statesmanship' was a setback at both the domestic and international level.[102] The *Post* was greatly troubled that the explanation
for this loss was that, in effect, Palmerston was too unpopular abroad.
'Public opinion will not be satisfied with light explanations of so
great a misfortune;' an article observed, 'still less with explanations
which attribute the result to unworthy or discreditable causes', more
especially since it was Palmerston above all others to whom the
longevity of the Russell government ought to be attributed.[103] To
remove a politician whose only fault was 'that he loves his country
so well, and serves his SOVEREIGN so faithfully, that he prefers the
independence of the one and the dignity of the other to the good or
ill pleasure of certain foreign politicians', was unjust indeed.[104] Peter
Borthwick, the editor of the *Post*, wrote personally to Palmerston
observing that 'You are entitled well to the hearty service of every
Englishman and I am desirous to be a faithful servant' and he even
organised a number of 'confidence meetings' for Palmerston 'to
express public gratitude for your administration of foreign affairs
and public admiration for your Character'.[105]

Significantly, it was not only the Palmerstonian papers that
expressed such sentiments. While adhering to the ministerial line,
which *The Times* had taken upon itself to present to the public, that
paper avoided the contention that Palmerston's removal was in the
country's best interests, and highlighted the abilities thus lost. In
the article which first announced the Foreign Secretary's fall, *The*

Times wrote of Palmerston (suspecting it had seen the last of him in office) commending his industry, courage and charm and steadfastly refrained from repeating the charges made against his foreign policy.[106] The *Morning Chronicle*, too, was sorry to lose the services of Palmerston. In an article on Christmas Day 1851, it chastised the Russell Cabinet for its inconsistency in dropping a minister whom the Government had heretofore dutifully defended, and described his dismissal as a 'national humiliation'. Palmerston had not only been 'the keystone of the arch' for the last five-and-a-half years, he was 'their only man of first-class ability; his policy, though dangerous always and injurious often, was at least bold, spirited, and not essentially un-English'.[107] The *Daily News*, too, acknowledged that Palmerston's policy was not always without its drawbacks, but saw his dismissal as dangerous in the present circumstances, and indeed, the only merit in his removal, it suggested, was that he had been 'for far too many years in possession of his late office' and that the country would be better served by a regular turn-around of foreign ministers every three years in order to elevate the standard of debate in Parliament.[108] The *Standard*, however, discerned a more sinister plot. Palmerston's dismissal was, it said, 'the reverse of satisfactory', and argued that, with an eye to the undercurrent of tension between Grey and Palmerston, 'as Lord Palmerston was certainly the most able, and on every account the least unpopular member of the administration, the retirement of Lord Grey was more generally anticipated'.[109] The Grey faction, the *Standard* maintained, were 'Radicals and Revolutionists', 'ultra pro-Papists', and the dismissal of the true Protestant, Palmerston, was interpreted as a Catholic scheme, underlined, surely, by the appointment in Palmerston's place, of Lord Granville, who was 'eminent for his pro-Romanist zeal'.[110] This served to illuminate further the potency of Palmerston's reputation for 'English' and Protestant foreign policy.

Alongside such wide-ranging newspaper support, Palmerston's going was also deeply regretted in the country at large. As with the national newspapers, in the provincial papers his fall was widely seen in terms of a personal loss, the loss of 'the English minister'. Apprehensive that the Foreign Secretary might be pushed out in favour of a Grey or a Peelite, *Bell's Life in London*, a sporting paper, warned in early December:

> No, Lord John Russell, you had better get rid of *twenty Lord Grey's*
> [Palmerston's emphasis], and preserve the respect, obedience and
> loyalty of the Colonies, than sacrifice one Lord Palmerston, and with
> him sacrifice the sense of England's national independence. There is
> in England, and in such as are worthy of the name of Englishmen
> (the intriguers who are trying to coerce Lord John on this point are
> not worthy of it), no inclination to truckle to foreign domination of
> any kind.[111]

Palmerston collected a variety of newspaper cuttings from this
period and, not surprisingly, all are from articles displaying a
sympathy for his cause, but it is interesting to note the diversity of
their origins, and the uniformity of their sentiments. The *Dundee
Courier* was alarmed to witness the ill-treatment of Palmerston,
suggesting that the real causes of his removal had been masked and
the Foreign Secretary's policy was not so out of line with the
sentiments expressed in other sections of the Government. In
Dublin, the *Warder*, an Orange newspaper clearly concerned about
France and the renewed threat posed by Catholicism, regarded the
events of December as 'the most unseasonable exhibition of "the
white feather," as of the most calamitous augury for the ultimate
interests of peace', while from London the *Morning Advertiser*, originally a publicans' paper, though by this time much more widely
read, asked: 'Will Englishmen submit to this?', finding it hard to
believe that they would acquiesce in the sacrifice of 'the most *English*
Minister' ever to hold the seals of the Foreign Office being '"basely"
sacrificed to the despotic Courts of the Continent'. A letter to the
Lincolnshire Times of February 1852 suggested that perhaps they
would not.[112]

Letters of support emphasised three crucial reasons for deplor-
ing Palmerston's removal: the threat to national honour, the
ill-treatment of the people's hero, and the precarious state of European affairs. His claims to represent England were unquestionable,
as a former Cambridge contemporary observed,[113] while the 'People's Minister' (as the Mayor of Southampton described him) was
the one upon whom 'the people' relied above all others.[114] As far as
Europe was concerned, such a veteran diplomat could ill be spared
at this moment.[115] On this solid basis of confidence Palmerston could
invert the traditional antagonism towards France – and in December

1851 with a Bonaparte at the head of the French government there was a good deal of suspicion and unease – and still be held up as the defender of liberty and peace. Having established himself, rhetorically, as the defender of these principles, public opinion could stoutly continue to believe that, however much the spectre of earlier Napoleonic menace might now be resurrected, Palmerston still stood as the defender of the national interest.

Palmerston had clearly won a popular victory in June 1850 and it was widely acknowledged that his political resiliency thereafter rested in no small part upon this popularity. Yet, that same popularity was in evidence at the end of 1851 and he was still dismissed. According to Donald Southgate, Palmerston's fall can be ascribed to his colleagues' growing weariness and unwillingness to tolerate him any longer, to a desire for poetic justice on Russell's part, and to a perception that the days of the Government were numbered and that without Palmerston in the Cabinet the chances of it being replaced by a Whig-Peelite one rather than a Tory administration seemed better.[116] On what grounds Russell would have believed that a Whig-Peelite alliance could be founded is unclear, however. When such a coalition had been proposed in February 1851 the Peelites had been adamant that no such grounds existed. There was a fundamental lack of agreement over basic policies, including an insuperable obstacle in the form of the Ecclesiastical Titles Bill, and the plan was not long entertained by the leading Peelites, Lord Aberdeen and Sir James Graham.[117]

It is true that, unlike June 1850, Palmerston was denied a platform because Parliament was not sitting at the time. There was consistency in his policy however – he had welcomed a new French government in 1848 on precisely the grounds he invoked in 1851: that despite his reservations about the government in Paris, stability and peace were above all more important to British policy than the right sort of government – and even senior colleagues accepted this.[118] In view of this consistency of policy, it is interesting to note that when in September 1848 the Queen had put pressure on Russell to remove Palmerston, the Prime Minister demurred on the grounds that Palmerston was important to the Government in Parliament, that his diplomacy was directed towards the preservation of British interests and he was popular with the public at large.[119]

Though all these elements remained in place, it would seem

that in December 1851 popular support was simply no longer enough to maintain Palmerston. However, the large extent to which Palmerston was able to manipulate and use public opinion to bolster his position should not be dismissed. By late 1851 not only was Russell resigned to the collapse of his government and looking to the Peelites rather than to Palmerston for an alliance, so too Palmerston himself saw grounds for welcoming change. He might have told Lansdowne that he had acquiesced in his removal in December 1851 so as to avoid compromising the position of the Queen, but he justified past conduct by repeated reference to popular approbation, as displayed particularly in June 1850.[120] Public opinion he felt was with him and in a private letter to his brother, Palmerston revealed clearly the extent to which good understanding had evaporated from his relationship with the Prime Minister:

> It is obvious that the Reason assigned for my Dismissal was a mere Pretext, eagerly caught at for want of any good Reason. The real Grounds were First a little petty narrowminded Jealousy which John Russell has long felt towards me, and Secondly a weak Truckling to the hostile Intrigues of the Orleans Family, Austria, Russia, Saxony & Bavaria & in some Degree also the present Prussian Govt ...
>
> John Russell's Jealousy is of long standing. When Ld Grey came in in 1830 John Russell wanted to be Foreign Secretary instead of me, during the Syrian Campaign when he was at the Home Office he was led by the Bear [Edward Ellice] & by Guizot into very active Endeavours to thwart me, but luckily Charlie Napier & others brought the matter to a successful Issue before these Cabals could operate. For some time he has been annoyed at finding my name more mentioned at home & abroad in Connection with our Foreign Policy than his, although he is Prime Minister, and his cold & reserved manner has rendered him less personally popular with our Party generally than I have happened to be.[121]

Palmerston was playing a longer game and was looking for an opportunity to steal a march on Russell. There was little reason for Palmerston to remain at his post, or to fight to remain there, if he no longer held sway over his most exalted apologist within the Government.

Having seen the Foreign Secretary dismissed, his supporters beyond Westminster were not wholly despondent. The *Leicestershire*

Mercury hoped that in time Palmerston's 'brilliancy' and 'genius' would once again be recognised and that 'then shall we speedily see his lordship carried back to office on the shoulders of the people'.[122] The *Morning Advertiser* suggested that the people of the City of London now had a duty to demonstrate their dissatisfaction with the holder of one of its parliamentary seats, Russell, by replacing him with Palmerston.[123] Indeed, Palmerston had already been approached by the City of London Tradesman's Club which proposed to nominate him for that constituency at the next election. Henry Berkeley, the liberal MP for the city of Bristol, asked Palmerston to join him in the next contest as a second liberal candidate for that constituency, and similarly Mr A. Drummond wrote inviting Palmerston to stand for the liberal interest in the city of Glasgow at the next election. To each of these requests, Palmerston gratefully acknowledged the honour of being approached, but answered that loyalty to the electors of Tiverton, with whom he enjoyed an intimate and friendly connection, prevented him accepting what would otherwise be a very tempting offer.[124]

Soon the shock wore off, and Palmerston's supporters began to hope for more than simply to secure his services as their representative. Eager to portray events in the best possible light, and recognising that this was an opportunity to undermine the Russell group in the Whig party, they began to see Palmerston's departure from the Cabinet not as a dismissal, but rather as a liberation. He was congratulated on his 'withdrawal' from the Government, and a London correspondent acquainted with that town's civic leaders observed that, less than a week after the news of his removal became known, all over the city, and especially in the Lord Mayor's house, Palmerston's name was widely mentioned ('"Long live Palmerston", "Palmerston for ever" – "Vive Palmerston"') and it was felt that it would not be long before Palmerston headed his own ministry.[125]

The Sheffield branch of the Rational Society welcomed Palmerston's dismissal on just these grounds. At a general meeting in January 1852, the society rejoiced 'in the liberation of Lord Palmerston from the thraldom of office', while Ambrose Brewin wrote from Palmerston's constituency in Tiverton to express the hope that 'a little cessation of intense labour will give you fresh strength and recruit the effect of past toils'.[126] There is a sense that Palmerston was being fêted as the saviour-in-waiting of his country. From Kent the Reverend Clotworthy Gillmor wrote to say that he believed that 'the talent, the energy, & the Protestantism of Lord Palmerston ... [will] come to the rescue of England', and another correspondent hoped that although he had 'only the Ace (the People) and Knave of Trumps in hand', he would be able to return to office as 'the Guardian of the Protestant Religion and the freedom of England'.[127] Here is a very clear invocation of the very essence of the patriotic hero: godly and determined in the maintenance of liberty and freedom. Clearly there was still a vibrant Protestant feeling into which Palmerston, or Palmerstonism, could tap. The Reverend Gillmor almost certainly was excited and concerned by 'papal aggression' which since 1850 had threatened to re-establish a Roman Catholic hierarchy in Britain, and which to those of his way of thinking meant absolutism and an end of religious liberty.[128] Anti-Catholic feeling was still widespread in the 1850s and so there was still a keen disposition within certain sections of society to celebrate the Protestantism of Britain over the Popery of the Continent.[129] Indeed these feelings were greatly strengthened by the fear of an enemy within the gates in the form of the Oxford Movement. It is significant, then, that in a street ballad proclaiming 'The Political Alphabet for 1855', 'P':

> Stands for Palmerstone [sic],
> Who will his duty do,
> Kill Puseyites and Jackabites [sic],
> And all the Russian crew.[130]

This prematurely raises the issue of Palmerston as Prime Minister, yet in early 1852, there were already voices advocating just such a role for Palmerston. And in championing the cause of Palmerston's claims to the premiership, supporters were urged to discount Palmerston's supposed anti-reform (even perhaps anti-democratic) tendencies and focus instead on the potential he promised for uniting the nation: in the shape of a hero-governor, such as Prime Minster Palmerston, national greatness and honour would be assured and the tacit and symbolic inclusion of the disenfranchised 'people' would more than compensate for any perceived lack of political reform. Indeed, would not the nation be freer under such a ruler? As 'an Edinburgh Elector' warned in a letter to the *Edinburgh News*:

Thus the *Daily News* writes – 'Lord John Russell promises us a new reform Bill. Let us see what it will be like before we try to upset him in favour of one whose opinions on reform are far less known than those of the present Premier.'

Electors, and people of Britain, beware of this piece of cunning and carry back Lord Palmerston as Premier to the Councils of Her Majesty and of the nation in favour of Kossuth, down-trodden nationalities, and the independence of this land from foreign dictation.[131]

Not everyone fully shared in these hearty aspirations for Palmerston's future career, however. The *Manchester Guardian*'s immediate reaction was one of 'regret if not alarm', and the leading article which first considered Palmerston's resignation declared that 'nothing but the triumph of principle [official disapprobation of recent events in France and support for 'the rights of abstract justice, and the interests of this country'] can reconcile us to his loss'.[132] Upon more mature reflection though, the *Guardian* tempered this view with the suggestion that Palmerston, aware of his great popularity in the nation at large, was perhaps becoming something of a liability: 'A long series of great successes', a leading article noted, 'had undoubtedly given to Lord PALMERSTON a confidence which, to say the least, was dangerous, in so delicate a matter as foreign diplomacy'.[133] Nevertheless, even those elements which saw some good in Palmerston's departure – with the exception of the more extreme interests such as the republican movement led by figures such as William James Linton [134] – still expected great things from Palmerston in the future. In the same article which criticised the over-confidence of the late minister, the *Guardian* concluded that: 'Lord PALMERSTON has acted with many sets of politicians; but there is one uniform characteristic of all his changes;– he always went forward;– he never took a step backward, and he will not do so now'. There was no reason to expect him to desert his principles and erstwhile sympathies – 'all of the most liberal kind' – and thus his contribution to Parliament would still be a force for good.[135]

Notes

1   Broadlands Papers, GC/RU/343/1–2, Russell to Palmerston, 22 May 1850.
2   Connell (ed.), *Regina v. Palmerston*, p. 115, Albert to Russell, 2 April 1850.
3   *Hansard*, 3rd ser., CXI, 1293–332 (17 June 1850).

4   *Hansard*, 3rd ser., CXI, 1332 (17 June 1850).

5   *Hansard*, 3rd ser., CXI, 1333 (17 June 1850).

6   *Hansard*, 3rd ser., CXI, 1333–50 (17 June 1850).

7   *Hansard*, 3rd ser., CXI, 1401–3 (17 June 1850). The voting figures for this debate were: Contents 169, Non-Contents 132.

8   Grey Papers (3rd Earl), C3/15, Grey, journal, 18 June 1850.

9   See J. Hogan, 'Party Management in the House of Lords, 1846–1865', *Parliamentary History*, 10: 1 (1991), esp. pp. 127–49.

10 Le May, *The Victorian Constitution*, p. 131.

11 Blake, *Disraeli*, p. 297, Stanley to Disraeli, 22 June 1850.

12 *Disraeli Letters*, V, 2013, n. 4, Londonderry to Disraeli, 20 June 1850.

13 *Hansard*, 3rd ser., CXII, 720 (28 June 1850).

14 *Hansard*, 3rd ser., CXII, 720–1 (28 June 1850).

15 *Hansard*, 3rd ser., CXII, 722 (28 June 1850).

16 *Hansard*, 3rd ser., CXII, 725 (28 June 1850).

17 *Hansard*, 3rd ser., CXII, 726–7 (28 June 1850).

18 *Hansard*, 3rd ser., CXII, 736–7 (28 June 1850); for Disraeli's examples of the Government's inconsistencies, see esp. 727–35.

19 *Hansard*, 3rd ser., CXII, 739 (28 June 1850).

20 Blake, *Disraeli*, pp. 297–8.

21 Smith, *Disraeli*, p. 185.

22 Stewart, *The Politics of Protection*, pp. 166–7.

23 Vincent (ed.), *Disraeli, Derby and the Conservative Party: Journals and Memoirs of Edward Henry, Lord Stanley, 1849–1869*, pp. 19–20 (9 June 1850).

24 *Ibid.*, pp. 40–1 (16 Feb. 1851).

25 Blake, *Disraeli*, pp. 301–3, 306, 308, 311–12.

26 Bodleian Library, Oxford, Hughenden Papers, dep. Hughenden 26/3, fols 18–20, 'Observations on men and things: Cobden and Bright'.

27 Taylor, *Trouble Makers*, p. 54.

28 N. McCord, 'Cobden and Bright in Politics, 1846–1857', in R. Robson (ed.), *Ideas and Institutions of Victorian Britain* (London, 1967), p. 90, Cobden to Bright, 24 Oct. 1846.

29 *Ibid.*, p. 91, Cobden to G. Wilson, 21 June 1847.

30 *Hansard*, 3rd ser., CXII, 673 (28 June 1850).

31 Taylor, *Trouble Makers*, p. 56.

32 *Hansard*, 3rd ser., CXII, 663 (28 June 1850).

33 *Hansard*, 3rd ser., CXII, 665 (28 June 1850).

34 *Hansard*, 3rd ser., CXII, 667–74 (28 June 1850).

35 *Hansard*, 3rd ser., CXII, 673 (28 June 1850).

36 Taylor, *Trouble Makers*, p. 57.

37 *Manchester Guardian*, 6 July 1850.

38 Quoted K. Robbins, *John Bright* (London, 1979), p. 89.

39 *Ibid.*, p. 72.

40 Taylor, *Trouble Makers*, p. 54.

41 See Gatrell, 'The Commercial Middle Class in Manchester', pp. 448–50 for

discussion of this 'accord between Palmerston's view of the world and that of the anti-Cobdenite opposition in Manchester'.

42   *Manchester Guardian*, 29 June 1850.

43   *Ibid.*, 3 July 1850.

44   *Ibid.*, 3 July 1850.

45   See R. M. Keeling, 'Palmerston and the Pacifico Debate' (unpublished PhD dissertation, University of Missouri, 1968), pp. 180–1.

46   Gatrell, 'The Commercial Middle Class in Manchester', p. 450.

47   Taylor, *Trouble Makers*, p. 57.

48   Broadlands Papers, GC/RU/343/enc. 1, from a minute, in Palmerston's hand, on a letter from Russell, 22 May 1850.

49   Smith, 'Cabinet and Constitution in the Age of Peel and Palmerston', p. 82, Prince Albert to Russell, 17 Aug. 1850.

50   See Keeling, 'Palmerston and the Pacifico Debate', pp. 62–6; ch. 4.

51   Greville, *The Greville Memoirs (second part)*, III, p. 347 (1 July 1850).

52   *Globe*, 29 June 1850.

53   *The Economist*, 16 March 1850, 15 June 1850.

54   *Globe*, 26 June 1850.

55   *Ibid.*, 27 June 1850.

56   *Daily News*, 24, 26 June, 1 July 1850.

57   *Ibid.*, 22 July 1850.

58   *Morning Post*, 27 June 1850.

59   *The Times*, 22 Feb., 20 May 1850.

60   *Ibid.*, 22 June 1850.

61   *Morning Chronicle*, 27 June 1850.

62   *Ibid.*, 29 June 1850.

63   *Standard*, 29 June, 1 July 1850.

64   *Ibid.*, 20 Aug. 1850.

65   *Morning Chronicle*, 1 July 1850; *The Times*, 1 July 1850.

66   Greville, *The Greville Memoirs (second part)*, III, 347–8 (1 July 1850).

67   Broadlands Papers, MM/GR/38, editor of the *Sun* to Col. Freeston, 30 May 1850 (copy).

68   *Ibid.*, MM/GR/47, James Aspinall to Palmerston, 26 June 1850; MM/GR/47/enc. 1, *Albion*, 24 June 1850.

69   *Illustrated London News*, 29 June 1850.

70   *On the Speech of Her Majesty's Foreign Secretary, delivered in the House of Commons June 25, 1850. A letter to the Right Hon. Viscount Palmerston, in reference to the Greek Question, exclusive of His Lordship's general foreign policy. By a Greek Gentleman* (1850), pp. 5, 6–8, 35.

71   See Keeling, 'Palmerston and the Pacifico Debate', ch. 4. Cf. H. Winston Barron's *Address to the Electors of Waterford* of 11 July 1850 in which he explained that he had voted against Palmerston and against his own personal feeling by way of 'showing my strong objection to the neglect of Irish interests' (Broadlands Papers, MM/GR/55).

72   Broadlands Papers, MM/GR/49, John Henderson [editor of the *Renfrewshire Reformer and Glasgow Saturday Post*] to Palmerston, 30 June 1850,

enclosing a copy of the paper; MM/GR/50, *Sligo Champion*, June 1850. It is interesting to note also that the *Sligo Champion* concluded its leading article thus: 'Honor [sic] where honor is due – honor to Lord Palmerston. Proud are we, indeed, that he is connected with Sligo by property; it gives us a kind of claim to him – imaginary it may be – but still it is gratifying to know that the Mind which governs the Foreign policy of the world some times thinks of our poor locality. That he has a wish to serve it we can readily believe, and we hope the time may come when he will have an opportunity of doing so'. It is surely significant thus to witness Irish Toryism buying into Palmerstonism.

73 *Ibid.*, MM/GR/52, R. O. Warwick [Pensioner of Greenwich Hospital] to Palmerston, 2 July 1850 refers to the way Palmerston has 'manfully ... like the Old Champions of old, stood forward for the Honour and Welfare, of the British nation, and the just rights of her subjects at Home and Abroad'; *ibid.*, MM/GR/54, Abraham Jones Le Gras[?] to Palmerston, 8 July 1850.

74 *Ibid.*, MM/GR/59/1, Edwin Budell to Palmerston, 24 July 1850.

75 *Illustrated London News*, 27 Sept. 1851.

76 *Standard*, 26 Dec. 1851.

77 Broadlands Papers, GC/RU/430/enc. 2, Palmerston to Russell, 24 Oct. 1851.

78 Russell Papers, PRO 30/22/9G(2), fols 143–4, Palmerston to Russell, 30 Oct. 1851.

79 Broadlands Papers, GC/RU/440/enc. 1(1)(2), Queen to Russell, 20 Nov. 1851 (copy).

80 *Ibid.*, GC/RU/449, GC/RU/450/1–2, Russell to Palmerston, 17 Dec. 1851.

81 *Ibid.*, GC/RU/1098, Palmerston to Russell, 18 Dec. 1851.

82 *Ibid.*, GC/RU/453, Russell to Palmerston, 19 Dec. 1851.

83 *Ibid.*, GC/RU/454, note by Palmerston on letter from Russell to Palmerston, 22 Dec. 1851.

84 Russell Papers, PRO 30/22/10A(1), fol. 80, Lord Truro to Russell, Jan. 1852.

85 Broadlands Papers, GC/MI/501, Minto to Palmerston, 13 Jan. 1852.

86 Minto papers, MS. 11998, Minto journal, 1, 3 Nov. 1851.

87 *Ibid.*, MS. 11998, 27 Nov. 1851.

88 'When the subject was brought before us I thought the cabinet showed great weakness for though I believe every member of it disapproved exceedingly of what had been done this feeling was scarcely expressed except by Labouchere and myself', Grey Papers, 3rd Earl, C3/15, Grey, journal, 'Retrospect written 6 March 1852'.

89 Minto Papers, MS. 11998, Minto journal, 19 Dec. 1851.

90 *Ibid.*, MS. 11998, Minto journal, 24 Dec. 1851.

91 Broadlands Papers, GMC/47/1–2, Peter Borthwick to Palmerston, 27 Dec. 1851.

92 Lansdowne Papers, Lans. 3/32, fol. 103, Clarendon to Lansdowne, 25 Dec. 1851; Grey Papers, 3rd Earl, C3/15, Grey journal, 'Retrospect written 6 March 1852'.

93 *LQV*, II, 325–7, Queen to Russell, 31 Oct. 1851.
94 *Ibid.*, II, 351–2, Queen to Russell, 28 Dec. 1851.
95 Connell (ed.), *Regina v. Palmerston*, p. 132, Queen's journal, 20 Dec. 1851.
96 Broadlands Papers, GMC/87, Grey to Palmerston, 23 Dec. 1851.
97 Brotherton Library, Leeds University, Hickleton Papers (microfilm), A4.55.1, Grey to Wood, 23 Dec. 1851.
98 Earl Russell, *Recollections and Suggestions, 1813–1873* (London, 1875), pp. 257–8. As G. P. Gooch suggests, however, it is likely that this 'judgement was inspired by the softening influence of time and by subsequent experience of harmonious co-operation' (G. P. Gooch (ed.), *The Later Correspondence of Lord John Russell, 1840–1878*, 2 vols (London, 1925), p. xxxv).
99 *Daily News*, 2 Dec. 1851.
100 Lansdowne Papers, Lans. 3/32, fol. 103, Clarendon to Lansdowne, 25 Dec. 1851.
101 Broadlands Papers, GC/RU/1006, Palmerston to Russell, 14 Nov. 1846.
102 *Morning Post*, 25 Dec. 1851.
103 *Ibid.*, 26 Dec. 1851.
104 *Ibid.*, 30 Dec. 1851.
105 Broadlands Papers, GMC/47/1–4, Peter Borthwick to Palmerston, 27 Dec. 1851.
106 *The Times*, 24 Dec. 1851.
107 *Morning Chronicle*, 25 Dec. 1851.
108 *Daily News*, 2, 25, 26 Dec. 1850.
109 *Standard*, 24 Dec. 1851.
110 *Ibid.*, 26, 30 Dec. 1850.
111 Broadlands Papers, GMC/49, *Bell's Life in London*, 7 Dec. 1851 (press cutting kept and annotated by Palmerston).
112 *Ibid.*, GMC/54/1–2, Dundee Courier, Feb. 1852; GMC/50, Warder, 26 Dec. 1851; GMC/51, *Morning Advertiser*, 31 Dec. 1851; GMC/53, *Lincolnshire Times*, Feb. 1852 (letter dated 20 Feb. 1852).
113 *Ibid.*, GMC/51, R. Alston to Palmerston, 27 Dec. 1851.
114 *Ibid.*, GMC/106, R. Andrews to Palmerston, 26 Jan. 1852. In a similar vein, also: Broadlands Papers, GMC/65, Henry Berkeley [MP for Bristol] to Palmerston, 27 Dec. 1851; GMC/73, George Coles [of Tiverton] to Palmerston, 2 Jan. 1852; GMC/77, Edward Dawes [MP for the Isle of Wight] to Palmerston, 13 Jan. 1852.
115 See J. Davidson, *The Fall of the Pope, and the Fate of the French President* (London and Aberdeen, 1852). Davidson sent this pamphlet to Palmerston on 17 Jan. 1852 (Broadlands Papers, GMC/76, GMC/76/enc. 1).
116 Southgate, 'Most English Minister ...', p. 291.
117 Aberdeen to Graham, 24 Feb. 1851; Aberdeen to Russell, 25 Feb. 1851, Walpole, *Russell*, II, 124–7. Indeed Palmerston had warned Russell in January 1849 when the topic had been raised then that: 'My impression as to Sidney Herbert is that he & others of the Peel Party look to forming a Govt of their own upon the Ruins of yours; and that neither He nor any of

the others will come over singly to be merged in your Cabinet' (Broadlands Papers, GC/RU/241/enc. 1, Palmerston to Russell, 5 Jan. 1849 [copy]).

118   On 1848 see G. J. Billy, *Palmerston's Foreign Policy: 1848* (New York, 1993), pp. 31–54.

119   *Ibid.*, pp. 141–2.

120   Ashley, *Palmerston*, II, p. 226, Palmerston to Lansdowne, Oct. 1852.

121   Broadlands Papers, GC/TE/341/3, Palmerston to Sir William Temple, 22 Jan. 1852.

122   *Ibid.*, GMC/52, *Leicestershire Mercury, 24 Jan. 1852.*

123   *Morning Advertiser*, 7 Feb. 1852.

124   Broadlands Papers, GMC/58, Mr Shaw (Honorary Secretary of the City of London Tradesman's Club) to Palmerston, 24 Jan. 1852 (with a copy of Palmerston's reply); GMC/66, Henry Berkeley to Palmerston, 6 Jan. 1852 (with a copy of Palmerston's reply); GMC/79, A. Drummond to Palmerston, 1 Jan. 1852 (with a copy of Palmerston's reply).

125   *Ibid.*, GMC/92/enc. 1, Address by the Members of the Working Men's Institution of Leamington Priors, Warwickshire, 1 Jan. 1852; GMC/97, A. Kirkaldy to Palmerston, 29 Dec. 1851.

126   *Ibid.*, GMC/57, Wm. Lawton (Secretary of the Sheffield Rational Society) to Palmerston, 7 Jan. 1852; GMC/70, Ambrose Brewin to Palmerston, 6 Jan. 1852.

127   *Ibid.*, GMC/85, Rev. Clotworthy Gillmor to Palmerston, 6 Jan. 1852; GMC/122, John Wallis to Palmerston, 5 Jan. 1852.

128   See D. E. D. Beales, *England and Italy, 1859–60* (1961), pp. 14, 19–20.

129   See G. F. A. Best, 'Popular Protestantism in Victorian Britain', in Robson (ed.), *Ideas and Institutions of Victorian Britain*, p. 119.

130   Bodleian Library, Harding Collection, B. 14 (355), 'The Political Alphabet for 1855'.

131   Broadlands Papers, GMC/86/enc. 2, letter 'To the Editor of the *Edinburgh News* from an Edinburgh Elector', 6 Jan. 1852, cut from the newspaper, with the quote from the *Daily News* highlighted [by Palmerston's pen?].

132   *Manchester Guardian*, 27 Dec. 1851.

133   *Ibid.*, 31 Dec. 1851.

134   The *English Republic*, a relatively short-lived republican paper under the editorship of Linton lamented the fall of the French Republic, but hoped that in the new year 1852, with Palmerston out, there were better prospects of England 'coming to the rescue' of the French (vol. 2 (1852/53), 1852, p. 4). See also F. B. Smith, *Radical Artisan: William James Linton, 1812–97* (Manchester, 1973), ch. 5.

135   *Manchester Guardian*, 31 Dec. 1851.

6

Palmerston, the Derby Government and the search for office, February to December 1852

When Parliament met again in the New Year, Lord Dufferin wrote that Palmerston 'is completely floored, and people seem to think he is not likely to rise again'.[1] Lord Truro rejoiced in the Foreign Secretary's dismissal: 'He is too fond of popularity hunting to fit the Foreign Office & when he makes the good men of Tiverton his Confidants, he incapacitates himself for that important situation', he told Russell.[2] Similarly Clarendon had been quick to reassure the Prime Minister that the ministry would not suffer as a result of the rupture with Palmerston,[3] adding in January 1852: 'His friends and newspapers put about that he is the victim of a cabal, and this sustains him for a time; but if he fails to prove it he will sink in public opinion'.[4] What Clarendon and others failed to appreciate was the effect Palmerston's recent dismissal had had on the political nation.

Palmerston successfully carried an amendment to the Militia Bill in February 1852 by a majority of 13 relying in large part upon an alliance of Protectionists and some Peelites and so brought down the Government. Russell, perhaps, had reason to welcome the vote: his administration was unquestionably tottering to its fall, and had it not been the militia question, it might have been something bigger – electoral reform for example – which might have had more damaging ramifications for the future careers of the ministers. Indeed, a defeat for the Government's colonial policy in the Cape loomed and as Palmerston himself observed, 'the cabinet were glad to make use of the militia question as a convenient parachute to avoid a ruder descent and a more dangerous one in Table Bay'.[5] As the Government collapsed, Palmerston reflected, with evident satisfaction, that he had now had his 'tit for tat' with Russell. He claimed

in a letter to his brother that he 'certainly did not expect to do so
nor did I intend to do anything more than to persuade the House
to reject his foolish Plan and to adopt a more sensible one',[6] but
such declarations of public spiritedness ring a little hollow. 'Lord
PALMERSTON now drives Lord JOHN from office', wrote the *Daily
News*, 'because he is not vigorous enough in the measure of military
defence. Of defence against whom? – against this very LOUIS NA-
POLEON. Great must be Lord PALMERSTON's organ of veneration.
He loves and fears the same object profoundly. He would embrace
this LOUIS NAPOLEON, but would put on defensive armour to obviate
the danger in the embrace'.[7] Palmerston had not only undermined
Russell's position, however, but also reinforced his own commitment
to the question of national defence and helped satisfy a growing
demand for a change of government. Palmerston was not yet in a
position to claim the premiership for himself, but he had reaffirmed
his political vitality. During the coming months he was able to play
factions and individuals off against each other at Westminster.
Possessing little real command of an efficient political party,
Palmerston had to exploit a reputation of being the national minister.

The Derby Government of 1852 which succeeded that of Russell
in February remained throughout a minority one. Even on the back
of the election held during the summer of that year in which the
Derbyites enlarged their representation in the House of Commons
from 280 to 310, there was still no clear majority in that chamber,
leaving the ministry vulnerable in Parliament. Furthermore, according to the Duke of Argyll at least, it seemed the Prime Minister
was not well suited to his task: 'He was too rollicking, too apt to
treat everything as a joke; the result was a Government obviously
provisional'.[8] Although, Argyll claimed, the 'Free Trade sections of
the House' preferred to 'watch and wait', there are signs that the
Whigs sought to regroup rapidly. Within days of the establishment
of the Derby Government Russell even wrote to Palmerston seeking
a common understanding in order more effectually to counter the
position adopted by Disraeli over foreign affairs on behalf of the
new ministry. 'At present I have no very settled opinion as to what
should be done', he wrote, 'but it is desirable that all who are for
free intercourse with foreign countries should know each other's
course before we confront Disraeli'.[9] Palmerston, however, replied

that it appeared to him scarcely consistent with the position in which he had been placed in December last to attend such a meeting as Russell proposed, and Russell was obliged to concede Palmerston had 'a perfect right' to adopt such an attitude.[10]

Palmerston's political force was clearly still not spent, something which was recognised on both sides of the House. When Palmerston had been dismissed in December 1851, rumours had begun to circulate at Westminster that he might now agree to a coalition with the Conservatives. Disraeli had been quick to give the lie to such suggestions however, as he told Derby, at the time, 'I ridiculed the rumour and reprobated the factiousness of such a sudden alliance, adding we hoped we were strong enough to carry on affairs without taking in the discarded partner of an insolvent firm, and thought that with fair play we should not be driven to such a course'.[11] 'There *was* a Palmerston', Disraeli is famously said to have remarked to Henry Bulwer having heard the parliamentary accounts of Palmerston's dismissal at the beginning of 1852.[12] Yet less than two months later, in the wake of Palmerston's 'tit-for-tat' with Russell, Disraeli wrote more seriously to Derby once he had replaced Russell as Prime Minister. 'It is everything for your Government that P. should be a member of it. His prestige in the House is very great; in the country considerable. He will not give you trouble about principles, but he may about *position*'.[13] In the event, Palmerston did give trouble about principles and refused to join the Derby government on the grounds of differences on the question of protection. While the greatest stress is laid on Palmerston's standing in the House, it is interesting that Disraeli did not fail to recognise Palmerston's 'considerable' prestige in the country. To Conservatives as well as Liberals, Palmerston's demonstrated strength with public opinion made him a figure to be reckoned with, and this was not the only overture made to Palmerston by the Protectionists in 1852.[14] No longer was anti-Palmerstonianism a 'possible common cause for fragmented Conservative opinion'.[15] Indeed, in the aftermath of the split with Russell and Russell's revival of the Reform question, there was good reason to believe that Palmerston might be receptive to Conservative overtures.

Palmerston's problem in 1852 was that while he retained a broad base of parliamentary and popular support, he still, as Roebuck noted, 'wants the support of the sedate portion of the politicians'.[16]

Greville went further, observing that 'though he is very popular, and can excite any amount of cheering in the House of Commons, he has no political adherents whatever'.[17] This independence from party affiliations, however, gave Palmerston not only relative freedom of action, but also the opportunity to capitalise on his perceived popular standing in the country at large.

Having offered to meet with Malmesbury, Derby's Foreign Secretary, in order to discuss the main principles of foreign policy, an offer which Malmesbury, who had been reluctant to take the Foreign Office, 'gratefully accepted', Palmerston impressed upon him the gravity of his new position: 'You have no idea until you know more of your office what a power of *prestige* England possesses abroad, and it will be your first duty to see that it does not wane … take care you yield nothing until you have well looked into every side of the question'.[18] Though he did voice criticisms of the new Government's foreign policy – as in the case of the maltreatment of a British subject in Tuscany by an Austrian officer in the summer of 1852, a stand reminiscent of his *civis Romanus sum* declaration – Palmerston adopted an attitude towards the ministry, according to Herbert Bell, of 'marked benevolence'.[19] He reserved for the Russell government of 1846–52 a degree of censure more personal, or at least so it appeared to contemporary observers. On 29 June Grey, on his way home, met Lansdowne 'who told us that Palmerston had been making a very bitter attack on the late govt. in the House of Commons with reference to Foreign Affairs, there being no one present to answer him'. On reading this speech, Grey observed that it was 'a very bitter attack principally on Lord John', which was 'most discreditable' to Palmerston.[20] Little wonder, then, that, presuming he would unite with anyone at all, it was the Conservatives it was believed Palmerston would join, and not Russell and the Whigs.

Throughout the ten-month life of the Derby administration, there was a constant search for a more stable government, a desire to do something given that 'Lord Derby's ship', was 'gradually going down'.[21] Significantly, in all of the combinations proposed to remedy this weakness, Palmerston's name was to be found in some regard.[22] Palmerston gave serious consideration to the notion that he might bolster the position of the Derby government and as late as the autumn of 1852, for instance, Charles Greville reported to Clarendon from Broadlands:

> I have had a long conversation with Palmerston and a good deal of
> desultory talk with Lady P. and Lord Shaftesbury, and the result is
> a strong conviction that it will end in P. joining Derby, provided the
> latter will give him a decent opportunity for so doing. She evidently
> wishes it very much ... He will not, however, join alone, whatever
> may happen, and I see that he will expect a good many changes and
> exclusions and that he should come in with some adherents.[23]

Quite what Palmerston might have regarded as a 'decent opportunity' remained unclear. Graham had already suggested that
Palmerston and Gladstone were waiting to join Derby on 'High
Tory Principles',[24] and the notion of a Palmerston–Peelite alliance
had some currency until November.[25] According to Greville, foreign
affairs continued to pre-occupy Palmerston and it appeared that
this was the area in which he would hope to contribute to the ailing
Derby administration: 'P. talks with the greatest contempt of
Malmesbury', he noted towards the end of the year, 'and seems fully
aware of the great danger of having our foreign relations in such
incompetent hands in the present state of Europe. Though he relies
much on Louis Napoleon's pacific professions, he seems a good deal
alarmed at the vast and matured preparations of France and at the
utterly defenceless position we are in'.[26] Palmerston's concern about
the current state of 'very imperfect security' signalled the end of
his so-called 'marked benevolence' towards the Government's
foreign policy.

However, Palmerston said he was reluctant to return to the
Foreign Office, which, he was to tell Aberdeen, perhaps somewhat
disingenuously, had 'become too much for him'.[27] Others thought
he was intriguing to satisfy different ambitions: Sir George Cornewall Lewis had no doubt for example, that Palmerston sought, or
at least would secure for himself, a commanding position, possibly
the lead in the Commons, which, Lewis pointed out, if he accepted,
'with his political standing, his official experience, his self-confi-
dence, his love of work, & his disregard for other men's feelings,
he would soon make himself the cabinet, in the midst of such a set
of colleagues, & Ld Derby would find not only that he had got a
master, but a master who made him feel his servitude every day –
& rode him with a sharp bit & a hard hand'.[28] Above all, Palmerston
was thought to want the premiership, as Lewis suggested to Sir

James Graham in late October. In a reconstructed Derby ministry, he wrote:

> Ld Derby might be first minister in name, but if Palmn. *not* being Foreign Secretary, were to lead the House of Commons, he wd be compelled to inform himself about all questions, & he wd in fact guide the policy of the govt. He would be the *real* Prime Minister, & it wd no longer be what it is at present – a Derby Dizzy affair. This is a change which it is easy to make in conversation, or on paper, but I doubt whether it wd be easily made in fact, or if made whether it wd last. Palmn. however will shortly become very impatient. Neither he nor Ld John will give way to the other, an intermediate ministry under Ld Lansdowne is an impossibility, & as he starts from the assumption that he must be in office *somehow*, it remains only that he shd join Ld Derby.[29]

While, as Lewis argued, Russell and Palmerston were ill-disposed to make concessions to each other in the interests of a new government, Palmerston's interest in an association with Derby was little more than a pragmatic response and did not signal a shift in him towards protectionism. So long as the prospect of a Lansdowne-led, 'Liberal' ministry had seemed a viable one, Lewis thought that Palmerston was keen to throw in his lot with the Whigs.[30] Palmerston looked above all for a chance to resume office and envisaged a central role for himself, yet there was a degree of flexibility, or ambiguity, in his sense of party allegiance.

It has been said that Palmerston by late 1852 was keen to take up office, or at least Lady Palmerston was keen that he should do so, for pecuniary reasons,[31] certainly she sought to encourage Lansdowne to persuade Palmerston to join Derby,[32] but if this were the case, he might have been expected to pursue more vigorously opportunities to join Derby's administration. Rather he waited for the elusive 'decent opportunity'. Palmerston had been unhappy about the Derby Government, and was to be less than sanguine about the prospects of an Aberdeen ministry, yet he joined the latter, reluctantly, while allowing the former to go to the wall. With neither did he have an obvious affiliation, although arguably he was more closely connected with the Whigs than any other 'party', and thus his conduct in the closing months of 1852 begs questions about his political motivations.

Although active in the search for an alternative to the Derby Government, the various factions sitting opposite the Treasury benches were not particularly well placed to challenge the Government. There was a need for some sort of re-alignment of parties, as the Duke of Newcastle argued in a letter to Aberdeen in August 1852 regarding the Peelite position. 'Union with Lord Derby is impossible', he suggested. 'Isolation is pleasant but not patriotic. Co-operation with other Liberals is requisite'.[33] The Peelites and the Protectionists were no longer united under the Conservative banner,[34] and the Whigs, who were led in opposition by Russell, were equally incapable of supplanting Derby themselves. Russell could not command the loyalty and respect of sufficient colleagues and Minto was forced to concede that his son-in-law could no longer claim to be able to carry the Whigs forward as a united body. 'Palmerston', he wrote in his journal, 'is I conceive the great difficulty at present; as he would not serve *under* tho he may be ready to serve *with* Ld John as a Colleague and it is to open the door for his return to us that some of our friends have desired to substitute Lansdowne for Lord John as Prime Minister'.[35] It was, then, in large measure a personal rivalry between Palmerston and Russell which damaged Whig prospects and the decent opportunity which Palmerston awaited was not to join Derby, but to return to his former colleagues under a different leadership, by playing Derby off against Russell throughout 1852.

Palmerston's confidence was misplaced as the political climate was not conducive at this time to such an enterprise. Now was the time when a new arrangement was called for, be that a union of the opposition members, or some sort of coalition. Newcastle imagined this was a watershed in British politics and sought, 'with a view to real fusion of all Liberals', to abandon the names 'Whig' and 'Peelite'. A new party, he believed, must be established 'not by one party joining another. With this view all old names as well as old jealousies must be abandoned'.[36] He was only expressing what Aberdeen himself had already said when he had written to Newcastle expressing his dissatisfaction with the Derby Administration: 'I cannot look to the continuance of the present Government in power with any degree of satisfaction', he said, concluding that, since Russell alone could not regain his old position:

I think therefore the time is come when we ought to act in cordial concert with Lord John and the Whigs. I am not aware of any real difference between us. Free Trade, with all its legitimate consequences, is quite safe; and I do not anticipate anything but agreement on the subject of our financial policy. Different views may be entertained respecting education, and the Church; but perhaps these are more theoretical than practical, and in which the necessity of mutual forbearance will be strongly felt. It is to be hoped, after the lesson of last year, that we shall have nothing to apprehend from any hostile interference on the part of the Whigs with religious freedom.[37]

Newcastle pressed on Aberdeen in August that in the present 'peculiar' circumstances, 'the state of parties [is] unprecedented, and I believe that, if *all* will lay aside selfish and personal views and wishes, you can better serve the Queen and the Country than any other person'.[38] At the same time, Russell told Graham that he was 'quite ready to support Lord Aberdeen as Prime Minister, if the Liberals prefer him to me'.[39] Aberdeen, however, displayed less confidence in his ability and prospects. There had been talk of him replacing Russell in 1848 which he had declared 'would be a dreadful affair, and I trust will never be realised', maintaining that if the Russell government did fail 'it is my determination to preserve my own freedom'.[40]

By 1852, however, the ground had shifted. Aberdeen was quite clearly the leading light among Peel's old colleagues and there was also considerable support within the Peelite ranks for an Aberdeen government. Still Aberdeen was a reluctant candidate, preferring a Russell-led administration which he could support though without being 'in office myself',[41] and even in the autumn he distanced himself from the attempts to supplant Derby. 'Shortly after the meeting of Parliament', he told Graham, 'we shall see more clearly what we have to expect. In the mean time, I am disposed to preserve my character of spectator; and as I have really no object of my own, I may do this the more easily'.[42] He would not attempt to construct a government which would stand little or no chance of survival purely for the sake of replacing Derby, and he seems not to have felt confident of his ability to do otherwise. Foreign affairs, as ever, continued to interest Aberdeen, and it was the poor management of this department which lay at the root of much of his frustration with Derby's government. However, he also maintained that 'the presence of Palmerston, as an influential member of any Govt, would create a serious difficulty; and this he must know perfectly well himself'.[43]

Palmerston, meanwhile, consolidated his own position and a certain detachment from party allegiance gave him an influential position in politics, perhaps something of a kingmaker, if not, indeed, a future leader-in-waiting himself.[44] As the Derby Administration stumbled in the autumn of 1852, attention in the press turned to the question of its replacement. Russell was dismissed as unfit again to become Prime Minister by the *Morning Post*: between him and that station were now 'raised up obstructions permanent and insurmountable', primarily popular and parliamentary distrust.[45] Palmerston, however, held a very strong hand, as one who 'in his present independent position, enjoys a wider popularity, and exercises a larger and more wholesome influence on the European mind, than any other living man'. On this ground, the *Post* argued, he need 'make no approaches to any party in the State ... for to him "*Tout vient à propos*", whether he wait or not'.[46] The *Post*, which was, according to Malmesbury, publishing articles paid for by the French Government, knew that Palmerston was well regarded in Paris, and particularly when he joined the Aberdeen Government Palmerston's known disposition to resort to war was a relief to Brünnow and Walewski.[47]

The *Globe* placed in Palmerston's hands the ability to turn out the Derby Government. Alluding to an old French caricature in which Calonne offered the Assembly of Notables the choice '*Mes chers animaux, à qu'elle sauce voulez-vous être mangés?*', the *Globe* asked the same question of the current British ministry, and helpfully outlined the options: 'The Chancellor of the Exchequer's, *à la financière*? – Mr VILLIER's Wolverhampton? – or Lord PALMERSTON's Tiverton sauce? It will be of little use for our poor Protective animals to reply, like CALONNE's – "Mais nous ne voulons pas être mangés!" ... That is a foregone conclusion'. The *Globe* believed it would be the Tiverton,[48] pointing out: 'As in the calculation of mechanical forces there always occurs the question, "Have you allowed for friction?" so in the anticipation of party divisions, there will henceforth occur the question, "Have you allowed for Palmerston?"'[49] Palmerston's standing no longer depended on his

day-to-day political activity and though his commitment to a free
trade government might be questionable, and for this, the *Globe*
admitted he was owed no 'gratitude for his conduct', and there
might thus be 'abundant grounds why Liberals should complain of
Lord PALMERSTON', this did not mean that his contributions in the
field of foreign policy to civil and religious liberty all over the world
should be ignored. Indeed 'it would be a scandalous injustice to
wreak our disappointment in slanders on the great achievements'
of his diplomatic career.[50]

In the closing month of the year the issue was brought to a
head when the Derby Government was defeated in the House of
Commons on a resolution for the increase of the House Tax.[51]
Although the Derbyites still out-numbered other factions at Westminster, combinations of these opposition groups now appeared
well-placed to supplant the Government. Derby himself reported
to the royal couple that he had heard that the Whigs and Peelites
would unite on Conservative principles under Aberdeen and,
'Although only 150 strong, they thought, that with all the talent
they had at their command, they would be able to obtain the
confidence of the country, and hold the balance between the two
extreme Parties in the House'.[52]

Derby advised the Queen to seek Lansdowne's advice and not
call upon Aberdeen straight away as such a move would be read
by Derbyites as having been prompted by Derby and lead those
among the ranks dissatisfied with Derby himself to with-hold
support from Aberdeen, while those Conservatives who felt betrayed
by the Peelites would ally themselves with the Radicals in a perverse
act of revenge. It was sensible advice and although Prince Albert
deemed it unconstitutional that an out-going premier should proffer
such a recommendation, it did not go altogether unheeded.

The Queen, after consulting Lansdowne and Aberdeen and
mooting the idea of some sort of ministry headed by the two of
them, was obliged to turn to the latter only as Lansdowne, prepared
to support a new 'liberal' administration, was not disposed to
attempt to lead one.[53] Aberdeen succeeded in forming a government,
and the new Cabinet comprised six each Whigs and Peelites and
one Radical and although it was not to everyone's taste, it was
workable. The Whigs especially were unhappy with the balance in
the Cabinet given the discrepancy in numbers in the House, but

Russell found that he could do little to remedy this fact.[54] Russell was vital to any Whig or Whig-Peelite Administration which might be established, and even though he had toyed with the idea of not joining at all, until Aberdeen had hinted that he would renounce the premiership in his favour sooner rather than later (an expensive hostage to fortune), Russell was unlikely to stand outside this new government. Minto had initially urged Russell to remain in opposition, telling him that by so doing 'you will recover your individuality instead of being seen as the impersonation of other mens errors',[55] but by October advised that though Russell should remain 'head of the great Whig party', there were 'only two men alive under whom you could submit to serve', one of whom was Lansdowne, the other Aberdeen.[56] Less certain, however, was Palmerston's position. He had successfully carved out something of an independent position during the previous ten months and it was not so clearly established that he would automatically join this Government; indeed there were those among his friends who believed he should not. But if the Aberdeen Government was to achieve anything, Palmerston, holding a certain balance between the Protectionists on the one hand and the Whigs and Peelites on the other, had to be brought on board.

When Palmerston accepted the Home Office under Aberdeen, the Peelite *Morning Chronicle* acknowledged that his 'great ability and long familiarity with affairs will add authority to his office as Secretary for the Home Department, while his influence in the House will, in case of need, be available for the assistance of a body of colleagues who will only be embarrassed by the absence of competent opponents'.[57] Palmerston wrote to make his peace with Russell, assuring him that 'we shall meet again as far as I am concerned just as good Friends as if we had never separated'.[58] Perhaps as Palmerston had told Lansdowne, he did not hold a grudge and could 'serve with him on equal Terms under a Third Person'.[59] So, Russell and Palmerston, it seemed, were reconciled, and Aberdeen and Palmerston, the 'Harrow Boys', were able to renew their school-boy friendship.[60]

Palmerston's accession to the Government was seen in some quarters however as a very expensive and submissive act. Argyll felt that Palmerston had made a great sacrifice 'of personal feeling to public duty'. Not only had the Foreign Office been given to

Russell ('the Minister who had summarily dismissed him from it'), but Palmerston now served 'under the leadership of a statesman whose arguments against his own policy he had described in the House of Commons as "antiquated imbecility"'.[61] Shaftesbury, too, confided in his diary at the time that Palmerston's acceptance of office, in direct contradiction of everything he had said previously, surprised him greatly, believing Palmerston had in some way been duped by Aberdeen and Russell, who had 'wanted to gag P.; and they have succeeded; they have bound the wild one between two tame elephants'.[62] Palmerston, however, suggested that after twelve months of 'acting the part of a Rope Dancer & much astonishing the public by my individual Performances and Feats', now was the time, for practical reasons, to cease playing the part of 'a reckless Adventurer' and commit to the cause of 'the great Liberal Party (not in the H. of Cms, nor at Brooks's nor at the Reform Club) but in the United Kingdom' and to fulfil his duty to his Tiverton constituents.[63]

There is a keen sense of realism running through Palmerston's correspondence at this time. Though he believed a ballot of the Whig party would return him (and not Russell) as 'their Chief', he also recognised that Russell was still seen as the Whigs' leader in the Commons: 'there he is, and he cannot be put down, nor put away'. To aim to become Prime Minister himself, he felt, was premature: 'that is not a thing a man can accomplish by willing it', he observed. 'He must first find himself the Head of some large party, and then must be chosen by the Sovereign, I could fulfill [sic] neither of those conditions.' His differences with Aberdeen over the years on matters of foreign policy similarly were not reason enough to refuse to serve with him (indeed Palmerston doubted how many people would remember such differences), and besides, there were in the new government those, notably Russell and Lansdowne, who had been parties to his own foreign policy in earlier governments. 'People must in this world take things as they find them', he wrote, 'and deal with them as best they can; and they who think they can have every thing their own way, generally find that every thing goes the way they wish it not to go'.[64]

The Queen was pleased to have a government 'so brilliant and strong', which she held 'deserves success, and will I think, command great support'.[65] The fact that Aberdeen was at the head of the

Government was 'a great happiness and comfort', but she was also greatly relieved to see that Palmerston's capacity to disrupt public affairs was much reduced. To her uncle she wrote: 'Lord Palmerston is terribly altered, and all his friends think him breaking. He walks with two sticks, and seemed in great suffering at the Council, I thought'.[66] It took more than a bit of gout to keep Palmerston down, however. His colleagues did not assume that he was a spent force, but they did take heart from the fact that his new public role seemed to distance him from his traditional sphere of influence. As the Government's new Lord Privy Seal observed: 'The only member of the Government who was considered a dangerous man, and who in very recent years had gone near to embroiling us with France, was safely tethered within the peaceful pastures of the Home Office'.[67]

Palmerston was not to see his public duties as being neatly confined within the arena of domestic affairs, but at the outset all signs augured well for a stable and effective new government. Aberdeen recognised that this Whig-Peelite 'coalition', was a 'great experiment, hitherto unattempted, and of which the success must be considered doubtful. In the meantime, the Public have regarded the new administration with singular favour'. Nevertheless, he could not deny that while the coming Parliamentary session would be difficult, 'I am sanguine in my belief, that our good measures will procure for us sufficient majorities in Parliament, as well as the support of the country'.[68] A fortnight later he was even more optimistic, telling Guizot, the former French ambassador: 'I have every reason to be satisfied with the disposition of my colleagues, and trust it may continue'.[69] Even the Whigs could find grounds for a small measure of optimism. As Clarendon told his wife, 'people were in better heart' now concerning the prospects of the ministry, even 'the Whig Chiefs who were so alarmed 2 or 3 days ago & if there is a rattling opposition to keep them all together the experiment may succeed but there is many a rock ahead'.[70] Minto was worried about the 'rival ambition of party distinction' undermining a government 'combining such an amount of talent, experience & high character' which on paper gave 'a promise of good government to the country', but he too was prepared to be positive: 'We must however hope for the best where so many men of sense & public virtue are combined for a common object and united by a common interest'. Such hopes, he believed, would be fulfilled provided the Peelites recognised the importance of not alienating Russell and the Whigs, numerically the mainstay of the new administration.[71] Walter Bagehot subsequently described the Aberdeen Cabinet as 'the ablest we have had, perhaps, since the Reform Act', but as he also noted, it was 'a cabinet not only adapted, but eminently adapted, for every sort of difficulty save the one that it had to meet'.[72] And that difficulty, significantly, was one of foreign affairs.

Notes

1　An observation made after the debate of 3 Feb. 1852 quoted in A. Lyall, *The Life of the Marquis of Dufferin and Ava* (London, 1905), p. 77.
2　Russell Papers, PRO, 30/22/10A(1), fol. 80, Truro to Russell, Jan. 1852.
3　Gooch (ed.), *Later Correspondence of Lord John Russell*, II, p. 94, Clarendon to Russell, 26 Dec. 1851.
4　*Ibid.*, II, p. 96, Clarendon to Russell, 4 Jan. 1852.
5　Bell, *Palmerston*, II, p. 58, Palmerston to Clarendon, 23 Feb. 1852.
6　Broadlands Papers, GC/TE/342, Palmerston to Sir William Temple, 24 Feb. 1852.
7　*Daily News*, 23 Feb. 1852.
8　George Douglas Campbell, Eighth Duke of Argyll, *Autobiography and Memoirs*, ed. Dowager Duchess of Argyll, 2 vols (London, 1906), I, p. 361. Cf. Angus Hawkins' more favourable assessment in 'Lord Derby and Victorian Conservatism: A Reappraisal', *Parliamentary History*, 6 (1987), 280–301.
9　Broadlands Papers, GC/RU/464, Russell to Palmerston, 4 March 1852.
10　*Ibid.*, GC/RU/464/enc.1, Palmerston to Russell, 5 March 1852; *ibid.*, GC/RU/465, Russell to Palmerston, 6 March 1852.
11　Quoted Monypenny and Buckle, *Disraeli*, I, p. 1155.
12　*Ibid.*, I, p. 1156.
13　*Ibid.*, I, p. 1158, Disraeli to Derby, 'Friday night' [Feb. 1852].
14　In July, for example, Lord Stanley agreeing with Disraeli and others that the Government needed to broaden its base, wrote, 'the ship requires fine steering; but she requires something else as well: an accession to the strength of the crew. There is an old helmsman who would be very useful in taking an occasional spell at the wheel'. There was no misunderstanding that this old helmsman was Palmerston, *ibid.*, I, p. 1196.
15　Hawkins, 'Lord Derby and Victorian Conservatism', p. 287.
16　Southgate, *'The Most English Minister ...'*, p. 310, Roebuck to Sir James Graham, 20 July 1852.
17　C. C. F. Greville, *The Greville Memoirs (third part): A Journal of the Reign of Queen Victoria, from 1852 to 1860*, ed. H. Reeve, 2 vols (London, 1887), I, p. 3 (22 Oct. 1852).

18 Lord Malmesbury, *Memoirs of an Ex-Minister, An Autobiography* 2 vols (London, 1884), I, pp. 305, 317.

19 Bell, *Palmerston*, II, p. 61; Southgate, '*The Most English Minister ...*', p. 310.

20 Grey Papers, 3rd Earl, C3/16, Grey, journal, 29 June 1852, 30 June 1852.

21 Bell, *Palmerston*, II, p. 64, Evelyn Denison [Speaker of the House of Commons] to Aberdeen, May 1852.

22 *Ibid.*, II, p. 64.

23 H. Maxwell, *The Life and Letters of George William Frederick Fourth Earl of Clarendon* 2 vols (London, 1913), I, p. 350, Charles Greville to Clarendon, 21 Oct. 1852.

24 Bodleian Library, Oxford, Graham Papers (microfilm), MS Film 124, Bundle 112, Graham to Russell, 6 Sept. 1852 (copy).

25 Eyck, *Prince Consort*, pp. 196–7.

26 Maxwell, *Clarendon*, I, p. 350, Charles Greville to Clarendon, 21 Oct. 1852.

27 Aberdeen Papers, Add. Mss. 43068, Aberdeen to Russell, 30 Nov. 1854. See also M. E. Chamberlain, *Lord Aberdeen* (Harlow, 1983), p. 434.

28 Graham Papers, MS Film 124, Bundle 112, G. C. Lewis to Graham, 8 Sept. 1852.

29 *Ibid.*, MS Film 124, Bundle 112, G. C. Lewis to Graham, 25 Oct. 1852.

30 *Ibid.*, MS Film 124, Bundle 112, G. C. Lewis to Graham, 11 Oct. 1852.

31 Ridley, *Palmerston*, p. 405. See also Bourne, *Palmerston: The Early Years*, esp. pp. 181–287 on Palmerston's financial situation. The *Standard* of 8 Feb. 1853 argued that in joining Aberdeen's government '"his poverty but not his will consented"' and in the light of the recent increase in the Palmerstons' income ('no less than 20,000*l* per annum') expected an apology for his joining the Government.

32 Lansdowne Papers, Lans 3/42, fol. 64, Lady Palmerston to Lansdowne, 'Wednesday', Dec. 1852. Palmerston was later to describe Lansdowne as 'the Person by whose advice I joined the present Government' (*ibid.*, Lans 3/42, fol. 37, Palmerston to Lansdowne, 22 April 1853). It is not possible to determine the extent to which Lady Palmerston had an impact upon Lansdowne's advice to Palmerston.

33 Aberdeen Papers, Add. Mss. 43197, fols 11–18, Newcastle to Aberdeen, 2 Aug. 1852.

34 See J. B. Conacher, *The Aberdeen Coalition, 1852–1855* (Cambridge, 1968), pp. 12–36; R. Blake, *The Conservative Party from Peel to Thatcher* (London, 1985), pp. 83–4.

35 Minto Papers, MS 11998, Minto, journal, 28 Aug. 1852.

36 Aberdeen Papers, Add. Mss. 43197, Newcastle to Aberdeen, 3 Aug. 1852.

37 *Ibid.*, Add. Mss. 43197, Aberdeen to Newcastle, 25 July 1852.

38 *Ibid.*, Add. Mss. 43197, Newcastle to Aberdeen, 2 Aug. 1852. Indeed, Newcastle had hoped to see Aberdeen at the head of the Peelites for some months (see H. J. Hanham (ed.), *The Nineteenth Century Constitution* (Cambridge, 1969), pp. 223–34, Newcastle to Sidney Herbert, 27 Oct. 1851).

39 C. S. Parker, *Life and Letters of Sir James Graham, Second Baronet of Netherby,*

1792–1861 2 vols (London, 1907), II, p. 174, Russell to Graham, 18 Aug. 1852.

40   Chamberlain, *Aberdeen*, p. 418, Aberdeen to Lady Haddo, 30 June, 8 July 1848.

41   Aberdeen Papers, Add. Mss. 43197, Aberdeen to Newcastle, 25 July 1852.

42   Graham Papers, MS Film 124, Bundle 112, Aberdeen to Graham, 7[?, poss. 8, or 2] Oct. 1852.

43   *Ibid.*, MS Film 124, Bundle 112, Aberdeen to Graham, 28 Oct. 1852.

44   As Algernon Borthwick wrote to his father at this time: 'Putting aside the ill-conduct question, the Russell Cabinet is evidently "done for". Stanley can't make a Cabinet and Graham can't make a Party. Coalition must be the order of the day. Now to say true, it seems to me that any Body may coalesce with any Body Else:

> Stanley and Graham
> Palmerston and Graham
> Graham and the Radicals
> Palmerston and the Radicals
> Palmerston and the Protectionists:

these may all join and interjoin if it suit them – I see no Principles that stand in the way, for the truth is that no one has any, except Lord P. I see no impediment to their *all* joining him'. He also reiterated his intention that 'the *Post* will always be Palmerston's true Friend' (Brotherton Library, Leeds University, Glenesk-Bathurst Papers, MS. Dep. 1990/1/1173, Algernon Borthwick to Peter Borthwick, 13 Dec. 1852).

45   *Morning Post*, 4 Oct. 1852.

46   *Ibid.*, 7 Oct. 1852.

47   Malmesbury, *Memoirs*, I, pp. 362 (4 and 5 Nov. 1852), 402 (3 June 1853).

48   *Globe*, 24 Nov. 1852.

49   *Ibid.*, 25 Nov. 1852.

50   *Ibid.*, 27 Nov. 1852.

51   *LQV*, II, pp. 499–500, Derby to Queen, 17 Dec. 1852.

52   *LQV*, II, pp. 500–2, memorandum by Prince Albert, 18 Dec. 1852. According to this memorandum, Derby calculated that the House was composed of 286 Government supporters, 150 Radicals, 50 'of the so-called Irish Brigade', 120 Whigs and 30 Peelites.

53   *LQV*, II, pp. 508–9, Queen to King of the Belgians, 21 Dec. 1852.

54   See C. H. Stuart, 'The Formation of the Coalition Cabinet of 1852', *Transactions of the Royal Historical Society*, 5th ser., IV (1954), 45–68 and Conacher, *The Aberdeen Coalition*, pp. 12–36.

55   Russell Papers, PRO 30/22/10E , Minto to Russell, 17 Sept. 1852.

56   *Ibid.*, PRO 30/22/10E, Minto to Russell, 4 Oct. 1852. Minto preferred Lansdowne to Aberdeen in such an arrangement.

57   *Morning Chronicle*, 24 Dec. 1852.

58   Russell Papers, PRO 30/22/10F, fols 117–18, Palmerston to Russell, 23 Dec. 1852.

59 Lansdowne Papers, Lans. 3/42, fol. 35, Palmerston to Lansdowne, 4 Oct. 1852.

60 'Lord Aberdeen said that when he saw Lord Palmerston, who then declined office, nothing could have exceeded the expressions of his cordiality; he had even reminded him that in fact they were great friends (!!!) of sixty years' standing, having been at school together. We could not help laughing heartily at the Harrow Boys and their friendship'. *LQV*, II, p. 511, memorandum by Prince Albert, 22 Dec. 1852.

61 Argyll, *Autobiography and Memoirs*, I, pp. 378–89.

62 Broadlands Papers, SHA/PD/6, Shaftesbury Diaries, 30 Dec. 1852.

63 *Ibid.*, GC/SU/34/2, Palmerston to Sulivan, 31 Dec. 1852. Contrast this with Lady Palmerston's brief notice of Palmerston's return at Tiverton in January: 'Election Tiverton everything prosperous. P's speech excellent. He did justice to Ld Derby's G[overnmen]t which [Sir James] Graham & John [Russell] absurdly cried down – a contrast that was very favourable to P' (Hatfield House, Hertfordshire, Lady Palmerston Papers, diary of Lady Palmerston, 3 Jan. 1853).

64 Broadlands Papers, GC/SU/34/1–4, Palmerston to Sulivan, 31 Dec. 1852.

65 *LQV*, II, p. 521, Queen to King of the Belgians, 28 Dec. 1852.

66 *LQV*, II, pp. 522–3, Queen to King of the Belgians, 31 Dec. 1852.

67 Argyll, *Autobiography and Memoirs*, I, p. 389.

68 Conacher, *The Aberdeen Coalition*, p. 49, Aberdeen to Edward Everett (U.S. cabinet minister and friend of Aberdeen), 13 Jan. 1853.

69 *Ibid.*, p. 49, Aberdeen to Guizot, 26 Jan. 1853.

70 Bodleian Library, English Manuscripts, MSS. Eng.c.2085, Clarendon to Lady Clarendon, 27 Dec. 1852.

71 Minto Papers, MS 11999, Minto, journal, 1, 2 & 3 Jan. 1853.

72 Bagehot, *English Constitution*, p. 20.

7

Palmerston, the Aberdeen Government and the politics of foreign policy: 1853 – hawks and doves

On taking up office in December 1852, Aberdeen felt it one of his first duties to address the question of the Government's foreign policy. Particularly with Palmerston sitting on the Treasury bench, it seemed requisite that some sort of declaration be made and Aberdeen played deftly upon a common belief that any future threat to the integrity of Britain would come from France. 'The truth is', he told the House of Lords, 'that for the last thirty years the principles of the foreign policy of this country have never varied. There may have been differences in the execution, according to the different hands intrusted with the direction of that policy: but the foundation of the foreign policy of this country has been, I repeat, for the last thirty years the same'. In particular, he said, there had always been 'an earnest desire to secure the general peace of Europe by all such means as were practicable and at our disposal'.[1] Muriel Chamberlain has said that this 'assertion of the essential continuity of British foreign policy caused understandable surprise, but he had worded the statement very carefully and there was, perhaps, an element of casuistry in it'.[2] Surprise it may have caused, but in emphasising the desire to assert British honour and interests, and to preserve European peace, Aberdeen simply drew out those factors which underpinned all foreign policies.

The question of the basis of British foreign policy and indeed, the manner of its implementation, is particularly important during this period. During the nineteenth century, at least down to the early 1880s, there are commonly held to be two distinct traditions, or schools, of foreign policy. On the one hand, Castlereagh, Aberdeen and Gladstone represented the 'European' approach, while Canning, Palmerston and Disraeli are seen to have pursued 'English' policies.

Each eulogised the younger Pitt's commitment to protect British interests, especially economic and commercial ones, through the preservation of a balance of power in Europe,[3] but it was the interpretation of this Pittite legacy, of course, that caused confusion. Castlereagh sought to bind the European Powers together, in a congress system, most obviously in 1814 and 1815, but when Canning followed him into the Foreign Office in 1822, he quickly set about changing such a 'new and very questionable policy', which would involve Britain 'deeply in all the politics of the Continent, whereas our true policy has always been not to interfere except in great emergencies, and then with commanding force'.[4] To contemporaries, at Westminster at least, the differences between these two approaches were fairly obvious, and in the 1850s there was an important clash between these two traditions, as Palmerston and Aberdeen fought to establish a supremacy in the Cabinet for their own strategies over the Crimean situation.

Meanwhile, Palmerston was safely ensconced at the Home Office where he set about his new duties with vigour and enthusiasm. Not only was he content to forego any claims to the Foreign Office, but he had told his constituents in Tiverton when they returned him in January 1853 that he had accepted 'that office which I was most desirous to fill'. In so far as he spoke of foreign affairs, he mentioned only the liberal instincts of the whole Government.[5] Palmerston continued to concern himself with questions of national defence, but, with regard to the threat from France, he told Aberdeen, 'I think that with common Prudence, & common Good Fortune we are safe for 1853 and I should hope for 1854', and thus the priority for the Government was 'to employ this interval in preparing actively permanent means of Defence'.[6] But this could, of course, be monitored easily from the Home Office.

During the life of the Government Palmerston oversaw the introduction of the Factory Act of 1853, which while not fulfilling all of the hopes of reformers such as Shaftesbury, did go some way towards improving industrial working conditions, especially for children. He also attempted to pass legislation which would have confirmed the rights of trade unions to combine for lawful purposes as laid down in an Act of 1825 (although he resisted trade union demands for the legalisation of peaceful picketing) and, more successfully, introduced the Truck Act under the terms of which workers were entitled to payment in money, rather than goods or tokens for employers' own shops. Palmerston also sought to improve the condition of society, both environmentally and morally. He pioneered legislation aimed at curbing pollution with the weak but well-intentioned Smoke Abatement Act in August 1853, for example, and throughout was a firm friend of the Temperance societies. Nor did he shy away from the thorny problems associated with prisons and their reform.[7]

Although the duties of the Home Office were great,[8] Palmerston's colleagues, or at least some of them, still wanted him to be involved in foreign politics. From the outset Palmerston was regarded as an important figure in foreign affairs, significantly being among the select group which met the diplomatic corps in January,[9] and the Government was not yet three months old when, at Clarendon's suggestion, Palmerston was invited to join Aberdeen, Russell, Graham and Clarendon for a meeting at the Admiralty to discuss affairs relating to Constantinople. With a crisis seemingly imminent in the Near East, by keeping Palmerston within the inner circle it was hoped to avoid him damaging the Government's foreign policy from without.

It is not insignificant that Palmerston's interest in home affairs, while sincere enough, was to wane as problems in the East developed and he could not disguise the fact that foreign affairs remained his first concern. When strikes broke out in the north of England as workers demanded a 10 per cent wage increase, *The Economist* asked with some justification, 'is Palmerston aware of these things?',[10] while the Home Secretary placed his faith in the market to resolve the problem.[11] When asked by the Queen whether he had any news about these strikes it is said that Palmerston replied: 'No, Madam, I have heard nothing; but it seems certain *the Turks have crossed the Danube*'.[12] Later, Shaftesbury was to complain when measures for various reforms seemed to be making little or no ground at Westminster, that: 'I have much to complain of in the sluggishness, indifference, & yet promises & professions of Palmerston. He undertakes every thing, performs nothing, but actually destroys a great deal'.[13]

It certainly took the newspapers a little while to adjust to Palmerston's new employment. As late as the summer of 1853, *The Times* still felt the need to make explicit this change and made a point of observing to its readers that 'though his heart may be on the Danube, his hand must be in the Holborn sewers'. Nonetheless, Palmerston had committed himself to numerous domestic measures which if executed with the same 'dexterity and fortune' that had characterised his foreign secretaryship, would give 'little reason for regretting the revolution which transferred such indefatigable energies to the peaceful fields of the Home-office'.[14] At the end of the first parliamentary session, the early positive forecasts about the ministry's potential looked well founded, and Palmerston's measures at the Home Office, especially those directed towards the improvement of towns and repression of crime, attracted favourable notice in certain sections of the press.[15]

Nevertheless, Palmerston was still seen first and foremost as a foreign minister, and there was no reason for this impression to be challenged given Palmerston's close involvement in Cabinet discussions of foreign policy from the very outset of this Government.[16] Protectionist journals persisted in complimenting Palmerston's abilities and suggesting that the conduct of the country's foreign policy would have been quite different had he been re-instated in his old station, indeed the *Standard* in February expected to see Palmerston leave the Government if he was not re-installed at the Foreign Office.[17] These assertions Palmerston strenuously denied in public speeches, but it is significant that in reporting one such speech, delivered in Perth, *The Economist* noted that there was no better judge of what is due to the country's honour than Palmerston, 'and he would neither continue to sit in the Cabinet, nor eulogise the Foreign Secretary, were he not perfectly convinced that the course pursued with respect to other countries is equally wise and spirited, calculated to preserve peace, ... and raise the national honour'.[18] Still, then, Palmerston's explicit support for Clarendon's management of foreign affairs was looked for even if he was not to handle matters himself.

But, with matters in the Ottoman Empire coming to a head, Palmerston had no desire to pass up an opportunity to engage once again in matters of foreign policy. Nor indeed, did the public want or expect him to do otherwise. When, by the summer, Palmerston still seemed to be playing second fiddle to the leadership of Aberdeen and Russell and relinquishing claims to the Foreign Office in favour of Clarendon, one correspondent asked:

What can have become of you? Your friends say that you are fright-
ened at Nicholas. Your Enemies, that you have sold the Liberties of
Europe to him and are preparing to become a Cossack.

I try to reassure both – that you are biding your time and may
shortly be expected to flash out as of yore ...

Oh, my Lord,! I did ever hope better Things of you and that whilst
you bind [?] Europe would not verify Napoleon's Prediction by
becoming a Cossack. But it is a sad Condition that you are placed
in! And your friends sorrowfully pray that you could emancipate
yourself from the tame elephants.[19]

While Palmerston may have been making progress in his domestic
reforms, attracting 'a new and widely extended public attention to
the subject' of smoke abatement, as Edwin Chadwick noted,[20] chief
among his identifiable attributes was his association with foreign
policy. In September 1853 he received honours from two sources
in Scotland. The Guild Incorporation of Perth bestowed on him the
freedom of the Corporation in recognition 'particularly of the firm,
manly, independent and truly British spirit uniformly displayed by
his Lordship, more especially when in the management of the foreign
relations of the United Kingdom'.[21] Still prominent were the symbolic images of heroic leadership: strong-willed, manly and in the
interests of the nation; and significantly, given the common feeling
that the main challenge of the Crimean War was as a test of the
abilities of the traditional ruling class to *manage* the war *efficiently*
(these terms are important),[22] Palmerston's standing as no less an
able manager than he was a member of the aristocratic elite is
important.

These sentiments were echoed at the same time in Glasgow
where Palmerston was awarded the freedom of the city. In his formal
speech presenting Palmerston with the freedom, the Lord Provost
referred to Palmerston being 'considered by your countrymen as
the greatest statesman of the age, and the most distinguished public
man of your day. (Loud cheers)' and highlighted 'the courage and
determination you have so often displayed in protecting the interests
and the privileges of your countrymen abroad – (loud cheers) – or
the manner in which you have upheld the honour and maintained
the dignity of your Sovereign and your country. (Loud cheers)'.
Even the one reference made to Palmerston's current tenure of the

Home Office was vague and emphasised still the national character of the value to the country of Palmerston still serving 'in so prominent place in her Majesty's Councils'.

In his acceptance speech, Palmerston praised the virtues of an enlightened and civilised society in which such honours as he was now in receipt of were all the more valuable, and then turned to Lord John Russell and Thomas Babington Macaulay who, as the Lord Provost had boasted in his speech, had also been similarly honoured. It perhaps jarred with Palmerston to be thus compared with Russell, but it is interesting to consider the qualities which he perceived he and Russell shared, describing Russell as 'the most energetic, the most consistent, the most persevering champion of the cause of civil and religious liberty in every quarter of the world'. On this basis, it was probably true that holding the freedom of the city in common with Russell added to the satisfaction of that honour. Likewise, Palmerston praised Macaulay's 'rare faculty of combining in his person the sagacity, the wisdom, and the practical experience of a statesman, with that intellectual distinction which qualifies him to be one of the greatest historians this country has ever produced'. By implication therefore, Palmerston was underlining his own libertarian and wise and sagacious conduct; appropriating the finer attributes of those with whom he was compared for his own self-enhancement. In common with those who bestowed the honour, Palmerston spoke primarily of his record in foreign affairs, and also made a good deal of his attempts to suppress the slave trade, which he surely knew would gratify non-conformist consciences and reinforce the notion that, as Colley puts it, 'Great Britain was still Israel, and its crusade against slavery was just one more vital proof and guarantee of its supremacy among the nations'.[23] Again, Palmerstonian foreign policy sought to appeal to a sense of a providentially-ordained national mission and Palmerston reiterated his belief in the principles which had underpinned the famous '*civis Romanus sum*' speech and talked of the responsibility he had felt to promote free and constitutional government throughout the world. By contrast, of his present employment he said simply: 'I can only say, in regard to the department which is now committed to my charge, that I shall always be thankful to any one who may suggest improvements, pointing out what may in their opinion be wrong, and enabling me to set that which is wrong right'.[24] Here was no pro-active manifesto: Palmerston it seemed had learned the value of courting popular support for his foreign policy and now sought also popular guidance for his domestic policy. It was, perhaps, a tacit admission that he had neither the desire nor the foresight to propose a grand scheme of domestic reforms.

Palmerston's real vision and grandiloquence, which swayed his extra-parliamentary audiences, found their expression in the domain of foreign affairs only. However sincere Palmerston might have been in the reforms he pursued at the Home Office it was still with foreign affairs that people most readily associated him and it was in this respect that, primarily, Palmerston regarded himself. Even when Palmerston offended Protestant feeling in his domestic measures – refusing, for example, to sanction a day of fast and prayer in the face of a request from Edinburgh presbyters concerned about the threat of cholera in October 1853, and, the following year, actually pleading for the pay of Roman Catholic prison chaplains [25] – he continued to stand, in many ways, as an important counter-point to a Catholic alternative, as a Protestant guardian of the nation.

He might have told Clarendon that it was 'a great Comfort and Satisfaction to me to know that the Conduct of our Foreign Relations is in such able Hands as yours; and your administration of your important Department is attended with this great advantage to the Country that, from a variety of Circumstances, you can say and do Things which could not so easily have been said or done by me',[26] but still he felt that a degree of guidance was required. After all, Palmerston pointed out to Clarendon in August 1853, the Foreign Secretary had been 'put into the position of a general who, having taken the command of an army one day, should be called upon to go into action the next, before he had made himself acquainted with the qualities, habits and dispositions of his officers, and before he had had time to sound the tactics of his opponents; and who, moreover, should find himself fettered by a council of war some of whose members were of the slow-march school.' [27] Clarendon's insistence that Palmerston be included within the inner Cabinet bore testimony to the importance of Palmerston's decade-and-a-half spent at the Foreign Office, but Palmerston's inclusion was also a safety device, as Aberdeen explained to the Queen on one occasion:

Unless he [Palmerston] should continue to be a cordial member of your Majesty's Government, he may very easily become the leader of the Opposition. Lord Aberdeen is, at this moment, ignorant of his real views and intentions. He has been recently more than once thwarted in his endeavours to press a warlike policy upon the Cabinet; and it has been reported to Lord Aberdeen, that he has expressed himself in terms of great hostility. This cannot perhaps be avoided, and is only the result of taking different views of the public interest; but it is very essential that Lord Palmerston should have no personal or private cause of complaint against Lord Aberdeen.[28]

Nevertheless, even Aberdeen was to find this ultimately unacceptable. Bell has written of the growing dissatisfaction which the Prime Minister felt as he saw the influence Palmerston had over Clarendon,[29] and by the autumn of 1853 Russell, who undoubtedly had ulterior motives in view, wished that Palmerston could, in some way, be ejected from the Government. Palmerston was an active Home Secretary, but he did not confine himself to domestic labours, and nor was this what influential members of the Cabinet wanted of him. However, Palmerston was not to be the steady counsellor which Aberdeen for one would have liked, but rather he was to seek to press upon the Cabinet a Palmerstonian outlook. The Eastern question brought the problem to the forefront of politics and the nature of the divisions within the British Cabinet did little to prevent the descent into war.

It has for a long time been commonplace to talk of the Ottoman Empire during the nineteenth century as moribund, decaying and weak. Without doubt, there was at Constantinople a lesser degree of stability than was to be found, perhaps, in the capital cities of the other Great Powers, but it was not inevitable that the particular sickness of that Empire in the 1850s would drag the others into a costly and damaging conflict.[30] The crisis of 1839–41 had done little to halt the disintegration of the Ottoman Empire, nor were antagonisms between the Great Powers of Europe which were centred around the Near East completely overcome. Rivalries were, however, noticeably less acute and the 1840s witnessed something of a rapprochement, most significantly in the agreement between Russia and Britain concluded in 1844. While the Tsar continued to regard the collapse of the Ottoman Empire as imminent, he was desirous of averting this problem for as long as possible, thus allowing provisions to be made for a stable partition of the territory. The nature of the balance of power meant that Russia would not, indeed could not, achieve this single-handed, but Franco-Russian relations were not conducive to an accord and overtures towards Metternich in 1843 had failed to bring Russia and Austria together on the issue. In Britain, Peel's Foreign Secretary, Aberdeen, had been more receptive to the Tsar's appeals and an agreement between Britain and Russia was forged in the summer of 1844 founded in no small measure upon a mutual dislike of France.[31] In effect it represented little more than a commitment to cooperate in the event of an attack upon, or a collapse of, the Ottoman Empire. There was no discussion of what constituted a genuine threat to Turkey's existence, nor was there any specific discussion of how Ottoman land would be disposed of in such a case. The Tsar, though, was satisfied. He saw to it that the agreement was 'formalised' in what has become known as the Nesselrode Memorandum, and in Britain, Peel and Aberdeen accepted this summary of the summer's dialogue as accurate.

It has been said that the Tsar mistakenly placed too much trust in this agreement and saw the Nesselrode communication as a symbol of a solid alliance. Certainly, the Russians placed a good deal more stock in the understanding than did the British, especially given that, not having been formalised by treaty but rather by more casual means it was not to survive in any meaningful way beyond the life of Peel's government when it fell in 1846. Events of the later 1840s served only to illustrate the great divide which separated Russia and Britain.[32] Nevertheless, when the dispute arose over the Holy Places in the late 1840s, the Tsar believed he could count on British support and by 1853, with Aberdeen back in office, now as Prime Minister, he perhaps had grounds to feel sanguine. Thus it was that in January 1853 Nicholas sought to revive the 'spirit of 1844' by opening conversations with Sir Hamilton Seymour, the British Ambassador to Russia.

The Tsar's approaches to Seymour 'provided apparent justification for British distrust by indulging in another venture in personal diplomacy'.[33] Indeed the role of Seymour points to the importance of personalities on both sides in exacerbating the tensions. With no telegraph to Constantinople, diplomats there exercised a good deal of personal influence, and, significantly, in the first half of 1853, according to Gavin Henderson, 'Seymour was ... anti-Russian at a time when the British Cabinet and the Russian Government were still on the most amicable terms: and, presuming that the Czar's assurances contained some real security against Russian aggression, Seymour had ceased to be a suitable minister for the maintenance of cordial relations'.[34] So the British Minister at St Petersburg was ill-suited to his task and the Tsar had dispatched to Constantinople, in an attempt to tie Russia and Turkey together against the western Powers, 'the perennially sarcastic, nationalist-minded, lackadaisical Minister of the Marine since 1830, Prince A. S. Menshikov, a man with questionable diplomatic credentials'.[35] It did not augur well for a peaceful year in the East.

In London these developments had far-reaching ramifications. The Duke of Argyll believed that there was reason initially to expect unity and firmness within the Cabinet, the Eastern question, he suggested, being the one foreign question which would not tear the new Aberdeen administration apart, pointing especially to Aberdeen's approbation of Palmerston's Eastern policy of 1839–41 as reason enough to trust that 'the basis of our policy in any revival of the Eastern Question rested on maxims of policy on which all the members of that Cabinet had long been thoroughly agreed'.[36] Furthermore, however dubious its status, the Nesselrode Memorandum gave the British Cabinet 'no reason to believe that ... [the Tsar] contemplated a different course of policy, we had every right to entertain that unsuspecting confidence in European peace which was undoubtedly the attitude of all our minds during the earlier months of 1853'.[37] Such was the attitude of the Cabinet indeed that in the opening few weeks of 1853, according to Argyll, the Eastern question impinged but little upon its meetings, given the faith placed in Aberdeen and Foreign Secretary Russell and the over-riding concern with the fate of Gladstone's budget. Only Palmerston, suggests Argyll, entertained any sympathy for Turkey although even this was little evident at the time.[38]

Palmerston recognised that this was a question above all of *Realpolitik*, and his Turcophile attitude was dictated largely by his conception of the British national interest. As he wrote to Clarendon in September 1853, 'the activity, spirit & the Energy, moral & Physical, military & political which the Turks have displayed in dealing with their present Crisis, must surely convince any impartial

& unprejudiced Person that Turkey is not a dead or dying Body, but that on the Contrary it possesses Powers of Life & national Resources which render it worth maintaining as a useful Element in the European Balance'.[39] In another letter to Clarendon a month later he elucidated further:

> We maintain the Integrity & Independence of Turkey not for the Love & affection for the Turks, but because we prefer the existing state of Things there, to any other state of Things which at present wd be humanly possible, and because the Interest political and Commercial of England & of Europe would be dangerously injured by the Destruction of that Integrity and Independence. For these Reasons we have undertaken to defend Turkey against Russia, and we could not sacrifice those great Interests by abandoning Turkey to her Fate merely because the Turkish Govt might not take our advice ... Things have in truth come to such a Pass that the real Conflict is between Russia on the one Hand & England & France on the other, much more than between Russia & Turkey, & unless England & France are prepared to sink down into the Condition of second Rate Powers they *must* prevail, by negotiation if possible, but by Force of arms if necessary.[40]

Soon foreign policy occupied a central role in politics and not only was Palmerston brought into the inner Cabinet in March, but by late April it is reported that every meeting of the full Cabinet was dominated by foreign affairs. Argyll records that at these meetings Palmerston was usually quiet and passive; that he concurred in the general thrust of the ministry's policy not wishing to undermine Clarendon.[41] This was partly due to his own standing. It was also, perhaps, the result of Stratford Canning directing affairs on the Government's behalf at Constantinople. There is much written on the extent to which Canning must shoulder the responsibility for embroiling Britain and indeed Russia and Turkey in war, but little on the way in which this impacted upon Palmerston's own position.

Initially, Stratford found favour with the new Government and Clarendon enthused on receipt of his first dispatches from Constantinople, 'We have a real jockey on our horse instead of a stable boy [Colonel Rose whom Canning replaced], and the odds are highest against the Czar'.[42] By May of 1853, however, the lustre was fading and Graham complained that the British ambassador 'is a Bashaw [i.e. a Pasha] – too long accustomed to rule alone. Such tempers and manners are not the pledges or emblems of peace'.[43] He was not the only member of the Cabinet to become frustrated with Stratford.

Throughout the year there was a feeling that Stratford was pursuing his own programme at Constantinople and by November Aberdeen declared, 'I have not the slightest confidence in him, I only feel some curiosity to see how he will contrive to defeat the objects of his government'.[44] Stratford was not necessarily intriguing to undermine the Government in London; as he acknowledged himself, in discussing policy in correspondence with ministers, it was his duty to confine himself 'to general intimations, conceiving that all beyond is the special domain of Her Majesty's Government',[45] but his actions did contribute to the division and fragmentation of that administration. Meanwhile Clarendon, at least, feared that a perception of Palmerstonian bellicosity within the Cabinet was fuelling Canning's forcefulness at Constantinople, and he and Aberdeen hoped, in early 1854, that 'Palmerston's resignation may make Lord Stratford more pacific'.[46] If neither Canning nor Palmerston directly encouraged the other, their outlooks still remained essentially concordant and frequently Stratford's actions were grist to Palmerston's mill, giving him grounds upon which to challenge the foreign policy of the Government, which he was to do in conjunction with Russell during 1853.

It is important to remember that in most areas other than foreign policy the Aberdeen Government enjoyed a particularly successful first year. The Cabinet was united on most issues and wherever divisions did occur, they were not along old party lines. As Aberdeen told Princess Lieven in the autumn: 'We have brought the Session of Parliament to a triumphant close; we have carried many useful and important measures; our majorities were numerous; and although a coalition of very different materials, we have adhered well together. For my part, I think I have done quite enough, but when *chained to the oar* it is difficult to escape'.[47] However, the omission of any reference to questions of foreign policy is striking for in this field there was anything but a sense of the Cabinet adhering well together. The roots of the coalition were exposed as Whigs and Peelites adopted differing stands over foreign policy, or at least over the Eastern question, and Greville recorded the observation made to him by Clarendon that far from the continuity in foreign affairs of which Aberdeen had initially spoken, the Foreign Secretary found himself, by the summer of 1853, 'mediating between Aberdeen and Palmerston, whose ancient and habitual ideas of foreign policy are brought by this business into antagonism'.[48]

The rivalry between Aberdeen and Palmerston was reflected more widely in the general division between Peelites and Whigs into doves and hawks respectively, though this is, of course, a simplification. During the spring and summer of 1853 the Aberdonian outlook gained ground within the Cabinet and frequently Palmerston was obliged to back down, as on one occasion in the summer, for example, when Palmerston, who had been advocating a forward policy through sending the fleet up to the Bosphorus, admitted the propriety of Aberdeen's hesitation and the Prime Minister rejoiced to think that now 'all *polémiques*' should cease between them.[49] Palmerston, though, had not given up in his attempts to influence foreign policy, and nor for that matter had Russell. To see the Cabinet as neatly divided between hawkish Whigs and dove-like Peelites with Aberdeen's approach in the ascendancy overstates the case and fails to convey the nature of the dynamics of the Cabinet over the affairs of the East.

Individual members of the Government viewed the priorities of the session differently. Aberdeen was concerned to preserve the unity of the Cabinet and to prove that a coalition could succeed. There was a full programme of domestic legislation planned and indeed followed through, and as a result of this, it was Gladstone, the Chancellor of the Exchequer, who emerged early on as the strong man in the Government.[50] But as Aberdeen had himself acknowledged, while all foreign policy was guided by national interest, there were differences in the methods and approaches of different Foreign Secretaries. What he had not paid sufficient attention to was the seriousness of this divide, for although there was a consensus even that in large part the Eastern question and its particular interest for Britain was as a balance of power question, there was not, significantly, a common view of what the balance of power meant.

For Aberdeen, preserving the balance of power meant focusing on the congress system of resolving disputes by negotiation. For Palmerston and Russell, while not speaking with one voice by any means, a more *Realpolitik* approach of checks and balances was the only way of preserving an equilibrium. Consequently, when Russia claimed rights over Ottoman territories, the Cabinet did not react in unison. There was, throughout the life of the Government, a contest between advocates of a forward policy which aimed at the preservation of Turkish independence as a brake on Russian expansionist tendencies, and a conciliatory approach arguing for a more accommodating attitude towards Russia given that British interests were not directly and materially affected.

Until the autumn of 1853 Aberdeen successfully held the various factions within the Cabinet together. While his views did not have currency all around the table, there was an unwillingness to pull the Government apart if this could be avoided. Early in September he convened a meeting with Clarendon, Russell and Palmerston, and though the mood was bellicose, Aberdeen's measured response to the situation carried the day. As the Prime Minister told his friend Sir James Graham:

> The present state of Eastern affairs was fully discussed, as well as plans for the future. There was no very great difference of opinion, except a strong desire on the part of my three companions to come to a decision that we should enter the Dardanelles, as soon as the state of the weather rendered it necessary to leave Besika Bay. I rejected this suggestion, partly as being premature, and partly because it was a measure of too great importance to be taken without the consent of the whole Cabinet ...
>
> Palmerston was not so warlike as Lord John; but neither of them was very unreasonably pugnacious. I thought the manner of both rather constrained.[51]

Furthermore, Aberdeen and Clarendon were able to out-manoeuvre Palmerston, presenting him with a *fait accompli* when the Home Secretary had objected to the wording of a despatch to Stratford, asserting that it laid the ground for the abandonment of Turkey, in which case, 'it is high time that another Government was formed'.[52] Yet, drawing partly on the advice of the Queen, who recognised Palmerston's bullying tactics of old, Clarendon sent the despatch off without attending to the alterations put forward by Palmerston, who later acknowledged that such a pragmatic approach was quite the most appropriate course. 'As your Despatch is gone, it is gone', he wrote to the Foreign Secretary, 'and I daresay no Harm will come of it, and our future Course will be determined by Events as they arise more than by what may from Time to Time have been written'; adding, 'I can quite imagine that you must have had a hard Task of it to get a Team which is disposed to go so many different ways to agree to any common Pull together'.[53]

Graham in particular was concerned about the impact Palmerston could have on proceedings should he gain ground within the Cabinet, and such fears weighed heavily with Aberdeen, and perhaps also account in part for Clarendon's loyalty to Aberdeen during the first three-quarters of the year. Two letters which Graham addressed to Clarendon illustrate clearly the nature of these concerns, which go to the very root of the Government's troubles during these months. In July he wrote that: 'Palmerston has seriously alarmed me by the eagerness and impatience of his tone and language. I am afraid that he may operate unfavorably [sic] on Walewski [the French minister in London] and thro' him on our Ally'.[54] A month later he raised the spectre of domestic troubles:

> I always foreboded mischief from a H. of Commons discussion on foreign affairs at this critical juncture. We have a stand-up fight between Cobden and Palmerston – the former the champion of Russia and Christianity – the latter the sworn ally of Turkey and Mahometanism. Both made very able speeches in opposite senses; but both pushed their doctrines to an extreme. Cobden, in the long run, will have England with him; but the Derbyites were enchanted with Palmerston and cheered him to the echo. So did young India, who were most offensive in their language towards Aberdeen. Fortunately it is the last night of the session; and before we meet again the Turkish affair, at least for the present, will probably be adjusted; otherwise the breach on our side of the House would soon spread into an open rupture.[55]

Aberdeen had a delicate balancing act to play. Palmerston, and Russell, were they allowed to exercise a commanding influence over the Cabinet would, it was believed, jeopardise the relationship with France; their isolation, however, would also be dangerous as there was a sufficiently large element within Parliament willing to unite under Palmerston should he break away from the coalition. Such a compromise policy served only to weaken the ministry, for in securing what was ultimately only grudging acceptance of Aberdonian policy from the vociferous Whigs, such attempted conciliation caused the policy of the Government to become vague and ill-defined.

Palmerston was keen that the Government's policy should be clearly directed towards checking the progress of Russia. By the summer of 1853 the Russian threat had become more pronounced when in May Menshikov had demanded of the Porte that Russia should be allowed to guarantee the position of the Orthodox Christians within the Ottoman Empire. Possibly encouraged by Stratford Canning, Turkey had rejected this as establishing a dangerous precedent for unchecked Russian interference in Ottoman domestic affairs. The failure of Menshikov's mission, however, raised the prospect of Russian occupation of the Ottoman Principalities. British warships were dispatched to Besika Bay, just outside the Dardanelles, at the beginning of June in an attempt to avert any potential Russian threat there, and along with a French squadron took up position by the middle of the month. This demonstration of solidarity steeled Turkish resolve, and Russian demands were finally rejected on 16 June. This led inevitably to direct Russian action, and on 3 July Russian forces crossed the Pruth into the Ottoman Empire. No power could afford now to stand down without loss of face, yet the positions adopted portended a confrontation.[56] Palmerston, prescient of this, urged on his colleagues that the British fleet should be ordered up to the Bosphorus. He was 'confident that this Country expects that we should pursue such a Course, and I cannot believe that we should receive anything but support in pursuing it, from the Party now in Opposition',[57] he told Aberdeen, who replied that he had,

> not the least doubt that the country, and the party of Opposition in the House of Commons, would be delighted if we took such a step. But the Country would not look to the consequences, and the Opposition would only anticipate our speedy overthrow. In a case of this kind I dread popular support. On some occasion, when the Athenian Assembly vehemently applauded Alcibiades, he asked if he had said anything particularly foolish![58]

Such differences lay at the heart of the tensions within the Government. Aberdeen distrusted Palmerston's motives and objectivity;

Palmerston saw Aberdeen as too hesitant and not sufficiently cavalier. Initially it had appeared that Palmerstonian and Aberdonian
policies would work together, and in Cabinet discussion, though
Palmerston frequently raised objections to the wording of diplomatic instructions, Aberdeen evidently felt that he could assuage
his colleague's reservations by adopting his suggestions, since they
were, as he commented on one occasion, 'not of sufficient importance
to make it worth while to contest them; although few of them appear
to me to be improvements'.[59] And even Palmerston, for a while,
was prepared to give the Prime Minister the benefit of the doubt.
In July, however, the Cabinet became the scene of squabbles over
the value or otherwise of sending the British fleet up to the Bosphorus, and it was Aberdeen who won the argument and pressed
on his colleagues the desirability of negotiated peace. 'I acquiesce
in Aberdeen's argument', wrote Palmerston, 'that it is better even
to submit to Insult than to Endanger the pending negotiation by
throwing into it any fresh Element of Difficulty which could afford
the Pettifogging & Quibbling Govt with which we have to deal any
Pretence for rejecting Proposals in themselves unobjectionable and
I am willing to share the Responsibility of such a Course though
contrary to my first opinions'.[60]

   This stalemate caused Palmerston, among others, to become
increasingly frustrated with the state of affairs. At the time that he
was making the concessions to Aberdeen over the fleet in the
Bosphorus, Palmerston was in reality far from contented. He argued
that Aberdeen was sending out signals which encouraged the
Russian government to believe the British Government timid and
in search of *la paix à tout prix*. Thus the Russians were, he argued,
arrogantly pretending to forbid the British and French fleets
from frequenting the waters of another Power, over whom the
Russians had absolutely no jurisdiction, and who had in fact invited
the British and French to be there. 'It is the Robber who declares
that he will not leave the House until the Policeman shall have first
retired from the Courtyard', he complained.[61] Palmerston was not
the only member of the Government becoming increasingly
frustrated with the progress of affairs and Russell, too, no longer
directly concerned with the impact of Palmerston's relations
with the Crown, became an ever more enthusiastic advocate of
Palmerston's policies.[62]

As the summer waned, however, even Russell and Palmerston grew discordant. They were, wrote Argyll, 'very far from being close allies. Sometimes their views coincided, but as often they disagreed, and it was evident from Palmerston's manner that old scores had been by no means forgotten'.[63] Russell, in writing to Clarendon late in September, did not suggest that he sought in conjunction with Palmerston to upset the Government, far from it in fact. 'I trust that when I have not wholly approved your course, I have not been wanting in the duty of fighting your battles, & sharing your responsibility', he said, but in thus defending a policy for which he entertained little sympathy 'you have made me feel my degradation more than I ever felt it before'.[64] If Russell did feel that he had been degraded by his association with the Government's foreign policy, he did not see the remedy for this condition in an alliance with Palmerston. That Palmerston had recommended a policy which the Cabinet had approved at this time, for example, failed to impress Russell.[65]

Palmerston saw little improvement in the conduct of affairs as the weeks passed, and was to write scathingly to protest about the weak and lacklustre leadership of Aberdeen: 'I will confess to you in Confidence', he wrote to Clarendon, 'that the Language I have heard on this matter in our Cabinet Discussions has often tried my Patience and led me to the Conclusion that we are in one Respect at least like Turkey, & have also our "wretched" Pasha'.[66] Thus two of the Government's chief sources of strength and inspiration, Palmerston and Russell, were dissatisfied with the ministry's approach to the most important issue of the day.

Though Aberdeen's policy was deemed inadequate, however, neither Russell nor Palmerston had the ability or the desire to push the point too far, offering only a sporadic and piece-meal alternative. In the middle of everything was Clarendon, striving to strike a balance between the competing factions in the Government. In early October, Clarendon complained to Aberdeen that the 'difficulty is very great of reconciling the opposite views held in the Cabt & of satisfying my own notions of moderation & firmness'.[67] From Sir Charles Wood, he was 'only too happy to receive your opinions for I feel the enormous responsibility of acting at this most critical moment without the entire Cabt', lamenting further that, 'no one but myself can have an idea of what I go through in endeavouring to reconcile the discordant views of Abn., J. R. & Palmn. but I never end by writing or doing exactly what I myself approve'.[68]

Aberdeen remained blind to the fragmentation of his Cabinet and when reporting on a meeting during which the Eastern question had been discussed on 7 October for instance, he told the Queen that although the 'meeting was very long, and considerable differ-ence of opinion prevailed in the course of the discussion', he had ultimately the satisfaction of seeing that 'there was such an agree-ment as ensured a certain degree of unanimity'.[69] The royal couple were not convinced, however. A letter from Aberdeen to Graham which had been submitted to the Queen revealed quite clearly the divisions within the Cabinet,[70] and following an interview with Graham, it seemed to the Queen and Prince 'evident that Lord Aberdeen was, against his better judgement, consenting to a course of policy which he inwardly condemned, that his desire to maintain unanimity at the Cabinet led to concessions which by degrees altered the whole character of the policy, while he held out no hope of being able permanently to secure agreement'.[71]

Matters had by now come to a head. On 4 October, Turkey had declared war on Russia and with no room left for vacillation, this development provoked important shifts within the British Cabinet. From Turin, Minto viewed the progress of events with little satis-faction:

> There is no doubt I fear that the feeble course of the English Government in its dealing with the Turkish question has tended greatly to lower us in the estimation of other nations and to deprive us of much of the influence we might have. For the impression is very general that the Aberdeenian [sic] policy prevails with us & that our aid is no longer to be counted on in the cause of freedom or independence. It will require some emphatic display of vigour to remove this impression & restore our old reputation.[72]

There was no doubt in Minto's mind that a 'higher tone' and 'more decided measures at an earlier period' would have prevented the Eastern question from descending into the troubled condition it was in by the autumn of 1853.[73] It was a view widely held within the Cabinet as well, where all members felt that a firmer and more decided line was needed. A few continued to believe that Aberdeen's plans for negotiated peace were still desirable,[74] but the heavyweights were beginning to see the value of a more aggressive Palmerstonian approach. Certainly Clarendon regarded Palmerston as the prime source of advice and support during the course of this month.[75] And perhaps even more ominous for the future of the Government, Graham noted that: 'The reunion of Ld John and Palmerston is certainly formidable; but much will after all depend on the righteousness of the Cause and on the purity of motives and of conduct. It is premature to form even an opinion: it would be most unwise to come to any decision'. Premature and unwise or not, even Aberdeen himself was forced to concede that Palmerston's interpretation of events had some merit. The outbreak of war forced a re-evaluation: 'It is very true that I may formerly have regarded with the utmost incredulity *the possibility of war between England and Russia* but for some time past', he told Palmerston, 'I have seen the desire for war increase so much, as to lead me to think that it is but too probable. At present therefore, *vous prêchez le Converti*'.[76] Aberdeen was not the only proselyte and a letter from Clarendon to the Prime Minister confirmed the ascendancy of Palmerston's opinions during the course of October.[77]

The fluctuations within the Government of October did not herald a new era of stability and clarity, however. Throughout November, divisions within the Cabinet grew ever more pronounced, and the split between Clarendon and Aberdeen particularly served to undermine the solidity of the Government at this critical juncture.[78] Heretofore, the majority of the Cabinet had, generally, concurred in the Aberdonian line, and opponents of this course had, to a large extent, suppressed their objections. Now, however, the Palmerstonian approach was increasingly attractive, but there was not the flexibility among the Aberdonians to adapt. The Government in late 1853 therefore was characterised by indecision and faction, and by the end of the year the pretence of a united Cabinet was impossible to maintain, and the coalition which had initially promised so much descended into rivalries between its component parts. While Aberdeen's faith in Clarendon had been somewhat restored, there was no denying that important divisions still existed. Russell had let Aberdeen know that he did not know what the Prime Minister aimed at; 'I say the same of him', Aberdeen told Clarendon, adding, 'The only real explanation is that which I have already given you, viz: that he intends war, and I intend peace'.[79]

Palmerston's growing influence within the Cabinet undoubtedly had something to do with the parliamentary context. Disraeli and the Protectionists were behind him and his policy. Though the formation of the Aberdeen ministry in December 1852 had effectively crushed hopes of a Protectionist reconciliation with the Peelites, a union with Palmerston, whose importance Disraeli had already impressed on Lord Derby, did still seem, if not immediately possible, at least ultimately desirable. Indeed, the *Daily News* had suggested at the formation of the Aberdeen government that Palmerston had intended to induce the Protectionists to join him and to be 'the means of adding an ex-Derbyite troop to the ministerial phalanx'.[80] Thus when called on to deliver a speech on foreign policy in February 1853, which he determined upon 'in a half apologetic tone, pleading the necessity of keeping his party in good humour',[81] Disraeli used this as an opportunity to underline the new alignments. He made a point of 'sparing Palmerston throughout', while criticising Wood, Graham and Aberdeen, outwardly three of Palmerston's potential antagonists or rivals in the new government.[82]

While there was a feeling that Palmerston would be disposed to unite with the Conservatives politically, their weak condition prohibited such a plan. Malmesbury told Derby in September that: 'If Palmerston left the Government there is no doubt that many of our staunchest supporters would follow him as leader of the Commons, but our present divisions are not likely to encourage him to leave his post'.[83] The disunity of the Cabinet, maintained Disraeli in the autumn, 'is one of the inevitable consequences of a coalition between statesmen of totally different systems',[84] yet even in this state of affairs, 'great as [is] the embroglio', it was insufficient grounds upon which to 'galvanise our party' and the Aberdeen government remained 'a necessity'.[85]

Meanwhile, from another part of the opposition benches, Cobden maintained a stout belief in the pacific disposition of the nation at large. 'The great mass of the people', he told J. B. Smith, an old friend from the Anti-Corn Law League, 'is always ready to hear the truth ... They have no interest in wrong-doing. Let us then by our great meetings in Edinburgh and elsewhere show that we are not afraid to appeal to the people against those who from ignorance, prejudice and sinister motives are trying to mislead them. We may roll back the tide of military enthusiasm whilst at its height if we will now make one great effort on behalf of the right'.[86]

On 16 August 1853, Cobden had given an early illustration of his view of events in the East. Russia, he agreed, had acted in a manner that was 'treacherous, overbearing, and violent', and should be compelled as swiftly as possible to evacuate the occupied principalities. But this was not a plea grounded in any special regard for Turkey: 'you cannot maintain Mahomedanism in Europe', he argued and while Russian invasion of Constantinople was to be regretted, the Ottoman Empire thus constituted was not an appropriate ally of Britain. And while it was the case that many subjects of Turkey in Europe, rayahs, were Christian, this did not necessarily demand an automatic defence of their interests against Russia; indeed, noted Cobden, 'I should prefer a Russian or any other government rather than a Mahomedan one'. Combining an unwillingness to over-stretch Britain in a cause for which there were no clear grounds, with a greater degree of admiration for Russian than Turkish culture, civilisation and commercial maturity, Cobden could find no compelling reason to go to war. He could, however, identify good reason not to. Commercial interests, he argued, were not threatened by Russian advances, but in any event, free trade principles did not require a military defence: 'I have too much faith in my principles to go to war for them', he said. 'I believe that free-trade principles will spread and make converts by means of peace'. Furthermore, a war of this nature, while stimulating industrial output in the short term to serve the campaign, would ultimately prove damaging to commerce: unknown numbers of markets stood to be lost or disrupted in case of war and as he observed in a remark addressed to Mr Blackett, the MP for Newcastle, 'there is no port which would suffer more severely, more in proportion to the magnitude of its commerce, than Newcastle would do, if we should go to war'.[87]

Indeed, within the very highest echelons of government, voices were to be heard praising the Cobdenite view. Aberdeen, for example, praised the desire for peace expressed at a conference of the Peace Society held in Edinburgh in mid-October. Suspecting that *The Times* was wavering in its support for peace, Aberdeen wrote to Delane of this meeting: 'I think that both the principal speakers [Cobden and Bright] uttered so much truth as to deserve a different treatment, by which the cause of peace might have been further advanced'.[88] Aberdeen, however, did not necessarily speak for the nation. Rather, the popular mood seemed quite at odds with the Cobdenite view. As Palmerston – significantly it was he who responded to Cobden's speech of August 1853 – argued, while Cobden's speech did not appear quite consistent, and while not accepting the Cobdenite denigration of the commercial importance of Turkey which was, he insisted, important 'as the channel through which our manufactures pass into Asia', it was all for nought when the views expressed ran so much counter to the prevailing mood: 'Nothing is so painful as to see a man of great ability labouring to bring about a conviction which he knows to be contrary to the opinions of the great majority of his fellow-countrymen, and which, therefore, he is afraid – I will not use a stronger expression – openly to express, but which he endeavours to conceal under every specious device which human ingenuity could afford to the precise orator'.[89]

While Cobden might maintain, somewhat hopelessly perhaps in December 1853, that he still carried the middle classes with him – that they were, as he put it 'fanatically devoted to peace' [90] – he eventually was drawn to admit some months later that this was not absolutely accurate. Retreating to his home in the country, Cobden tacitly admitted the defeat of his approach, asking an old friend:

> how can I better escape from the humbling spectacle of a nation given up to the dominion of its fiercest animal passions, *whilst flattering itself that it is wielding the sceptre of justice*, than in taking refuge in my nursery, where the children, if not more logical, are at least less hypocritical than those of a larger growth whose 'fe, fa, fi, fo, fum' is now resounding from our streets, theatres, churches and chapels? To confess the truth, I am afraid I am growing cynical, and I am half disposed to take to my tub, let my beard grow, and pass a vote of want of confidence in mankind.[91]

Having presented to the House of Commons, on two notable occasions, his view of events in the East and the Government's handling of those events, all that Cobden held dear and believed about the sagacity of the people he thought he represented was controverted when his counsel was not heeded. Yet these parliamentary speeches demonstrate not only the rational approach adopted by the Cobdenites, but also, in this case, its bankruptcy.

Outside Parliament, too, criticism of Palmerston had little impact. Having failed to make an impression on Parliament, David Urquhart had fallen back on the extra-parliamentary constituency in order to renew his attacks on Palmerston. Over the Crimean War he was an early and vociferous opponent of British intervention on behalf of Turkey and in September and October of 1853 he began delivering a series of speeches around the country calling for a greater involvement of 'the people' in foreign affairs. He couched his attacks on the Government in terms of challenging the evil of 'secret diplomacy', but he meant to condemn the whole of the Cabinet for going to war with Russia with a Russian agent in their midst.

The logic of Urquhart's attacks was tortuous, as indeed it had to be in order to prove that Palmerston, the Cabinet's Russian agent, was now the foremost advocate of a forward policy against Russia. But in the event this was perhaps of little consequence. His oratorical skills were poor and it is reported, for instance, that at a meeting at the London Tavern the man who rose to second Urquhart's resolution admitted that he could not understand the second part of it and when this particular meeting moved its resolutions, among the names most loudly cheered was still that of Palmerston.[92] This is an important point, which partly explains why Palmerston was able to overcome opposition to his policies at the grass roots level. For while these issues had national implications, and while Palmerston was keen to win over provincial interests such as the Manchester commercial classes, the debate over key foreign policy questions, and especially in the case of the Crimean situation in 1853 and 1854, was London-centric. As Antony Taylor has demonstrated, pro-Palmerston feeling was particularly strong in London, if only because the opposition to him there was so weak.[93] Urquhart might have courted popular support all over the country, but the foundation of his support was pre-eminently northern,[94] and in terms of popular politics, relying on strong oratorical performances and wide-ranging reporting of the same, the bias was definitely towards the capital.

More than this, it seems Urquhart's closest allies were not the working classes Urquhart himself liked to claim he represented, but in fact were typically middle-class figures such as Charles Attwood, George Crawshay and Isaac Ironside – three of Urquhart's 'staunchest colleagues' – who had 'inherited the manufacturing and mercantile wealth of their fathers', and Stewart Rolland who was a newspaper proprietor.[95] Even at its height, the Urquhartite movement's hold over the hearts of the working classes was thin, and it does not appear to have established any meaningful sense of solidarity with the constituency it aimed at and thus failed to negate a feeling of middle-class patronage of the workers.[96] Letters from Urquhart's friends and agents around the country suggest even more clearly the mis-direction (or mis-interpretation) of Urquhart's addresses. In Manchester, S. Langley told Urquhart, there was a lack of direction and 'I am every day more and more convinced that a meeting here got up merely by a few working men would be damaging'.[97] Indeed, the potential of the working classes in Manchester seemed especially poor: 'For twenty years there has been a political organisation here', wrote Langley again, but, 'during the last two years it has disappeared and nearly every leading man amongst the working classes, disgusted at the apathy and ingratitude of those for whom he had laboured has retired altogether from public life'.[98] Elsewhere, the prospects of rousing support seemed just as bleak. In Wolverhampton and Birmingham, reported William Peplow, 'there is no life in those towns' and on Urquhart's behalf, Peplow wrote to an un-named source to ask if 'you cannot do something in Macclesfield towards arousing the nation to a sense of its Duty at this important crisis, while the honour & the Dearest interests of it are being swamped by a Corrupt and imbecile Govt!' [99] According to Miles Taylor, Urquhartism was not a movement concerned with activating the working classes, nor indeed was it primarily concerned with foreign policy. Rather, the free trade liberalism that lay at the heart of Urquhart's programme particularly attracted radical support. Commerce, Urquhart had stressed throughout, should be a major determinant of British external policy: peace and retrenchment were the ideals Urquhart promoted and in this, then, he was courting the commercial classes in the manufacturing districts he visited and not the working classes.[100] Here, indeed, suspicion of Palmerston was a common cause between Urquhart and Cobden.[101]

It was Palmerston whom radicals saw as best able to guarantee an upright and true foreign policy. In fact it was Louis Kossuth, when he visited Britain in 1854, who charmed the people whom

Urquhart sought to win over and in meetings across the Midlands and in London, in which he eulogised Palmerstonian policy, he consistently overshadowed Urquhart's earlier performances in those districts.[102]

Thus, with little by way of an effective alternative to the Government's foreign policy presented in Parliament and the continued resonance of Palmerston's image of the most English minister beyond Westminster, the main site for contests over foreign policy continued to be the Cabinet. By December, however, government unity appeared distant. On the 16th, the Peelite members of the Cabinet – Aberdeen, Graham, Newcastle and Gladstone – met at the Admiralty to discuss the Eastern question and the course to be pressed upon the rest of the Cabinet the following day, thus further establishing the Peelites as a distinct group within the ministry.[103] At the meeting the next day Aberdeen believed that everything went off well, evidently the solidarity among the Peelites had given him renewed confidence. Russell, though, was less pleased. 'I confess I was surprised & mortified', he wrote, 'it is obvious I cannot trust to any compromise, & must henceforth state fully my own views in the Cabinet and press for a positive decision. If it is against me I must consider what is due to my own character & the reputation of the country'.[104]

However, Palmerston was now 'out' of the Government. Aberdeen took this as an opportunity to break what ties there might have been between Russell and Palmerston, for while only allies of convenience, they were, nonetheless, united in their desire to upset the Government. However, alone they were unlikely to be able to achieve this, certainly of the two Russell was not well placed to supplant Aberdeen, and Aberdeen used the opportunity to appease Russell. As Graham explained to Lord John: 'I can bear witness to Ld Aberdeen's constant and anxious desire to act in concert with you on Foreign Affairs to the utmost limit consistent with his strong sense of public duty. It would be a great calamity, if there were any serious misunderstanding in spite of such a friendly disposition: I cannot believe that it will occur'.[105]

Notes

1   *Hansard*, 3rd ser., CXXIII, 1724 (27 Dec. 1852).
2   Chamberlain, *Aberdeen*, p. 451.
3   See K. Bourne, *The Foreign Policy of Victorian England, 1830–1902* (Oxford, 1970), pp. 197–8, Pitt's 'Memorandum on the Deliverance and Security of Europe' (19 Jan. 1805).
4   Quoted Chamberlain, *'Pax Britannica'?*, p. 63.
5   *Daily News*, 4 Jan. 1853.
6   Aberdeen Papers, Add. Mss. 43069, Palmerston to Aberdeen, 10 Jan. 1853.
7   See D. Roberts, 'Lord Palmerston at the Home Office', *The Historian*, 21:1 (1958), 63–81, and Ridley, *Palmerston*, pp. 406–12 for detail about these and other measures which occupied Palmerston's time at the Home Office.
8   Roberts, 'Lord Palmerston at the Home Office', p. 68: 'Besides planning reforms Palmerston had to perform the regular duties of the Home Office, in detail and number quite harassing. Though in April [1853] he wrote that work at the Home Office was lighter than at the Foreign Office, by July he confessed "I have never found time to read these [prison] reports and despair of being able to do so"'.
9   When a dinner was held at the beginning of the ministry's life to meet diplomatic staff Lady Palmerston recorded that: 'Paln. dined at Ld Aberdeen's to meet Corps Diplomatique. 4 English Secys of State present Ld A[berdeen], P[almerston] (past), [Lord] John [Russell] (present), Clarendon (future)' (Lady Palmerston Papers, diary of Lady Palmerston, 10 Jan. 1853). Note that Clarendon is already recognised as the heir apparent to the Foreign Office.
10 *The Economist*, 26 Nov. 1853.
11 Roberts, 'Lord Palmerston at the Home Office', pp. 69–70.
12 Greville, *The Greville Memoirs (third part)*, I, p. 106 (15 Nov. 1853).
13 Broadlands Papers, SHA/PD/6, Shaftesbury Diaries, 28 June 1854.
14 *The Times*, 26 July 1853.
15 See, for example, *The Economist*, 20 Aug. 1853.
16 *The Times*, for example, was well aware of Palmerston's involvement in the conduct of foreign policy, in no small measure due to the letters from Clarendon to Reeve (see for example, Clarendon Deposit, MS.Clar.dep.c.535, fols 87–8, Clarendon to Reeve, 16 Dec. 1853). See also Delane Papers, Times Newspapers Ltd Archive, News International Record Office, London, T.N.L., 5/39, J. T. Delane to G. [Dasent], 4 Oct. 1853.
17 *Standard*, 9 Feb. 1853.
18 *The Economist*, 1 Oct. 1853.
19 Broadlands Papers, MPC/1554, 'Cadux' to Palmerston, 12 July 1853.
20 *Ibid.*, GC/CH/51, Edwin Chadwick to Palmerston, 3 Dec. 1853.
21 *Ibid.*, GC/RO/20, David Ross (Dean of the Guild Incorporation of Perth) to Palmerston, 21 Sept. 1853.
22 See O. Anderson, *A Liberal State at War: English Politics and Economics during*

the Crimean War (London, 1967), pp. 23–4. As Anderson demonstrates throughout this book, the war represented an important test of the British system of government and the sense of a premature and inconclusive peace settlement, imposed on Britain by the determination of France, prevented the complete fulfilment of this promise (see esp. pp. 275–83).

23   Colley, *Britons*, p. 380.

24   Broadlands Papers, SP/B/3/1–4 (the presentation of the freedom of the city of Glasgow and the associated speeches reported in the *Glasgow Constitutional*).

25   Roberts, 'Lord Palmerston at the Home Office', pp. 71, 78. For contemporary arguments addressed to Palmerston on the subject of Catholic freedoms, and in particular religious freedom for Catholic prisoners, see Frederick Oakley, *The Religious Disabilities of our Catholic Prisoners Considered, with a view to their removal, in a letter to the Viscount Palmerston, M.P., &c, &c, &c* (London, 1854) which advocated religious freedom on moral grounds but which was heartily contradicted by Joseph Kingsmill, *Roman Catholic Chaplains to Gaols. A letter to the Rt. Hon. Viscount Palmerston, M.P., Secretary of State for the Home Department, on this Subject; occasioned by a letter of the Rev. Frederick Oakley, M.A., entitled, 'The Religious Disabilities of our Catholic Prisoners considered, with a view to their removal'* (London, 1854).

26   Clarendon Deposit, MSS.Clar.dep.c.3, fols 108–9, Palmerston to Clarendon, 31 July 1853.

27   Maxwell, *Clarendon*, II, p. 18, Palmerston to Clarendon, 26 Aug. 1853.

28   *LQV*, II, p. 548, Aberdeen to the Queen, 11 Sept. 1853.

29   Bell, *Palmerston*, II, p. 90.

30   See M. S. Anderson, *The Eastern Question, 1774–1923* (London, 1966), esp. pp. 110–49; D. M. Goldfrank, *The Origins of the Crimean War* (Harlow, 1994); and G. B. Henderson, *Crimean War Diplomacy and Other Historical Essays* (Glasgow, 1947).

31   Anderson, *The Eastern Question*, p. 111.

32   *Ibid.*, pp. 112–14. For example, Britain and France came together to support the Sultan against Russian demands that Polish revolutionaries in Turkey be extradited. Russia did not take kindly to finding the British fleet in the Straits during this crisis. It was yet one more example of how far Britain and Russia were from genuine cooperation over the Near East.

33   *Ibid.*, p. 118.

34   Henderson, *Crimean War Diplomacy*, p. 9.

35   Goldfrank, *The Origins of the Crimean War*, p. 117.

36   Argyll, *Autobiography and Memoirs*, I, p. 441. Cf. Chamberlain's view that the Crimean War was to see 'a disastrous clash between the two traditions, now represented by Aberdeen and Palmerston' (*'Pax Britannica'?*, p. 102).

37   Argyll, *Autobiography and Memoirs*, I, pp. 442–3.

38   *Ibid.*, I, pp. 445–6. Russell was Foreign Secretary until February 1853, at which point he was replaced by Clarendon.

39   Broadlands Papers, GC/CL/523/enc. 1, Palmerston to Clarendon, 12 Sept. 1853.

40 *Ibid.*, GC/CL/1371/1, Palmerston to Clarendon, 14 Oct. 1853.

41 Argyll, *Autobiography and Memoirs*, I, pp. 455–6.

42 Goldfrank, *The Origins of the Crimean War*, pp. 147–8, Clarendon to Cowley, 29 April 1853.

43 Maxwell, *Clarendon*, II, p. 12, Graham to Clarendon, 9 May 1853.

44 Aberdeen Papers, Add. Mss. 43188, Aberdeen to Clarendon, 20 Nov. 1853. See also J. L. Herkless, 'Stratford, the Cabinet and the Outbreak of the Crimean War', *Historical Journal*, 18: 3 (1975), 497–523.

45 Aberdeen Papers, Add. Mss. 43355, Stratford Canning (Lord Stratford de Redcliffe) to Clarendon, 3 Feb. 1853.

46 *Ibid.*, Add. Mss. 43188, Clarendon to Aberdeen, 8 Jan. 1854. The quote is Aberdeen's who made this note on the letter.

47 Conacher, *The Aberdeen Coalition*, pp. 172–3, Aberdeen to Madame Lieven, 8 Sept. 1853. See pp. 119–20 for Conacher's own observations on the success of the Government's first session.

48 Greville, *The Greville Memoirs (third part)*, I, p. 71 (22 June 1853).

49 Conacher, *The Aberdeen Coalition*, p. 160, Aberdeen to Palmerston, 15 July 1853.

50 *Ibid.*, p. 119. In addition to the various fiscal measures which Gladstone proposed, the Government was also committed to bringing railways more under governmental control, to reform of universities and of the civil service, and of, course, to parliamentary reform, Russell's own favourite cause.

51 Graham Papers, MS Film 124, Bundle 114, Aberdeen to Graham, 4 Sept. 1853.

52 Conacher, *The Aberdeen Coalition*, p. 204, Palmerston to Clarendon, 20 Oct. 1853.

53 Clarendon Deposit, MSS.Clar.dep.c.3, fols 209–12, Palmerston to Clarendon, 27 Oct. 1853.

54 *Ibid.*, MSS.Clar.dep.c.4, fols 178–9, Graham to Clarendon, 14 July 1853.

55 Maxwell, *Clarendon*, II, p. 16, Graham to Clarendon, 16 Aug. 1853.

56 Anderson, *The Eastern Question*, pp. 120–5.

57 Aberdeen Papers, Add. Mss. 43069, Palmerston to Aberdeen, 4 July 1853.

58 *Ibid.*, Add. Mss. 43069, Aberdeen to Palmerston, 4 July 1853.

59 *Ibid.*, Add. Mss. 43188, Aberdeen to Clarendon, 15 July 1853.

60 Clarendon Deposit, MSS.Clar.dep.c.3, fols 98–9, Palmerston to Clarendon, 15 July 1853.

61 Broadlands Papers, GC/AB/304, memorandum circulated to members of the Cabinet by Palmerston, 12 July 1853.

62 Bell, *Palmerston*, II, p. 92.

63 Argyll, *Autobiography and Memoirs*, I, p. 459. See also a satirical description of 'A Card Party at the Foreign Office' in the *Press*, 10 Sept. 1853.

64 Clarendon Deposit, MSS.Clar.dep.c.3, fols 425–7, Russell to Clarendon, 23 Sept. 1853.

65 Aberdeen Papers. Add. Mss. 43067, Russell to Aberdeen, 24 Sept. 1853.

66 Clarendon Deposit, MSS.Clar.dep.c.3, fols 187–92, Palmerston to Clarendon, 14 Oct. 1853.

67   Aberdeen Papers, Add. Mss. 43188, Clarendon to Aberdeen, 8 Oct. 1853.

68   Hickleton Papers, A4.57, Clarendon to Wood, 20 Oct. 1853.

69   *LQV*, II, pp. 551–2, Aberdeen to Queen, 7 Oct. 1853.

70   Although the letter sought to play down the differences, that they were described at all is significant. In reporting the course of a Cabinet summoned to discuss the Eastern question, Aberdeen wrote: 'The aspect of the Cabinet was, on the whole, very good. Gladstone, active and energetic for Peace; Argyll, Herbert, C. Wood, and Granville, all in the same sense. Newcastle, not quite so much so, but good; Lansdowne, not so warlike as formerly; Lord John warlike enough, but subdued in tone; Palmerston urged his views perseveringly, but not disagreeably. The Chancellor said little, but was cordially peaceful. Molesworth was not present, there having been some mistake in sending the notice' (Aberdeen Papers, Add. Mss. 43191, Aberdeen to Graham, 8 Oct. 1853).

71   *LQV*, II, pp. 552–4, memorandum by Albert, 10 Oct. 1853.

72   Minto Papers, MS 12000, Minto, journal, 8 Oct. 1853.

73   *Ibid.*, MS 12000, Minto, journal, 7 Nov. 1853.

74   Wood, for example, wrote to Russell in December: 'Now I hold it to be the worst & most discreditable course of conduct to alter a course once deliberately adopted. We must I think steadily pursue the attempt to settle by negociation. We must follow up the attempt which we have made to bring the two parties to a meeting in the presence of a conference. If we fail in that, a change of circumstances will have taken place which may justify, & even call for a change of conduct' (Hickleton Papers, A4.56.5, Wood to Russell, 13 Dec. 1853).

75   Broadlands Papers, GC/CL/540/1–5, Clarendon to Palmerston, 20 Oct. 1853. The letter opens: 'I must ask you to read these papers & to give me your opinion for I am not justified in acting singly upon such important matters, & my difficulties are of course much increased by the different views held in the Cabinet as to the best mode of proceeding'.

76   Aberdeen Papers, Add. Mss. 43069, Aberdeen to Palmerston, 5 Oct. 1853.

77   *Ibid.*, Add. Mss. 43188, Clarendon to Aberdeen, 4 Nov. 1853.

78   See Conacher, *The Aberdeen Coalition*, pp. 207–12.

79   Clarendon Deposit, MSS.Clar.dep.c.4, fol. 35, Aberdeen to Clarendon, 3 Dec. 1853.

80   *Daily News*, 5 Jan. 1853.

81   Vincent (ed.), *Disraeli, Derby and the Conservative Party: Journals and Memoirs of Edward Henry, Lord Stanley, 1849–1869*, p. 98 (16 Feb. 1853).

82   *Ibid.*, pp. 98–9 (17 Feb. 1853).

83   *Disraeli Letters*, VI, 2549 n. 2, Malmesbury to Derby, 8 Sept. 1853.

84   *Ibid.*, VI, 2558, Disraeli to Lord Londonderry, 26 Sept. 1853.

85   *Ibid.*, VI, 2561, Disraeli to Lord Stanley, 2 Oct. 1853.

86   W. Hinde, *Richard Cobden: A Victorian Outsider* (New Haven and London, 1987), pp. 244–5, Cobden to J. B. Smith, 5 Sept. 1853.

87   *Hansard*, 3rd ser., CXXIX, 1798–1806 (16 Aug. 1853).

88   Martin, *The Triumph of Lord Palmerston*, p. 168, Aberdeen to J. T. Delane,
     15 Oct. 1853.
89   *Hansard*, 3rd ser., CXXIX, 1806–10 (16 Aug. 1853).
90   Hinde, *Richard Cobden*, p. 247, Cobden to Hargreaves, 23 Dec. 1852.
91   *Ibid.*, p. 250, Cobden to Hargreaves, 7 Oct. 1854.
92   Jenks, 'The Activities and Influence of David Urquhart', pp. 301–2.
93   Taylor, 'Palmerston and Radicalism, 1847–1865', pp. 167–8.
94   See, for example, Balliol College Library, Oxford, David Urquhart Papers,
     I:G25, 'List of Addresses of the Foreign Affairs Committees', which dates
     from the late 1850s but which demonstrates a clear north of England bias
     in the geographical distribution of Urquhartite support.
95   Taylor, 'The Old Radicalism and the New', p. 26.
96   Shannon, 'David Urquhart and the Foreign Affairs Committees', pp. 252–3,
     255. See also the lofty tone of Urquhart's pamphlets at this time, such as
     The War of Ignorance: A Prognostication (London, 1854).
97   Urquhart Papers, I:E3, S. Langley to David Urquhart, 25 Oct. [?1853].
98   *Ibid.*, I:E3, S. Langley to David Urquhart, 26 Oct. [?1853].
99   *Ibid.*, I:E3, William Peplow to David Urquhart, 'Friday night' [?1853];
     William Peplow to ?, 11 Oct. 1853.
100 Taylor, 'The Old Radicalism and the New', pp. 26, 31, 32.
101 Howe, *Free Trade*, p. 71.
102 Taylor, 'The Old Radicalism and the New', p. 35.
103 Conacher, *The Aberdeen Coalition*, p. 238.
104 *Ibid.*, p. 239, Russell to Graham [?], 18 Dec. 1853. This was not the first
     time Russell had been unhappy with the Cabinet discussion of foreign affairs.
     Only a little over a week before this episode, he had written to Graham to
     say: 'I cannot help telling you that I was sorely disappointed at the result
     of the Cabinet of yesterday'. (Graham Papers, MS. Film 124, Bundle 115,
     Russell to Graham, 9 Dec. 1853).
105 Russell Papers, PRO 30/22/11B , Graham to Russell, 20 Dec. 1853.

8

Rivalry with Russell and Palmerston's ascendancy, December 1853 to February 1855

Palmerston had made no secret of his opposition to Russell's various plans for Reform. Throughout his career he had been lukewarm on the question of franchise extension, certainly he regarded the 1832 Act as 'final',[1] yet Reform was again brought forward, by Russell, in December 1853. While British participation in the war in the Near East was looking increasingly likely, it was not yet inevitable, and there was a return within the Government to some consideration of domestic questions and particularly of franchise reform, if only, as Albert suggested, 'pour les beaux yeux de Master Johnny'.[2] In a letter to Lansdowne, Palmerston explained that he could no longer bring himself to serve the Government. Despite having 'Matters in Hand which I should much wish to bring to a Conclusion', at the Home Office and believing that he could offer a valuable counter-point in the Cabinet to those advocates of a foreign policy injurious 'to the Interests & Dignity of the Country', he concluded that he could not 'consent to stand forward as one of the authors and supporters of John Russell's sweeping alterations'.[3] This caused great consternation and Prince Albert wrote from Osborne to Aberdeen urging him to seek an accommodation with Palmerston. Not only did Palmerston have a legitimate departmental right to offer criticism of the proposed Reform measure, but it was important also 'to balance the probable value of the modification with the risk of allowing Lord Palmerston to put himself at the head of the Opposition Party, entailing as it does the possibility of his forcing himself back upon ... [the Queen] as leader of that Party'.[4] Accordingly, and despite 'a sincere desire to ... meet your views, and if possible obviate your objections', Russell, Graham and Aberdeen, having met to discuss the problem, told Palmerston they could not

avoid concluding that these objections 'appear to be so serious as
to strike at the most essential principles of the measure. Under
these circumstances, we fear it would be impossible to make such
alterations as could be expected to afford you satisfaction'.[5] Palmerston asked then that his resignation be placed before Her Majesty
and a few days later, once Palmerston's resignation had become
public knowledge, Albert wrote that there could 'be no doubt that
Lord Palmerston will at once try to put himself at the head of the
late Protectionist party'.[6]

It was a source of some surprise to certain observers that Reform
should cause such turmoil within the Government. Shaftesbury felt
that the 'indifference in many cases, & the antipathy in others, to
Reform is singular; not a meeting, not a letter, not a speech, scarcely
an article in behalf of it!'[7] Yet there was a considerable body of
feeling that Reform was not the issue at stake. To the majority of
his colleagues, Palmerston's resignation appeared to be motivated
by considerations of foreign policy: certainly, they believed that his
going would have ramifications for that area of business.

Earl Grey, who disclosed in his diary that though 'it seems to
be given as from authority that Palmerston's resignat'n had
reference only to the plan of Reform the world will believe (as I
confess I shall too) that it has some connect'n at least with foreign
politics',[8] was not alone in this view. Clarendon wrote immediately
to Cowley, admitting that while the resignation was said to be
founded on the Reform question, and had nothing to do with the
Eastern question, 'we may swear that till we are black in the face
and nobody will believe either at home or abroad'. The *Standard*
and the *Daily News*, for example, at different points of the political
spectrum, both refused to accept the official line.[9] Not only did
Clarendon regret the loss of an 'invaluable colleague' on the Eastern
question, but he feared that, 'our difficulties abroad will be increased
by the notion that we shall be more disposed than hitherto to tolerate
Russian encroachment on Turkey or Russian insolence to England'.
He pressed upon Cowley the importance of not allowing Princess
Lieven to report to the Tsar that, 'Palmerston's resignation is a
letter of licence to the Czar, or that there will be any change of
policy here or less union with France'.[10] While he acknowledged
politely Palmerston's help over the past year, Clarendon could not
help worrying about the future prospects of the Government.[11]

Russell concurred: 'It increases all our difficulties, at home and abroad'.[12] The *Standard* reported, for example, that sections of the French press, such as the *Moniteur*, attributed 'in great measure the good understanding now happily existing between France and England' directly to Palmerston and thus regretted his resignation.[13] Moreover, as Charles Wood observed: 'Palmerston out of the Govt wd lead or support such an attack [on the Government's foreign policy], & many of those who wd shrink from voting against us on Reform itself, wd gladly & eagerly avail themselves of the opportunity of voting against us on such a question, not sorry to ward off or postpone Reform by so doing'.[14]

To Aberdeen, Palmerston's resignation appeared to present a good opportunity to remove a troublesome interference over foreign affairs. At the outset, Graham had impressed on the Prime Minister the need to steal this march on Palmerston. The letter which Palmerston had initially addressed to Lansdowne and which had come into Aberdeen's possession, Graham pointed out, 'touches very lightly on the Eastern question and puts Reform prominently forward. For this reason it suits our purpose best; and I would advise strongly, that you should confine your observations in answer principally, if not exclusively, to that letter, and make the difference on the Foreign Question secondary in your estimation'.[15] When the 'mis-understanding' was exposed and Palmerston was allowed to withdraw his resignation – on the grounds that he had framed it on an erroneous assumption that a definite decision had been reached regarding Reform (though he may have been stung by suggestions in the *Daily News* that there was 'the most philosophic indifference' to his resignation in the country[16]) – the Prime Minister was keen to keep foreign affairs out of the picture as far as possible. Palmerston had let it be known that his decision to return to the Government was due in no small part to a Cabinet decision made in his absence to accede to French proposals about sending the fleets to the Black Sea.[17] It may also have been significant that Lansdowne, with whom Palmerston had consulted over his resignation and who also, furthermore, enjoyed 'public respect' and 'confidence', had not followed Palmerston out of the Government as had been anticipated in some quarters.[18] Aberdeen welcomed Palmerston's approval of the Government's policy, but remarked pointedly: 'Although not connected with the cause of your resignation, I am glad to find that you approve of a recent decision of the Cabinet, with respect to the British and French fleets, adopted in your absence'. Nor could he resist adding, 'I feel assured you will have learnt with pleasure that whether absent, or present, the Government are duly careful to preserve from all inquiry the interests and dignity of the country'.[19]

To read Palmerston's resignation of December 1853 simply as a disagreement over Reform is erroneous – whether Palmerston genuinely resigned over this issue alone is almost immaterial, for the perception was that the Eastern question was just as, if not more, important – and yet also, to see it as a clever manoeuvre over foreign affairs, similarly misses the essence of the matter. Palmerston's resignation was, in a sense, a personal contest; it was as much about a rivalry between Palmerston and Russell as between Palmerston and the Aberdeen Government, something the *Daily News* hinted at almost as soon as the breach was known.[20] As Albert later noted, Palmerston had 'been playing a deep game all along'.[21]

Heretofore, Palmerston and Russell had acted in unison inasmuch as they had both opposed the general Aberdonian tone of British foreign policy. However, while there was indeed a genuine concern with the issues at stake, both were fully aware that this Government was a coalition. Newcastle's earlier hopes that the terms 'Whig' and 'Peelite' be dropped in favour of something of a more general 'liberal' nature had not been fulfilled. The differences between the groups had been subsumed by the coalition, but not eradicated and, whatever this might mean for the stability of the Cabinet as a whole, it also kept alive questions about political leadership. By virtue of having led a Whig government, and a Whig opposition, as well as leading the Whigs into the Aberdeen administration, Russell was, whether *de jure* or *de facto*, the head of the parliamentary Whig faction. Yet, as a subordinate member of the Aberdeen ministry, Russell feared that he risked losing his hold over the great Whig legacy. Palmerston, meanwhile had little doubt that only circumstance, and not ability, deprived him of the Whig leadership. Both, then, had cause to make whatever political capital they could during the life of the Government.

There were fears throughout the life of this Government that Palmerston and Russell sought to, or at least might, leave the Government and supplant it. Aberdeen's initial intimations that he would renounce the lead in favour of Russell, 'when the time was right', had raised Russell's expectations, and the failure to fulfil them did little to fortify the Government. Consequently, the tussles between Palmerston, Russell and the Cabinet over foreign policy and the Eastern question, were significant not only for their own sake, but also as symptoms of a struggle, never made explicit, between Russell and Palmerston for the leadership of the Whigs and Liberals at Westminster. Neither could afford the charge of wilfully engineering the overthrow of the Aberdeen Government and needed an issue which would neatly polarise the Cabinet and if the ministry fell as a result (not something to be aimed at straight away), they had to appear as the Government's saviour, not the root of its downfall.

Russell appears to have been the first to attempt to use foreign affairs to this end. As Aberdeen wrote to Graham in September 1853:

> it seems to me pretty clear that Lord John is determined to go. It is probable that on reflection, he found that the intention of leaving a Government with whom he entirely agreed, and a place, which however exceptional, was of his own making, would put him in a ridiculous point of view, and was in fact an untenable position. It was therefore necessary to have some ground of difference; and this Turkish affair presented one, out of which some capital might be made into the bargain. He has made a bad hit this time; but he may be more successful on the next occasion.[22]

Russell, however, had not the means to make a more successful hit. While he was popular among the Whig grandees, it was Palmerston to whom those outside the present Government – and upon whose support a replacement would draw – looked for inspiration. He, too, however was obliged to await a suitable opportunity.

The re-introduction of Reform to the political arena did much to appease Russell, giving him an opportunity to pursue a policy with which his name was clearly and commonly identified. The same was not to be said of Palmerston, as his correspondence of December 1853 demonstrates and in this sense he did resign over Reform. While Palmerston could have resigned exclusively over Eastern affairs, have carried the country with him, undermined Aberdeen's government and established good claims to lead his own administration, he would have remained politically shackled to Russell. However, in making Reform the cause of his resignation, while allowing foreign affairs to be cited in the country at large, Palmerston could secure popularity for removing himself from an unpopular government, without giving Russell an opportunity to join him in the venture and share in the credit.[23]

Palmerston called the Government's bluff: the Cabinet could not afford to allow him to stand outside the Government, and Kingsley Martin is perhaps right that Palmerston would have failed had he attempted to take the lead of the Tories in opposition,[24] but he had made, as Aberdeen saw early on, 'a very dextrous move'.[25] He had established an ascendancy over the rest of the Government regarding the Eastern question – that the rest of the Cabinet wanted him back on the grounds that he posed a serious threat in this field (above and perhaps to the exclusion of all others) is evidence of this [26] – but by implication in so doing he had also stolen a march on Russell. He was shown to be, as he had always liked to believe, the real strength of the Government. 'Now Palmerston is again in his seat and all is quiet', observed Albert. 'The best of the joke is, that, because he went out, the Opposition journals extolled him to the skies, in order to damage the Ministry, and now the Ministerial journals have to do so, in order to justify the reconciliation'.[27]

In the first instance, as *The Times* originally reported, it was believed that Palmerston's resignation was wholly unconnected with the foreign policy of the Government, and especially that relating to the Eastern question.[28] Whig and Peelite titles such as *The Economist*, the *Globe* and the *Morning Chronicle* all strenuously denied a link between the Home Secretary's action and the conduct of foreign policy. On the basis that, as the *Globe* had it, no step had been taken by the Foreign Office without Palmerston's 'previous knowledge, and perfect concurrence', it upheld the official account.[29] By that token the same could be said of the Reform issue up to that point, but whether it was true or not – and the Palmerstonian (and Protectionist) *Morning Post* maintained throughout that foreign policy disagreements were just as important as any over Reform [30] – there was agreement that Palmerston's membership of the Government was beneficial to the effectual execution of foreign policy. On his return to the Cabinet, once the 'mis-understanding' had been cleared up, the *Post*, for example, saw that this would guarantee that British policy in the East would henceforth be 'of a more worthy and active nature'.[31] More telling still was the response of the *Morning Chronicle*. Having assured readers that Reform was the only question at issue, the *Chronicle* welcomed his return and couched this relief exclusively in terms of its implications for foreign affairs. Significantly, the *Chronicle* wrote: 'To a large class of politicians, who feel rather than reason – who admire rather than understand – the name of Palmerston is a symbol of pluck and public spirit – a sort of epitome of all that is most English in the English character. It was, indeed, amusing to see the pertinacity with which, for some time after the formation of the present Government, people refused to recognise him in his new post of Home Secretary'.[32] No less importantly, Palmerston's return would, the *Chronicle* added, display to foreign governments, especially those of Russia and Turkey, 'his approval of the foreign policy of the Government'.[33] The *Standard* argued that Palmerston's 'true English spirit' distanced him from the rest of the Cabinet (suggesting that if he did return it would be as Prime Minister), while on his return, it affirmed the popularity of Palmerston's foreign policy with the country.[34]

Significantly, Palmerston's long-standing rivalry with the Palace also featured, to his advantage, in the popular interpretation of his resignation. Although the Court had generally endorsed government policy throughout 1853,[35] Albert's ties with continental royal houses, with which he maintained a correspondence (often clandestine) throughout his life in England,[36] made him personally, and by implication the Crown generally, unpopular and suspect at this critical juncture. Ironically, the Court in late 1853 was starting to move closer to an explicitly Palmerstonian position on the Eastern question,[37] but in the country Albert was seen as not only unduly conciliatory to Russian interests, but positively to be colluding with the forces of continental despotism. In January 1854 rumours circulated in the press, primarily in the *Morning Advertiser*, but also other titles of varied political persuasions, that Albert had been directly responsible for Palmerston's resignation.[38] Although Palmerston used the *Morning Post* to deny these suggestions, such was the growing distrust of the Prince that claims that he had been arrested for treason and imprisoned in the Tower were for a time taken seriously. Indeed, crowds assembled outside the Tower on

29 January, waiting to witness Albert's committal to that place (along with Aberdeen), actually burnt effigies of the Prince and Prime Minister.[39]

When Palmerston resigned from the Cabinet in December 1853, then, he did so in the knowledge that outside Parliament he was still widely, though not universally,[40] apprehended as the Government's ablest manager of foreign policy, particularly significant at a time when the country appeared to be on the point of going to war in the East. Concurrently, he was, as certain sources within Parliament attested at this time, riding high at Westminster. C. H. Frewen, an independent Member of Parliament, suggested that seven eighths of the Conservative party in the Commons and many independents such as himself, would support Palmerston as Prime Minister.[41]

Earl Grey was not at all sanguine about the prospects for harmony within the Cabinet as letters from friends including Ellice and Charles Wood persuaded him, 'that there can never be a good understanding again between Palmerston & some of his colleagues, & it will be difficult indeed for a Cabinet so avowedly divided to go on'.[42] Good understanding or not, however, Palmerston was to exert considerable influence over the course of affairs throughout 1854.

In the opening few weeks of the new year, the likelihood of Britain becoming involved in the fighting in the Near East became ever greater. At the very beginning of the year, Clarendon wrote to his wife, 'for my part, I am getting *in favor of war*'.[43] Aberdeen continued to hope for peace, but his hold over Cabinet opinion was weakening. Even those members of the Government previously identified as being on the peace wing of the Cabinet – Gladstone, Argyll, and Granville – by January were endeavouring to justify British participation in the war, should it become necessary.[44] Aberdeen's growing separation from his ministers is perhaps implicit in his admission to Clarendon that war did not seem inevitable, 'unless indeed we are determined to have it, which perhaps for aught I know, may be the case'.[45]

Fresh from his resignation 'triumph', Palmerston assumed a central role in the direction of foreign policy at this crucial moment. Significantly, even Russell was drawn to conclude a letter to Clarendon on the nature of Russia's intentions and possible responses of France and Britain with the observation: 'Mighty questions these,

& I should like to hear Palmerston's opinion upon them; no one sees so quickly & so clearly in these matters'.[46] It was Palmerston who took it upon himself in March when a declaration of war appeared imminent to lay out formally Britain's aims in which his 'beau Ideal' aimed at a far-reaching re-casting of Europe designed not only to preserve peace and under-pin the balance of power, but also to add to British prestige,[47] and Clarendon observed in May that he was 'perpetually making new maps of Europe'.[48]

The great problem was that, even with Palmerston attempting to drive the Government on, and a disposition within the Cabinet to pursue the war (which Britain entered on 27–28 March), there still remained a lack of leadership from Aberdeen. From the initial approach of war, Aberdeen had indulged in morbid reflections on the state of affairs, and Russell observed that 'the late meetings of the Cabinet have shown so much indecision, & there is so great a reluctance to adopt those measures which would force the Emperor of Russia to consent to a speedy peace that I can feel no such confidence. Indeed the sooner I can be relieved from my share of the responsibility the better'.[49] To Clarendon, Russell argued that the 'great want of all is a head of the English Cabinet', concluding later in the year that, 'I by no means admit that he [Aberdeen] has at any time adequately performed the duties of Prime Minister'.[50] Calls in the newspapers, especially the Tory press, for Aberdeen's removal, which had been heard since the beginning of the year, became steadily more forceful.[51] The Duke of Argyll, typical of many of his colleagues, wrote:

> What I dread is our going on without some purpose more definitely recognised – afraid of public opinion because we do not try to lead or guide it;– shy of each other because we do not know exactly each others' views. I do not believe that there is any difference which will prevent a practical conclusion, provided we try to come to it. But there is quite enough variety of *tendency* & of *feeling*, if we do not try, to keep our language various – our course unsteady – perhaps I ought rather to say, to prevent any definite course from being shaped at all. We shall then be at the mercy of tides; and our motion becomes a mere drift.[52]

At Court, too, the erstwhile favourite was losing favour, as Albert told Stockmar in March: 'Even yet Aberdeen cannot rise to the level of the situation, the war in his eyes "like a civil war, like a war between England and Scotland"!'.[53]

In Parliament Cobden's continued attachment to a pacific foreign policy failed to resonate with any significant body of opinion. In February 1854 with Britain poised to go to war, Cobden questioned the benefit to the Ottoman Empire of sustaining it, its ability to reform itself, and the extent to which the Ottoman Christians were suited to Ottoman, rather than Russian, rule. But ultimately, he admitted he was less concerned with whether or not the proposed war was right or wrong, than with the material consequences of it. Placing before the House his calculations of the value of Russian trade with Britain, he argued:

> Compare the Russian and Turkish trades together, and you will find that in the former you have one of three times the importance of the other. There is no one foreign country whose trade is so important to us as Russia, excepting the United States; and it is well to remember that all the carrying trade between our ports and Russia is in our hands. Now, is there any ground for urging this country into a war with Russia, for the purpose of protecting our commercial and trading interests? None whatever. The advantage is all on the other side.[54]

Cobden himself admitted in this speech that it was 'not to speak upon abstract principles of non-interference, or upon abstract questions of peace, that I rise to address the House; but with reference to the points at issue between Turkey and Russia, and of the war between England and France on the one side, and Russia upon the other'.[55] Yet herein lay the weakness of his case. For in the war with Russia the calculations were not those of balance sheets and account books, but of perceived violations of liberties and affronts to national honour and interest. Only once the war started to go badly did John Bright's initial questions about the nobility and popularity of the endeavour have any real resonance.[56]

Cobdenism had some currency in Parliament where speeches were cheered and applauded in certain quarters although were never actually put to the test directly in the division lobbies, but it lacked sympathy in the country at large. Certainly the Cobdenite perspective failed to chime with the popular anti-Russianism of public outrage over Albert's perceived intrigues, for example.

Fundamentally, it also lacked the support of its traditional constituency. Cobdenite opposition to the war not only offended Whig
and Tory sensibilities, but with many Radicals viewing the war as
a crusade against a tyrannical Russia in defence of the peoples of
Europe, it also alienated much parliamentary radical feeling.[57]
Former allies from the League turned on their erstwhile leaders and
denounced their anti-war stand while Cobden regretted their adherence to 'an absurd policy'.[58] In fact Cobden and Bright had already
alienated much radical feeling in 1850 over Don Pacifico,[59] and now
the backing, such as it was, that they would have liked to receive
from radical leaders such as John Roebuck in 1853 and 1854 went
instead to Palmerston.[60]

Palmerston, furthermore, remained attractive to the Protectionists, serving to underline his position as broker of parliamentary
power. Even though Disraeli claimed in the wake of his resignation
'that P. has lost caste terribly with the country by his levity of
conduct',[61] there is little reason to accept that this was an accurate
reflection of Disraeli's own estimation of the situation. Since 1850,
Disraeli had been much concerned with improving the Conservatives' record with public opinion pursuing various schemes to
produce a party-newspaper, which finally resulted in the emergence
of the *Press* in 1853.[62] This paper displayed a great admiration for
Palmerston and significantly, although he sought to keep his connection hidden, it is well known that Disraeli's contributions to its
pages were frequent and full. When Palmerston had walked out of
the Cabinet in December 1853, the *Press* had expressed regret at
the loss of 'the most eminent member of the Administration',[63] and
a few days later in a satirical piece on the 'Downing Street Christmas
Playbill', 'Mr Stone Palmer' appeared as 'The Genius of the Cabinet'.
The end result, significantly, was promised as 'DESTRUCTION OF
THE CABINET, AND TRIUMPH OF BRITISH POLICY'.[64] Furthermore,
not only was the *Press* loudly singing Palmerston's praises, but in
the new year clearly hinted at a natural and positive connection
between the genius of the Cabinet and Disraeli, if only party
connection did not stand in the way. A satirical verse imagined
Palmerston telling Gladstone, 'DISRAELI's charms my bosom feels,/
Whose name suggests the thought unpleasant,/That some have
held Exchequer seals,/When funds were higher than at present'
and that 'Though he is versed in Tory arts,/And thou'rt, I fear, a

ratting Raddy,/Still, *till our Coalition parts,*/I'll live and die collea-
gued with GLADDY.'[65]

By this point, though Disraeli was losing ground within the
Conservative party, many others in that party are said to have been
looking warmly at Palmerston. Throughout the year the *Standard,*
for instance, referred to Palmerston's good claims to replace Aberdeen, arguing on one occasion that although Derby was the obvious
candidate to lead a Protectionist ministry, the Conservative party
would be equally 'well contented' with Palmerston.[66] Disraeli denied
that he was intriguing with Palmerston to form a union between
themselves,[67] but he was widely believed to be closely connected
and associated with Palmerston, to the extent that in March 1854
Lord Stanley felt that in making attacks on the Government's
handling of the Eastern question, Disraeli 'relies, as before, on
Palmerston's secret support'.[68] Palmerston indeed appears to have
been prepared in 1854 to cooperate with certain members of the
opposition in order to foster criticism of the Government's foreign
policy. Malmesbury records in his *Memoirs* that in May of that year
he 'had a long and confidential conversation with Palmerston, whom
I met at dinner at the Walewskis, and we agreed perfectly on all
points of foreign policy'. Palmerston supplied Malmesbury with
information about the fleets at Odessa which Malmesbury was able
to use as the basis for a question about the orders sent to Admiral
Dundas regarding the bombardment of that port (which the 'Duke
of Newcastle refused to answer') in the House of Lords the following
week.[69]

This Protectionist support for Palmerston combined with
the divisions within the Government served only to emphasise the
importance to the ministry of Palmerston remaining within its
bounds, particularly now that, as Prince Albert observed, 'the
Country' thought him 'the only able War Minister'.[70] Palmerston's
advocacy throughout 1853 of a firm line towards Russia had
identified him very clearly with the 'war party' and consequently
it was now in a way inevitable that he should enjoy an ascendancy
within the Cabinet as a result. It is said that Palmerston was 'furious'
to have been passed over in favour of the Duke of Newcastle for
the War Office,[71] though the Peelite *Morning Chronicle,* perhaps not
surprisingly, claimed that there was no real evidence that Palmerston wanted the post and that he and Newcastle had 'always acted

together with perfect cordiality'.[72] As long ago as 1846 the *Standard* had suggested that Newcastle (then Lord Lincoln) was quite a suitable candidate for the War Office (then in the more junior post of Secretary at War) being 'so very plastic a person',[73] and perhaps such perceived malleability was still seen as an important qualification for office. There is, in the absence of evidence of a definite resistance to the War Office on Palmerston's part, reason to suggest that he saw Newcastle as a suitable minister for the role (significantly, he did not seek to replace Newcastle at the War Office later in the year either when the change was again mooted) and was happy to plough his Home Office furrow. The *Daily News* wondered at Palmerston not becoming War Secretary, however. 'Was it Court or Cabinet influence, or was it the Duke of NEWCASTLE's amour-propre, that had stood in the way of so natural arrangement?', it asked. Certainly, it seemed to the *News* that Newcastle's appointment implied a reluctance to prosecute the war vigorously.[74]

With Britain fighting in the war, arguments over foreign policy gave way to concern over how to manage the war itself. With unprecedented press coverage of the conflict, the conduct of the military campaigns was a matter of immediate concern and belief in Palmerston's ability to direct the war was recognised far and wide, from the Court to the popular press. Significantly, though, at this crucial juncture, Palmerston used his ability to manipulate the press to portray himself outside the bounds of government in quite a different light.[75] Though he was still held up as the most able minister for the direction of British foreign policy in the East, it is striking that most press attention in 1854 concerning Palmerston focused on his domestic politics and his work at the Home Office. The *Standard*, indeed, implied Palmerston should avoid speaking on foreign policy questions in Parliament.[76] The *Morning Post* was one of the few newspapers in this year, particularly once Britain had gone to war, to continue to peddle the line that a more determined and consistent Palmerstonian approach from the outset would have avoided this conflict.[77]

Whatever might have been the value of Palmerston's support for the Government's foreign policy, it is notable that as soon as he had been re-admitted to the Cabinet, it was to his domestic reforms that the attention of the press was directed.[78] Newspaper coverage of Palmerston's political activities in 1854 was concerned primarily with issues such as the work of the Board of Health; the poor law; smoke abatement; the reforms of prisons, universities, and police; and town improvements such as sewage systems.[79] The absence of meaningful connections between Palmerston and foreign policy in newspaper articles during this year and a far greater preponderance of articles discussing his domestic undertakings is remarkable. In the summer, indeed, the *Standard* commented on Palmerston's 'ominous silence' in the principal debates of the parliamentary session (perceiving a bid for the premiership).[80] Towards the end of the year, *The Times* observed how Palmerston was no longer at the forefront of diplomatic debates, at least those before the public gaze, and wondered at his propensity to busy himself with other issues:

> So now, if people have time to look back – and the long intervals of the intelligence give us time for almost anything – it is likely the question is now and then asked, 'What is Lord PALMERSTON doing? What does he think of the war? Would he have averted it? Would he have brought it earlier to a crisis? Is he gathering friends and concerting measures with a view to his old post?' We cannot undertake to answer all those questions, but the world may see at once one thing that Lord PALMERSTON is doing. Deep in the heart of the country, somewhere between the New Forest and Salisbury Plain, he is presiding over innocent rustic celebrities, delivering prizes to bucolic excellence, and teaching labourers how to be happy, and merry and wise.[81]

Meanwhile, the debate over the correct course in the war raged on at Westminster. Crucially, however, whereas it had been Palmerston as much as, if not more so than Russell, who had challenged the Aberdonian approach, the contest was now, in 1854, presented in the press as being between Russell and Aberdeen. In the *Morning Post* an article appeared in July highly critical of the leadership of the Prime Minister, or 'Lord FEEBLEMIND' as it dubbed him. Significantly though, in discussing the merits of the Aberdonian versus the alternative policy, the *Post*, while accepting that many in the Cabinet were losing faith in the premier's approach (although these were not named), identified Lord John Russell and Lord Clarendon as the leading lights among those 'expressing and acting on directly opposite opinions'. In the same edition Palmerston was mentioned in the following leading article, but solely in connection with police reform.[82]

Three days later the *Post* returned to its attacks on the Government, this time critical of its performance in all areas of public business, condemning the ministry as susceptible to parliamentary majorities not its own, indeed majorities resulting 'from chance combinations, which appear to have been formed rather without than within the walls of Parliament'. Unacceptable by any measure of ministerial conduct, the *Post* was especially critical of this situation in the face of the current turbulent foreign context, arguing that weak government at home would send out obscure signals to foreign powers about British policy. A firm hand was required, but again, it was not Palmerston, to whom a reading of the press prior to 1854 might have suggested an appeal would be made. Rather, on the question of who directed policy, the *Post* asked; 'Is it the Earl of ABERDEEN or Lord JOHN RUSSELL?'.[83] Not that Palmerston was completely silent on the subject of the Eastern question – as the *Post* again reported, a month after this attack, Palmerston's recent speech on this subject had contained 'manly and English declarations',[84] – but he was not being put forward as the statesman who should be given the opportunity to take up the reins of the Foreign Office and execute his 'beau Ideal'. There was, of course, a risk involved in such a strategy, as the *Morning Herald*, suggested in June:

> Where is he now, when the destinies of the world are trembling in the balance? Pottering over sewers and squabbling about a county police. Let the noble lord the member for Tiverton beware; the favour of a great nation is never slighted with impunity, and the vexed people of England, however unwillingly, may be compelled to adopt the explanations tendered by Mr. Urquhart, and say that the greatest man at the present day in Britain does not dare to place himself at the head of his countrymen, because he fears to face the revelations which his promotion would render inevitable.[85]

Only once the war could be seen to be going badly did the press seek to tie Palmerston's fortunes in with those of his colleagues. Of a meeting at the Horn's Tavern in Kennington in December, for example, in which a resolution was passed critical of Aberdeen's handling of the Eastern question and war, the *Morning Chronicle* noted that 'Lord PALMERSTON and Lord JOHN RUSSELL have been equally guilty of the "extreme folly" which is denounced; and they are equally responsible for the "alarm and disgust" which the Ministerial policy may call forth'.[86] It was an implicit recognition of the careful manoeuvring on the part of Palmerston which had allowed him to present himself after December 1853 as the Government's ablest foreign and subsequently war minister without having to put those claims to the test. Thus the Peelite press by the end of the year was clearly concerned lest he win, by default, the credit for his wise, though unheeded, counsels in this matter. As the speeches made by Louis Kossuth during his visit to Britain in 1854 demonstrate, it was Palmerstonian interventionism that enjoyed the broadest popular support at this time:

> I am led to believe that, as well from a natural sympathy for liberty, justice and right, as also from the instinctive knowledge of the fact that the welfare, interest, and honour of England go all that way, the people did and does not shrink from all the dangers and sacrifices of a great war, by the only reason, because it means to fight for freedom; because it believes that a real advantage to the cause of oppressed nationalities will be the issue. I am led to believe that it is by this reason, that the war is popular with the people of England. Is it so, or is it not so? Please answer me. Am I right or am I wrong in my supposition? (Cries of 'yes') ... How is it that England is leaning just the other way, and her statesmen straining every diplomatic nerve to ally despotic Austria to you? Why, it is simply because the people of England has not pronounced its will until now. Let that will be spoken, and, I trust, there shall not be wanting good and true men in Parliament to represent it, and to make the people's will efficient.[87]

It was Palmerston who, it was hoped, would make this will efficient. By the autumn of 1854 most titles were advocating a Palmerstonian line, whether they had supported his approach from the outset or been converted by witnessing the progress of events. *The Times*, for instance, had been initially a reliable Aberdonian journal, but by the end of the 1853 the Prime Minister was already starting to lose its support while intelligence received from Clarendon revealed the divisions which were carving up the Cabinet, and *The Times* became increasingly bellicose.[88] *The Times* in 1854 acted increasingly independently of Aberdeen and was no longer swayed by his counsel, printing articles on a regular basis which the Prime Minister deeply regretted. But as the paper's owner, John Walter, told John Bright in March, 'when the country would go for war, it was not worth while to oppose it, hurting themselves and doing no good'.[89] Yet it was not a purely political decision. Delane, the editor of *The Times*, visited the Crimea in August and September and foresaw the coming winter hardships facing British soldiers there. When the Duke of Newcastle, at the War Department, took no notice, Delane became more vocal in his criticism of the Government, and, significantly, joined the campaign behind Palmerston.[90] But by late 1854, there was no reason for Palmerston to fear that his name might be attached to the ministry's: he had made his stand, been vindicated in his view of the Eastern question and had contrived to steal a march on his nearest Whig rival, Russell. As Albert recorded, by December the breach between Palmerston and Russell had become insurmountable and, furthermore, though Aberdeen may have been willing to yield the premiership to Russell, the Prime Minister was also 'certain that not one of the present Cabinet could now serve under Lord John'.[91]

Palmerston's avoidance of the limelight during the critical months of 1854 is interesting. Clearly, in contrast to earlier periods, he did not court press attention for his opinions on foreign policy. Even in the *Morning Post*, 'which is notoriously his [Palmerston's] paper' Aberdeen complained in February,[92] Russell, not Palmerston was represented as the Cabinet's chief anti-Aberdonian. This was not coincidental and whether Palmerston guided this editorial policy or not, it suited the 'deep game' he was playing. His resignation of December 1853 had been, arguably, an attempt to gain political ground at Russell's expense. He returned at the beginning of 1854 having given the impression that he disliked the Government's foreign policy and that he could offer a better alternative, but had suppressed these for reasons of national stability. Apparently weak, however, hopes for the Government's long-term survival were slim and Palmerston was presented with an opportunity of laying the foundations for his 'inevitable' accession to the premiership within a year.

He had two main tasks: firstly to undermine Russell; and secondly to secure or confirm a broad base of popular support. His correspondence with Russell at this time suggests a desire to limit Russell's position, and to check any popularity-hunting by him. Over Reform, for example, Palmerston counselled caution. Not only would it be dangerous at the present moment to bring into question the future of the Government, he said, but:

> Your measure may possibly give you some small & fleeting Popularity among the lower Classes, though there seems good Reason to doubt whether the Balance of Feeling would not be against you for not giving to all that which you would grant to a few. But your intentioned Course is openly disapproved by all the intelligent & respectable Classes whose good opinion is most to be valued, & you can hardly be aware of the Feelings of personal Hostility towards you which are daily spreading through all the Party which has hitherto acknowledged you as their Leader.[93]

At this point, in January 1854, Palmerston was ready neither to assume Russell's mantle as leader of the Whigs, nor to mount a challenge for the premiership should the Government fall. Palmerston needed to re-establish his credibility with the rest of the Cabinet, having done much in the previous December to win popular support, but also consolidate this support outside Westminster. Were Russell to gain the upper hand now by either passing Reform and winning popular acclaim, or upsetting the Government, Palmerston's domestic policies were not enough to win popular support and the Eastern question was not yet far enough advanced for his bellicose stand to justify him dis-associating himself from the ministry; indeed, it was still thought possible in early 1854 that war could be avoided. The most effective way for Palmerston to usurp Russell's position was to allow Russell to undermine himself. If the anti-Aberdonian policy was not to gain widespread currency within the Cabinet, there seemed little prospect of a happy outcome in the war, and better then that Russell go down as the minister who compromised Aberdeen's leadership, than Palmerston. Thus, attention in the press, and especially the pro-Palmerston journals, recognised Palmerston's diplomatic ability but did not attribute to him responsibility for the current divisions: Russell was presented as the disloyal one.

Focusing on Palmerston's domestic policies was not a wasted enterprise. The new Palmerston, socially aware, reforming, even philanthropic, was designed to appeal to the middle classes whose concerns, especially in the growing industrial regions, were heavily focused on public health and social conditions. And as the war, through Gladstone's budgets, imposed financially on the middle classes in particular,[94] it was important to be seen as their ally. Furthermore, the nature of the Eastern question, as it related to Britain, by 1854 was not exclusively a foreign policy issue. Whatever Palmerston might have said in his Cabinet memorandum outlining his 'beau Ideal', at home the Crimean war was seen as essentially a test of Britain's greatness; of British institutions faced with the despotic menace of Russian absolutism and of the fitness of the British government to execute successfully what was expected to be 'a long and global war'.[95] For Palmerston to be associated with these institutions, indeed as a reformer and improver of them, was no impediment to his growing popularity, indeed it was essential, however misplaced such expectations might ultimately prove to have been.[96]

Russell, by contrast, although during 1853 a consistent advocate of a more assertive foreign policy was now being left behind. As Minto, who had discussed the matter with Russell recorded in June 1854:

> He is almost without support in the Cabinet. On great questions of foreign policy indeed Lansdowne, Palmerston and he, and I may add Granville, heartily agree, and in recent questions some of the Peelite members of the Cabinet entirely go with them. But as regards general support of him individually as the head of their party he can count upon none I think except Granville & I believe the Chancellor, & probably now George Grey, but on questions of foreign affairs the latter will bring him weakness rather than strength, and his most wretched speech at his election at Morpeth, as well as his conversation since has greatly lowered the estimate of the value of his accession to the government.[97]

Russell weakened his own position in the course of 1854 by persisting in making attacks on the Government's foreign policy and on Aberdeen specifically. Throughout the year, although himself becoming frustrated and disappointed with Aberdeen's lack of leadership, Clarendon defended the Prime Minister against Russell's attacks, accusing Russell of disloyalty and arguing that disparaging

Aberdeen would not alleviate the Government's problems.[98] Russell's attacks on Aberdeen, however, became more frequent, almost comically so, and Albert was even moved to arrange a special file, 'Concerning the part which Lord John Russell took in breaking up Lord Aberdeen's Governmt, Nov 1854–Feby 1855'.[99]

Palmerston sought to capitalise on this, assisted by the general lack of vitality among his colleagues. On the Cabinet's decision to order Raglan to lay siege to Sebastopol at the end of June, for example, Russell claimed that, 'the expedition had occupied the anxious thoughts of the members of the Cabinet for several months and that it had been discussed very carefully and maturely', but he did not deny the claim made by Kinglake in *The Invasion of the Crimea* that the ministers slept while the despatch was read out to them by Newcastle. In fact, such ministerial somnolence appears to have been not at all uncommon.[100] It was not difficult then for Palmerston to exercise very considerable influence over the Cabinet in matters relating to the strategy and tactics to be adopted in the war.

The decision to press an early attack on Sebastopol was, without doubt, Palmerston's doing. The Cabinet papers relating to this resolution remain among Palmerston's private papers and show how he persuaded his colleagues that having entered the war at great expense and for a great purpose, Britain and France would, 'lose Caste in the world if they concluded the war with only a small Result'.[101] Aberdeen noted that on this resolution to destroy Sebastopol and the Russian fleet, 'there appears to be very little difference of opinion'.[102] When, at Russell's injunction, Palmerston sent 'this Box around again in order that Each member of the Cabinet may see the observations made by his Colleagues', he was gratified to find that they all shared his concerns.[103]

In late 1854 it was again proposed that Palmerston should take charge of the War Office. Russell wrote to Aberdeen in November, stressing 'the necessity of having in that office a man, who from experience of military details, from inherent vigour of mind, & from weight with the H. of Commons can be expected to guide the great operations of war with authority and success'. He believed that there was 'only one person belonging to the Govt who combines these advantages', and that was Palmerston, who should therefore 'be entrusted with the seals of the War Department'.[104] Aberdeen feared that the duties would be unduly onerous for one who 'possesses no immunity from the effects of age',[105] but there were hints of party intrigue in this objection to Palmerston. As Palmerston noted, such a change at the War Office would have unavoidable repercussions:

> Clarendon said that as the matter now stands, Aberdeen declares that if Newcastle is forced out he Aberdeen will resign, while on the other Hand he Clarendon fears that John Russell will say that he will leave the Govt if Newcastle does not give up the Conduct of the War. Clarendon seemed to think this an Intrigue got up for the Purpose of breaking up the Govt and getting John Russell back as Prime Minister.[106]

Russell's claims to the premiership were not as strong as they had been in 1853, however, if only because with the war now the central issue in politics it was Palmerston who had won over the Cabinet and the public, not Russell. Thus it was Palmerston, not Russell, of whom Clarendon wrote to his wife in December, that much 'if not all will depend' on what he determined since if 'he says that any change at this moment wd be detrimental to the public service the thing will fall to the ground as Johnny wd have no support at all, but if P (wch is not likely) was to condemn Newcastle then I see nothing for it but a break up & as that wd destroy the confidence of France & crush the nascent vitality of Austria & be worth a dozen victories to Russia it wd I think fulfill [sic] all the conditions of treason'.[107]

Yet, as Clarendon supposed, Palmerston was not likely to condemn Newcastle. Throughout the year, Palmerston and Newcastle had enjoyed a good understanding on matters pertaining to the war while his position at the Home Office suited his personal ambitions. Only when Russell threatened to resign over Roebuck's motion in January 1855 did Palmerston put himself forward for the War Department, pointing out that he did not believe that he could do the job as well as Newcastle, but hoping that if necessary this might be one way of saving the Government from dissolution.[108]

Ultimately, however, the Government could not be saved. Roebuck's motion for a committee of inquiry into the conduct of the war, effectively a question of confidence in the ministry, was carried by a vote of 305 to 148 against the Government and the Ministers resigned on 30 January 1855. The search for a successor was not straightforward. Derby was called for but he was not able to form his second government just yet. The Queen and Prince, who were 'resolved to exhaust everything before they send for Palmerston',[109] were eventually forced to do just that. Even Russell was obliged to concede that, 'the country wanted Lord Palmerston either as War Minister or Prime Minister'.[110] It seemed in many cases as the latter. Throughout 1854, while the talk around the Cabinet table might have been about replacing Newcastle with Palmerston as War Secretary, outside those closed quarters the debate was whether (perhaps even when) Palmerston should become the Prime Minister. Certainly there was little regard for Aberdeen's 'unstatesman-like views' among the 'Inhabitants of London' who had addressed a protest to the Lord Mayor about Aberdeen's speech in the House of Lords of 19 June 1854 which, they felt, stood in stark contrast to the 'manly and truly British declarations' of the Cabinet's anti-Aberdonians, Russell and Clarendon.[111] In September 1854 E. Davies sent Palmerston a letter enclosing a copy of a pen portrait which he had composed and published in an un-named London weekly journal. The sketch of Palmerston's character acknowledged the difficulty in seeking to label Palmerston's political affiliations (without engaging in the debate) and praised his abilities and his industry. 'His importance is felt so much in the whole kingdom, by almost all parties', it continued, 'that he is looked upon as the only one to be an efficient English premier'. He was free from party ties (though able to unite a broad spectrum of opinion), his character 'peculiarly masculine' and English, and his habits gentlemanly. 'The country expects much from him', the article concluded: 'We believe that he is "the coming man" in the legislature. It is possible that circumstances may shortly bring about such changes as to place him where he ought to be, in the government of this great country'.[112] There were dissentient voices, of course, as found in pamphlets such as *Palmerston for Premier!* (1854) which attacked Palmerston's claim to that office, tracing an Urquhartite line through the history of Palmerston's foreign policy and concluding that Palmerston had been intriguing throughout for 'the union of England and Russia'. Palmerston as Prime Minister, it maintained, would only encourage Russia 'to strike her grand blow for universal empire!'[113] But Urquhartite approaches have already been seen to have had little purchase on the popular imagination. Washington Wilks' pamphlet *Palmerston in Three Epochs* (1854) similarly failed to strike a chord with what appears to have been the over-arching popular mood in charging Palmerston with pursuing 'an un-English policy', that he was, in short, the purveyor of 'false Liberalism', and a 'Captain of Shams'.[114]

When John Bright needed a police escort to defend him against protesters in his own Manchester constituency angry at his anti-interventionist stance, it was only further evidence of the extent to which Palmerston had secured the support of the Manchester commercial classes.[115] According to Antony Taylor, the 'body of disenfranchised in Manchester was not renowned for its positive level of commitment to the war effort', although the old Anti-Corn Law League was now solidly pro-Palmerston. Thus, the opposition to Palmerston (or at least lack of positive support) which Taylor identifies in Manchester was not the most visible popular sentiment, and winning over the commercial classes was far more valuable.[116] The problem for those opposing Palmerstonian policies was that in London, where the debate was liveliest, opposition was weakest. And so the Queen's hand was forced – Palmerston had to be offered the premiership:

> I know this would be very objectionable in many respects, and personally not agreeable to me, [she wrote] but *I* think of *nothing* but the country, and the preservation of its institutions, and *my own* personal feelings would be sunk if only the efficiency of the government could be obtained. *If* the *Peelites* and *Whigs* would serve *under* Lord Palmerston, *I should not* apprehend the consequences – for they would restrain him from mischief, and Palmerston *himself* in *that position* would feel the weight and responsibility of *such a position* in a manner that would make him feel very differently to what he has hitherto done, as a subordinate.[117]

The Queen claimed that in appointing Palmerston, she 'had *no* other alternative',[118] and was supported by Albert (who now closed the files he had been keeping on Palmerston since 1848 [119]) while Palmerston believed that he was *l'inévitable*. The *Morning Post* observed in January 1855 that 'the people of England at this important juncture, when the fate of England and Europe hangs in the balance, require and will have for Minister the only Statesman to whose great spirit, far-seeing wisdom, and thoroughly English character, they are ready to confide their destinies, and the issue, under PROVIDENCE, of this great war. That Statesman is Lord PALMERSTON'.[120] The *Globe* echoed this sentiment: 'Out of doors', it claimed, 'there is not a part of the country that has not contributed spontaneous expressions of the wish for Lord PALMERSTON to untake [?undertake] the chief conduct of affairs'.[121] Even the *Morning Chronicle* was forced to admit that, on account of the damage that would have been caused to Britain's foreign relations, had Palmerston not been able to form a government, 'his failure would have been a national misfortune'.[122] In this sense, then, he was indeed, *l'inévitable.*

Notes

1 As the *Daily News* had once observed, Palmerston 'was considered as rather yielding to the inevitable necessity of parliamentary reform than zealously supporting it' (29 Dec. 1851).

2 Prest, *Russell,* p. 361, memorandum by Prince Albert, 16 Dec. 1853.

3 Lansdowne Papers Lans. 3/42, fol. 39, Palmerston to Lansdowne, 8 Dec. 1853.

4 *LQV*, II, pp. 568–9, Prince Albert to Aberdeen, 9 Dec. 1853.

5 Broadlands Papers, GC/AB/302, Aberdeen to Palmerston, 14 Dec. 1853.

6 *LQV*, II, pp. 569–70, memorandum by Prince Albert, 16 Dec. 1853.

7 Broadlands Papers, SHA/PD/6, Shaftesbury Diaries, 21 Dec. 1853.

8 Grey Papers, 3rd Earl, C3/17, Grey, journal, 17 Dec. 1853.

9 *Standard,* 16 Dec. 1853; *Daily News,* 19 Dec. 1853.

10 Maxwell, *Clarendon,* II, p. 35, Clarendon to Cowley, 16 Dec. 1853.

11 Broadlands Papers, GC/CL/549, Clarendon to Palmerston, 14 Dec. 1853.

12 Clarendon Deposit, MSS.Clar.dep.c.3, fols 562–3, Russell to Clarendon, 15 Dec. 1853.

13 *Standard,* 19 Dec. 1853.

14 Hickleton Papers, A4.56, Wood to Russell, 25 Dec. 1853.

15 Aberdeen Papers, Add. Mss. 43191, Graham to Aberdeen, 10 Dec. 1853.

16 *Daily News,* 22 Dec. 1853.

17 Palmerston wrote to Lansdowne on 22 December 1853 that: 'The Decision of the Cabinet to accede to the French Proposal, which I took Care to have confirmed by Walewsky before I wrote my Letter to Aberdeen places our future Course in regard to Turkish affairs in a proper Direction & was a great Inducement to me to comply with the wishes which had been so strongly expressed to me [by Newcastle, Gladstone, Sidney Herbert, Molesworth and Charles Wood, that Palmerston should continue as a member of the Government]' (Broadlands Papers, GC/LA/112). Similarly to Aberdeen, he wrote: 'You will perhaps allow me to add that the Decision which I am informed the Cabinet came to yesterday to accede to the Proposal of the

French Government, whereby the British and French Squadrons will have the Command of the Black Sea, greatly enters into the Considerations which have led me to address this Letter to you' (Aberdeen Papers, Add. Mss. 43069, Palmerston to Aberdeen, 23 Dec. 1853).

18 *Standard*, 17 Dec. 1853.

19 Aberdeen Papers, Add. Mss. 43069, Aberdeen to Palmerston, 24 Dec. 1853.

20 *Daily News*, 19 Dec. 1853.

21 Eyck, *Prince Consort*, p. 233, memorandum by Albert, 26 Feb. 1854.

22 Graham Papers, MS Film 124, Bundle 114, Aberdeen to Graham, 22 Sept. 1853.

23 Martin, *The Triumph of Lord Palmerston*, pp. 159–60.

24 *Ibid.*, p. 160.

25 Conacher, *The Aberdeen Coalition*, p. 221, Aberdeen to Graham, 10 Dec. 1853.

26 Palmerston reported to Lansdowne that several members of the Cabinet, primarily Newcastle, Gladstone, Sidney Herbert, Molesworth and Sir Charles Wood, actively sought an arrangement at this time with the aim of securing Palmerston's return to the Government (Broadlands Papers, GC/LA/112, Palmerston to Lansdowne, 22 Dec. 1853).

27 Bell, *Palmerston*, II, p. 101, Prince Albert, 24 Dec. 1853 [?].

28 *The Times*, 16 Dec. 1853.

29 *The Economist*, 17 Dec. 1853; *Globe*, 16, 17 Dec. 1853 (quote from 17 Dec.); *Morning Chronicle*, 16 Dec. 1853.

30 *Morning Post*, 17, 19 Dec. 1853.

31 *Ibid.*, 26 Dec. 1853.

32 *Morning Chronicle*, 26 Dec. 1853.

33 *Ibid.*, 27 Dec. 1853.

34 *Standard*, 23, 26 Dec. 1853.

35 See, for example, *LQV*, II, p. 549, Queen to Clarendon, 24 Sept. 1853.

36 S. Weintraub, *Albert. Uncrowned King* (London, 1997), pp. 270–1.

37 Eyck, *Prince Consort*, p. 225.

38 See R. Williams, *The Contentious Crown: Public Discussion of the British Monarchy in the Reign of Queen Victoria* (Aldershot, 1997), pp. 99–103.

39 Weintraub, *Albert*, pp. 296–301.

40 Cf. *Daily News*, 27 Dec. 1853.

41 Broadlands Papers, GC/FR/7, C. H. Frewen to Palmerston, 19 Dec. 1853.

42 Grey Papers, 3rd Earl, C3/17, Grey, journal, 31 Dec. 1853.

43 Clarendon to Lady Clarendon, 2 Jan. 1854, Maxwell, *Clarendon*, II, p. 37.

44 Conacher, *The Aberdeen Coalition*, pp. 245, 261–3.

45 Clarendon Deposit, MSS.Clar.dep.c.14, fol. 12, Aberdeen to Clarendon, 12 Feb. 1854.

46 *Ibid.*, MSS.Clar.dep.c.15, fols 311–12, Russell to Clarendon, 15 Jan. 1854.

47 Russell Papers, PRO 30/22/11/C, fols 267–8, memorandum by Palmerston, 19 March 1854.

48 *Later Correspondence of Lord John Russell*, II, p. 164, Clarendon to Russell, 7 May 1854.

49 Russell Papers, PRO 30/22/11D , Russell to Aberdeen, 5 May 1854.

50 Clarendon Deposit, MSS.Clar.dep.c.15, fols 485–8, Russell to Clarendon, 12 May 1854; *ibid.*, MSS.Clar.dep.c.15, fols 679–80, Russell to Clarendon, 12 Oct. 1854.

51 *Standard*, 9 Jan., 13 July, 2 Aug., 25 Sept. 1854.

52 Clarendon Deposit, MSS.Clar.dep.c.14, fols 706–15, Argyll to Clarendon, 25 Oct. 1854.

53 Henderson, *Crimean War Diplomacy*, p. 72. Cf. Graham's report to Aberdeen from Balmoral in October 1853: 'On one thing you may rely, and that is, the utmost support, which the Crown can give. While you are willing to fight the battle and to remain at the Head of Affairs, I am confident, that the man does not live, who can supplant you in Royal Favor. What is far better than Favor, you possess a willing and well-grounded Confidence' (Aberdeen Papers, Add. Mss. 43191, Graham to Aberdeen, 8 Oct. 1853).

54 *Hansard*, 3rd ser., CXXX, 917–44 (20 Feb. 1854).

55 *Hansard*, 3rd ser., CXXX, 917 (20 Feb. 1854).

56 *Hansard*, 3rd ser., CXXXII, 243–67 (31 March 1854).

57 McCord, 'Cobden and Bright', pp. 104–5.

58 *Ibid.*, p. 105, J. P. Thompson to Cobden, 18 Aug. 1853; Cobden to Bright, 9 Nov. 1854.

59 D. Read, *Cobden and Bright: A Victorian Political Partnership* (London, 1967), pp. 118–19.

60 In fact Roebuck, due to ill-health, was able to offer little effective parliamentary support to even Palmerston by 1854. R. E. Leader (ed.), *Life and Letters of John Arthur Roebuck* (London, 1897), p. 258.

61 *Disraeli Letters*, VI, 2610, Disraeli to Lord Stanley, 30 Dec. 1853.

62 See Smith, *Disraeli*, p. 117.

63 *Press*, 17 Dec. 1853.

64 *Ibid.*, 24 Dec. 1853.

65 'CARMEN AMŒBÆUM BY MR GLADSTONE AND LORD PALMERSTON' *ibid.*, 7 Jan. 1854. The emphasis is that of the *Press*.

66 *Standard*, 2 Aug. 1854.

67 *Disraeli Letters*, VI, 2624, Disraeli to Ponsonby, 22 Jan. 1854.

68 Vincent (ed.), *Disraeli, Derby and the Conservative Party: Journals and Memoirs of Edward Henry, Lord Stanley, 1849–1869*, p. 123 (24 March 1854).

69 Malmesbury, *Memoirs*, I, p. 433 (3, 11 May 1854); *Hansard*, 3rd ser., CXXXIII, 142–4 (11 May 1854).

70 *LQV*, III, pp. 27–8, memorandum by Prince Albert, 10 April 1854.

71 Malmesbury, *Memoirs*, I, pp. 435–6.

72 *Morning Chronicle*, 3, 12 June 1854.

73 *Standard*, 3 July 1846.

74 *Daily News*, 18, 17 July 1854.

75 On Palmerston's ability to manipulate the press, see Brown, 'Compelling but not Controlling?', 41–61.

76 *Standard*, 21 Feb. 1854.

77 *Morning Post*, 3 April 1854.

78 See, for example, the *Globe*, 2 Feb. 1854.

79 See articles in: the *Globe*, 10 March, 3 April, 11, 31 July, 5 Oct., 2 Nov. 1854; *Morning Chronicle*, 7, 11 Jan., 7 Feb., 17 April, 27 June, 8, 13, 20 July, 1, 3 Aug., 11 Sept. 1854; *Daily News*, 27 Jan., 24 March, 30 Aug., 18 Nov. 1854; *Standard*, 30, 31 March 1854.

80 *Standard*, 1 Aug. 1854.

81 *The Times*, 2 Nov. 1854.

82 *Morning Post*, 21 June 1854.

83 *Ibid.*, 24 June 1854.

84 *Ibid.*, 26 July 1854.

85 Quoted (approvingly) in the *Globe*, 10 June 1854.

86 *Morning Chronicle*, 7 Dec. 1854. Nevertheless, the Peelites did still see Russell as more important than Palmerston in this Government's foreign policy debates, as a letter from Newcastle to Gladstone in February 1855 illustrates in which Newcastle clearly labels the anti-Aberdonian faction within the Cabinet as 'the Russell section' (Nottingham University Library, Newcastle Papers, NeC 10851/1/2, Newcastle to Gladstone, 5 Feb. 1855).

87 *Authentic Report of Kossuth's Speeches on the War in the East and the Alliance with Austria, at Sheffield, June 5, and at Nottingham, June 12, 1854. Published by Himself* (London, 1854), p. 5.

88 See Clarendon Deposit, MS.Clar.dep.c.535, letters from Clarendon to Reeve for 1853. Also, Koss, S., *The Rise and Fall of the Political Press in Britain: Vol. I The Nineteenth Century* (London, 1981), pp. 101–2.

89 For the changing attitudes of *The Times* in this period, see Koss, *The Rise and Fall of the Political Press: Vol. I*, pp. 102–6.

90 L. Brown, *Victorian News and Newspapers* (Oxford, 1985), p. 235.

91 *LQV*, II, p. 76, memorandum by Albert, 9 Dec. 1854.

92 Koss, *The Rise and Fall of the Political Press: Vol. I*, p. 103.

93 Russell Papers, PRO 30/22/11C, fols 110A–12, Palmerston to Russell, 29 Jan. 1854.

94 H. C. G. Matthew, *Gladstone 1809–1874* (Oxford, 1986), pp. 121–4.

95 See O. Anderson, *A Liberal State at War: English Politics and Economics during the Crimean War* (London, 1967), p. 1.

96 *Ibid.*, p. 35.

97 Minto Papers, MS 12001, Minto, journal, 30 June 1854.

98 See Conacher, *The Aberdeen Coalition*, p. 492.

99 Henderson, *Crimean War Diplomacy*, p. 34.

100 Conacher, *The Aberdeen Coalition*, p. 453 and n. 2.

101 Broadlands Papers, CAB/65, memorandum by Palmerston 'on the measures to be adopted against Russia', 15 June 1854.

102 *Ibid.*, CAB/66, memorandum by Aberdeen, n.d. Argyll, for example, believed Palmerston's proposals 'wd go far to settle the war at once, and command an immediate & advantageous peace' (CAB/67); Sir George Grey agreed 'in the general views expressed by Lord Palmerston' (CAB/72); as did Clarendon (CAB/68), Granville (CAB/71) and Molesworth (CAB/75).

103 *Ibid.*, CAB/79/2, memorandum by Palmerston, 22 June 1854.

104   Newcastle Papers, NeC 10295/1–2, Russell to Aberdeen, 17 Nov. 1854 (copy).

105   Aberdeen Papers, Add. Mss. 43068, Aberdeen to Russell, 21 Nov. 1854.

106   Broadlands Papers, GC/CL/582, minute by Palmerston, 2 Dec. 1854 on letter from Clarendon to Palmerston, 30 Nov. 1854.

107   Bodleian Library, MSS.Eng.c.2085, Clarendon to Lady Clarendon, 5 Dec. 1854.

108   See F. D. Munsell, *The Unfortunate Duke: Henry Pelham, Fifth Duke of Newcastle, 1811–1864* (Columbia, 1985), pp. 209–10.

109   Broadlands Papers, SHA/PD/6, Shaftesbury Diaries, 2 Feb. 1855.

110   *LQV*, III, pp. 118–19, memorandum by the Queen, [3 Feb. 1855?].

111   Aberdeen Papers, Add. Mss. 43068, letter 'To the Right Honourable the Lord Mayor of the City of London', from 'Inhabitants of London'. A copy of this letter was sent to Aberdeen on 23 June 1854 by Russell who had received it himself on 22 June. Russell's note to the Prime Minister observes: 'It is right that you should know what is going on. The position of the Govt has become very precarious'.

112   Broadlands Papers, MPC/1561 and enc. 1, E. Davies to Palmerston, 16 Sept. 1854, enclosing newspaper cutting entitled 'Portrait Gallery of Eminent Living Men. Lord Palmerston, MP'.

113   [Anon], *Palmerston for Premier! The claims of Lord Palmerston to fill the post of Prime Minister of England considered* (London, 1854), p. 42. For details of the charges made against Palmerston indicated, see esp. pp. 6–37.

114   Washington Wilks, *Palmerston in Three Epochs: a comparison of facts with opinions* (London, 1854), pp. 62–3.

115   Broadlands Papers, GC/HU/53, J. W. Hudson to Palmerston, 23 Dec. 1854.

116   Taylor, 'Modes of Political Expression and Working Class Radicalism', pp. 267–70.

117   Henderson, *Crimean War Diplomacy*, p. 81, memorandum by the Queen, 1 Feb. 1855.

118   *LQV*, III, p. 128, Queen to the King of the Belgians, 6 Feb. 1855.

119   Eyck, *Prince Consort*, p. 235.

120   *Morning Post*, 30 Jan. 1855.

121   *Globe*, 5 Feb. 1855.

122   *Morning Chronicle*, 7 Feb. 1855.

9

Conclusion

'He [Palmerston] a little degraded us by preaching a doctrine just below our own standard – a doctrine not enough below us to repel us much, but yet enough below us to harm us by augmenting a worldliness which needed no addition and by diminishing a love of principle and philosophy which did not want deduction'.[1]

The basis of Palmerston's political potency and ultimately of his accession to the highest office of state rested on more than his ability to play forces off against each other at Westminster. Throughout the life of the Russell Government he had set the Court against the Cabinet over his policy, with some degree of success until the end of 1851, and during Aberdeen's ministry, from his position at the Home Office, he offered a compelling alternative foreign policy to that of Aberdeen and simultaneously used this as a means of overcoming Russell in the campaign to claim the leadership of the Whigs and Liberals. His base of support and his political standing, widely acknowledged as 'popular', were taken as tacit justifications for his manoeuvrings at the political centre. Thus Gladstone observed in 1856 that while Palmerston's foreign policy since 1834 had 'scarcely had the approbation of a single British statesman', nonetheless, 'whether from its manliness or from the sound and affectation of it, it has beyond all doubt been eminently agreeable to those who form the masses of the ten-pound constituency, and to those who reflect that constituency in the press'.[2]

The importance of 'popular support' and indeed the strength conferred by the approbation of 'public opinion' was commonly acknowledged throughout the political world. Prince Albert, indeed, maintained that the people 'will, even if they in the beginning lend their hands willingly, deny their hearts and in the course of the struggle they will obey the great moral law which governs this earth more than their governments',[3] yet he also later suggested that it was perhaps possible for a minister still to guide the feeling of these peoples. 'Lord Palmerston', he wrote in 1852 in a survey of Palmerston's foreign policy, 'could bring no counter poise except that which he always declares to be stronger than any material force, *"the public opinion of England"'*. Significantly, Albert argued that Palmerston 'had to create this opinion, however'.[4]

It may have been that there were many people with an interest in foreign policy but little time in which to study it, and that this 'large class of persons take for granted any specious statement connected with a subject they do not understand, and are ready to re-echo every popular cry that is raised in connection with it',[5] but Palmerston had still been able to exploit this disposition to express opinions (however much they were simply uncritical echoes of vociferous interests) to his own ends. In the face of Whig disorganisation, indeed what Angus Hawkins has called 'the bankruptcy of Whig doctrine' as uniformity of purpose gave way to 'a series of shifts and compromises',[6] Palmerston was able to supply leadership which ultimately placed him at the very heart of government. The Times had complained in October 1846 that Peel had failed to supply clear leadership and purpose and that there remained an absence of a great man now to lead the country.[7] As Lord John Russell also failed to provide the required leadership, Palmerston sought to impress direction on the Government in his stead.

Palmerston's manoeuvring at Westminster can be studied and indeed to a certain extent explained by an examination of the course of high politics, but only when underpinned by an appreciation of Palmerston's highly effective invocation of a wide and very general popular support – to forge the reputation of the national minister – do his political career and the nature of mid-century politics acquire a convincing gloss. While not dissenting, therefore, from Hawkins' broader argument that both 'the distinction and relation between Palmerstonian language and parliamentary circumstance are crucial to an understanding of the true nature of Palmerston's pre-eminence during 1855 and 1856',[8] this book urges an important qualification of that view. It was during the period 1846–55 that Palmerstonism was really established and building upon the legacy of George Canning it infused political life with a greater appreciation of the role and importance of public opinion and a more responsible attitude to a system of virtual representation. Palmerston, however, did not regard himself as the servant of public opinion: Palmerstonism required a mastery over that opinion in order to channel it towards Palmerston's own ends. To a large extent, arguably, he succeeded in demonstrating such mastery, although this may have been as much the result of the inability of his rivals to articulate the view of a contrary public opinion. Thus, whereas after 1855 Palmerston's rhetoric might fail adequately to elucidate the nature of Palmerston's parliamentary position, before he became Prime Minister it was precisely this rhetoric and, more widely, Palmerston's invocation of extra-parliamentary pillars of support, that gave his parliamentary position much of the strength that it had.

Palmerston in 1846 was already sixty-two years old and by the time he became Prime Minister he was seventy. No one at the time really expected him to achieve very much politically and indeed, as *The Times* observed on the occasion of his death in 1865: 'Had he died at seventy he would have left a second class reputation. It was his great and peculiar fortune to live to right himself'.[9] In the sense that a retrospective review of his career in 1855 would have revealed a curmudgeonly Cabinet colleague who served in the important offices of Foreign Secretary and Home Secretary, his career would have appeared solid, respectable, occasionally noteworthy and inflammatory, but perhaps not unduly remarkable. However, it would be wrong to judge Palmerston's career in the fashion of *The Times*. By 1855 Palmerston's place in political life (and history) was already more than second class and indeed his career, especially his association with foreign affairs before 1855 has attracted considerably more historical interest than his career after that date. He had not only secured for himself a prominent role in Westminster politics but had done much to place foreign affairs at the centre of political debate and had used this not only to advance his own position but to help change the face of parliamentary and extra-parliamentary politics in the mid-nineteenth century.

Traditionally foreign policy has been discussed in terms of an abstract concern of the political elite. Diplomatic history as a discipline focused on the discourse between governments and diplomats and while this resulted in many important studies, the historiographical trend in the later twentieth century has been to seek to place foreign policy in a much broader context; to regard it as illuminating domestic political situations as much (if not more than) external ones.[10] Diplomatic business – dry, intricate and frequently legalistic – was the preserve of an educated clique, capable not only of understanding the issues but of discussing them in a foreign language. There is something to be said for this view – perhaps more than any other area of public life, foreign policy demanded a specialist interest – and Palmerston believed, when he returned to the Foreign Office in 1846 that his expertise should be relied upon in the conduct of that business. However, the Crown and the Cabinet both laid claims to a role in foreign policy as well. In an age of constitutional ambiguity, Palmerston had to defend himself against these interventions, if he was to preserve for himself the independence he sought, through a series of bluffs and threats. In terms of foreign affairs, this made British policy frequently vague and ambiguous; for Palmerston himself it was the means by which he could use a particular area of political business to carve out a pre-eminent position for himself.

As this book has argued, Palmerston used his 'expertise' to confound the Court and the Cabinet, and his conduct, especially during the fragile administration of Russell, was tolerated largely because he was perceived to be 'popular' with the country. There was little contemporary examination of the nature and dynamics of this popularity, however, and Palmerston was able, until the Government ceased to regard tolerance of him as a necessary price to pay for office, to use this popularity to make himself politically indispensable, or at least central to politics, by the early 1850s. As Greville observed of Palmerston in 1851, 'He thinks to make himself too formidable, by having the masses at his back, for his colleagues to dare to quarrel with him, and by this audacious defiance of them he intends to make himself once for all master of the situation'.[11]

After he had accepted the Home Office under Lord Aberdeen, it was not long before Palmerston made explicit his continuing pre-occupation with foreign affairs. Neither did his colleagues in this Government pretend that Palmerston was really retired from foreign policy debates and if he was kept in largely because he was too dangerous to be left outside, this reflected again Palmerston's perceived strengths in the field of foreign policy. It is significant that from the Home Office, Palmerston was able to engineer his accession to the premiership, or at least lay the foundations for such an appointment, on the grounds that he was the one best qualified to take charge of a question of foreign policy.

If it is true that Palmerston believed in December 1852 that his obligations were to 'the great Liberal party', not in Parliament, but, essentially, in the country at large, pre-figuring, perhaps, the more familiar association of an appeal to provincial liberalism with Gladstone, then it needs also to be considered how far this points to the importance of 'the country' in the selection of ministers. Certainly, conventional Whig and Bagehotian models of parliamentary government failed to account for such an influence for extra-parliamentary forces. Palmerston's use of popular support aimed at more than establishing an ascendancy for his views of foreign policy. He cultivated an extra-parliamentary constituency of support which extended beyond the traditional political nation in order to underwrite his own political position and through which he could steal a march on rivals within the party. Through the newspapers and periodicals Palmerston could appeal (primarily) to the middle classes and lay the Palmerstonian view before them. Such publicity was important but in this, while he was arguably one of the period's most skilful manipulators of the press, he was not unique. Other politicians could similarly speak through the press to the burgeoning middle classes and campaign for their approbation. Palmerston needed to establish a rapport with a community possessing political weight but over which he could exercise a more individual mastery. Enjoying little real dominance or control of a political party and being the object of antagonism for the Crown and the Cabinet, Palmerston looked to a more broadly defined political nation for support.

Here his association with foreign policy was significant. Uniquely this could be presented as an area of business of pre-eminently national significance in which even the most oppressed inhabitants of a London slum could share in the reflected 'glory' of the *pax Britannica*. Indeed, Palmerstonian foreign policy can be seen, to a degree, to have exploited a sense of Protestant, and liberal, providentialism. Palmerston frequently played upon notions of Britain as a model of constitutional freedom and commercial prosperity able, and in certain cases perhaps obliged, to elevate the condition of less favoured parts of the world. Thus Palmerston's foreign policy could appeal to a sense of a higher purpose, transcending domestic difficulties and offering a rallying point for national cohesion. However superficial it might have been, Palmerstonian foreign policy and Palmerston's conduct, especially, in 1854, for example, suggested he was the figure best able to articulate and guide this national mission. Whatever the paradoxes of Palmerston's foreign policy and the inconsistencies of his attempts to present that policy as directed in the interests of liberalism all over the world, these flaws were not always apparent to a population easily swayed by an emotive Palmerstonian rhetoric. The force of Palmerston's popular support was felt throughout the high political world. Not that Palmerston was universally applauded, but in the absence of a more effective interpreter of popular feeling, he was able to present (and substantiate) the image of himself that he wanted to. Here arguably was his greatest contribution to the evolution of a new political style, something recognised after his death by both Disraeli and Gladstone. Disraeli quickly sought to appropriate the Palmerstonian mantle after 1865 and even Gladstone, however much the words must have stuck in his throat, appreciated in 1879 the necessity of identifying himself with Palmerston, whose name, he declared at the end of his third Midlothian speech 'will ever be honoured by those who recollect the erection of the kingdom of Belgium, and the union of the disjointed provinces of Italy'.[12]

Sympathy for Palmerston had been, after all, one of the causes of weakness in the opposition to Palmerston between 1846 and 1855, at least in the case of Disraeli: the success and value of Palmerston's popularising foreign policy, Disraeli realised, could not justifiably be criticised. As Robert Blake has suggested, after the death of Palmerston ('whose patriotism in foreign policy could hardly be challenged'), Disraeli was finally able to acquire the 'national' colours for his own party in foreign as well as domestic affairs.[13] More than this, indeed, throughout the 1870s, according to John Vincent, Palmerston more than any other figure, including Derby, was Disraeli's role model.[14] During the 1840s and 1850s, then, Disraeli had been struggling in the face of Palmerston's pre-eminence to reconcile the conflict between his supposed party-political obligations and his personal faith in Palmerston, or at least Palmerstonism. Palmerstonism had not achieved its final victory over the minds of all politicians (witness for example the opposition led by Urquhart and Cobden), but the inability of parliamentary opponents to make a telling strike against Palmerston (due to their own shortcomings as much as to Palmerston's strengths) strengthened, or at least, did not weaken, Palmerston's hand.

John Vincent argues that in 1857 'the old school in the Cabinet', including Palmerston, came 'to regard the public as a millstone', and that 'the participation of the public in the making of foreign policy, or even their support, was hardly canvassed because they were presumed to be hostile, wrong, or ignorant'.[15] Palmerston had never looked to the public for guidance in the making of policy, only for its approval in the execution, but even if Vincent's argument holds true for the specific instance he is concerned with in 1857 (the Persian war), it is hollow when reflected back to the period prior to Palmerston's becoming Prime Minister.

Palmerston established foreign policy as central to popular politics and he put himself forward as one of its key exponents. He brought the role of public opinion into sharper focus and illustrated the political capital to be made from efficient representation of popular interests (significantly he remained throughout an opponent of more direct representative government). Political success in the mid-nineteenth century was determined now not solely in terms of tenure of office and the confidence of the high political elite but in the support more widely of the country. The Peelite *Morning Chronicle* declared in February 1855 that if Palmerston had been unable to form a government, 'his failure would have been a national misfortune'; the *Globe* attributed his success in large part to the force of opinion 'out of doors'.[16] Palmerston's particular achievement in the mid-nineteenth century was to court popular interest in politics, and, particularly, foreign affairs. *The Times* was not far wide of the mark in its obituary of Palmerston in October 1865 writing that he 'was a patriot in this sense: that he had the art to find out what the country wished to do, and the will to assist it ... He saw in Public Opinion a force and a meaning which no statesman before him had realized ... all through his political life Lord Palmerston bowed to this deity, recognized its power, and used it as he could'.[17]

Notes

1 Bagehot, *English Constitution*, p. 118.
2 W. E. Gladstone, 'The Declining Efficiency of Parliament', *Quarterly Review*, 99 (1856), 557.
3 Eyck, *Prince Consort*, p. 47, Albert to King of Prussia, 21 Dec. 1846.
4 *Ibid.*, p. 53, Albert's memorandum on Palmerston's foreign policy, 14 July 1852.
5 [Anon], *Palmerston for Premier! The claims of Lord Palmerston to fill the post of Prime Minister of England considered* (London, 1854), p. 5.
6 Hawkins, *Parliament, Party and the Art of Politics*, p. 6.
7 Read, *Peel and the Victorians*, p. 20.
8 Hawkins, *Parliament, Party and the Art of Politics*, p. 23.
9 *The Times*, 21 Oct. 1865.
10 For example, P. Kennedy, *The Realities Behind Diplomacy: Background Influences on British External Policy, 1865–1980* (London, 1981); M. Swartz, *The Politics of British Foreign Policy in the Era of Disraeli and Gladstone* (London, 1985); Chamberlain, *'Pax Britannica'?*.
11 Greville, *Greville Memoirs (second part)*, III, p. 416 (22 Nov. 1851).
12 Bourne, *The Foreign Policy of Victorian England*, p. 422, Gladstone's third Midlothian speech, 27 Nov. 1879.
13 Blake, *Disraeli*, p. 283.
14 Vincent, *Disraeli*, p. 12.
15 Vincent, *The Formation of the British Liberal Party*, pp. 248–9.
16 *Morning Chronicle*, 7 Feb. 1855; *Globe*, 5 Feb. 1855.
17 *The Times*, 19, 21 Oct. 1865.

Bibliography

Primary sources

MANUSCRIPTS

Balliol College Library, Oxford
David Urquhart Papers

Bodleian Library, Oxford
Clarendon Deposit
English Manuscripts (MSS.Eng.c.2085: correspondence of Lady Clarendon)
Firth Collection
Sir James Graham Papers (microfilm)
Harding Collection
Hughenden Deposit
John Johnson Collection

British Library
Aberdeen Papers
Broughton Diaries
Lansdowne Papers
Palmerston Letter Books

Brotherton Library, Leeds University
Glenesk-Bathurst Papers (Peter and Algernon Borthwick)
Hickleton Papers (Sir Charles Wood) (microfilm)

Duke University Special Collections Library, North Carolina, USA
Sir John Easthope Papers
Westmoreland Papers (11th Earl)

Durham University Library
Grey Papers (3rd Earl)

Hatfield House, Hertfordshire
Lady Palmerston Papers

National Library of Scotland
Minto Papers

Nottingham University Library
Newcastle Papers

Public Record Office, Kew
Russell Papers

Southampton University Library
Broadlands Papers (Palmerston and Shaftesbury)

Times Newspapers Ltd Archive, News International Record Office, London
Delane Papers

OFFICIAL PUBLICATIONS
Hansard's Parliamentary Debates, second series
Hansard's Parliamentary Debates, third series

NEWSPAPERS AND PERIODICALS
Daily News
The Economist
English Republic
Globe
Illustrated London News
Manchester Guardian
Morning Chronicle
Morning Post
Press
Quarterly Review
Standard
The Times

PAMPHLETS (IN ORDER OF PUBLICATION)
*Lord Grey and Lord Palmerston. A letter addressed to the Right Honourable T. B.
    Macaulay, M.P. on the occasion of his letter to Mr M'Farlane, from a Free Trader*
    (London, 1846)
De la Pryme, C., *The Roman Embassy. A Letter to Viscount Palmerston, M.P.*, 2nd
    edn (London, corrected, 1847)
*Speech of Lord Viscount Palmerston, Secretary of State for Foreign Affairs, to the Electors
    of Tiverton, on the 31st July 1847*, 2nd edn (London, 1847)
*The Trial and Condemnation of Lord Viscount Palmerston, at Tiverton, July 30, 1847,
    containing a verbatim report of the speech of G. Julian Harney, the People's Member
    for Tiverton* (London, 1847)
Snooks (pseud.), *A letter to Lord Palmerston, on the 'Condition of England Question,'
    elicited by his speech to the electors of Tiverton* (London, 1847)
Granville, A. B., *On the Formation and Constitution of a Kingdom of Upper Italy. In
    a letter to the Right Hon. Viscount Palmerston.* (London, 1848)

Granville, A. B., *The Italian Question. A second letter to Lord Palmerston, G.C.B, M.P.,* *etc. etc; with a refutation of certain misrepresentations by Lord Brougham, Mr D'Israeli,* *and the Quarterly Review, respecting the rights of Austria and the Lombardo Venetians* (London, 1848)

MacFarlane, C., *Sicily; her constitutions, and Viscount Palmerston's Sicilian Blue-Book.* *Being an appendix to 'A Glance at Revolutionized Italy'* (London, 1849)

Verney, H., *Some Observations on the affairs of Germany, in a letter addressed to the* *Right Hon. Viscount Palmerston* (London, 1849)

Lloyd, T., *A letter to Lord Viscount Palmerston. Containing a refutation of Mr Turnbull's* *statements that the British merchants are implicated in the slave-trade* (Printed for private circulation, [1850])

On the Speech of Her Majesty's Foreign Secretary, delivered in the House of Commons *June 25, 1850. A letter to the Right Hon. Viscount Palmerston, in reference to the* *Greek Question, exclusive of His Lordship's general foreign policy. By a Greek Gentle-*man (London, 1850)

Germanicus Vindex, *A Letter to Viscount Palmerston concerning the question of Schles-*swig-Holstein (London, 1850)

Aiton, J., *Letter to the Right Honourable Lord Palmerston. Principal Secretary of State* *for Foreign Affairs, on the Political Imprisonments and Present Condition of Naples* (Edinburgh, 1851)

Thomson, J., *British Religious Liberty Abroad, and General Religious Liberty in all* *Nations: in a letter to the Right Honourable Viscount Palmerston* (London, 1851)

Davidson, J., *The Fall of the Pope, and the Fate of the French President* (London and Aberdeen, 1852)

Opinions and Policy of the Right Honourable Viscount Palmerston, G.C.B., M.P., &c., *as Minister, Diplomatist, and Statesman, during more than Forty Years of Public* *Life. With a memoir by George Henry Francis, Esq.* (London, 1852)

Wilson, T., *England's Foreign Policy, or, Grey-Whigs and Cotton-Whigs, with Lord* *Palmerston's Pet Belgian Constitution of Catholics and Liberals* (London, [1852])

Blackwell, J. K., *Explosions in Coal Mines, their causes, and the means available for* *their prevention or control; containing a review of the report of the committee of 1852* *on this subject; A letter addressed to Lord Palmerston on the late explosions and on* *mining inspection; and notes on various forms of the Davy Lamp and their relative* *value* (London, 1853)

The Flag List and its Prospects. A letter to the Right Hon. Lord Palmerston, Secretary *for Home Affairs, by An Enquirer* (Edinburgh, 1853)

Vaughan, C. J., *A Letter to the Viscount Palmerston, M.P. on the Monitorial System of* *Harrow School* (Privately printed, not published, 1853)

Eardley-Wilmot, A. P., *A Letter to the Right Honourable Viscount Palmerston, M.P.,* *one of Her Majesty's Secretaries of State, &C, on the present state of the African Slave* *Trade and on the necessity of increasing the African Squadron* (London, 1853)

Bailey, T., *Village Reform: The Great Social Necessity of Britain. A letter to Viscount* *Palmerston, M.P., Her Majesty's Principal Secretary of State for the Home Department* (London and Nottingham, 1854)

Broun, R., *Metropolitan Extramural Sepulture. London Necropolis & National Mau-*soleum Company. Letter to the Right Hon. Lord Palmerston, M.P., Secretary of State *for the Home Department; with a copy of a letter to Messrs Rotheray, Dakin, Chatterton, Hinds, Croll, Wilkinson, and others, advertising themselves as Directors of the above named Company; reviewing the* PROSPECTUS *recently issued by them to the Public, and exposing its numerous Misrepresentations* (London, 1854)

Burnell, G. R., *Letter to the Right Honourable Viscount Palmerston, G.C.B., M.P., &c, Her Most Gracious Majesty's Secretary of State for the Home Department, in reply to the Report of the General Board of Health, on the Administration of the Public Health Act, and the Nuisances Removal and Diseases Prevention Act, from 1848 to 1854* (London, 1854)

Coningham, W., *Lord Palmerston and Prince Albert* (London, 1854)

[Fortesque, H.], *Representative Self-Government for the Metropolis. A letter to Viscount Palmerston, from Viscount Ebrington* (London, 1854)

Oakley, F., *The Religious Disabilities of our Catholic Prisoners Considered, with a view to their removal, in a letter to the Viscount Palmerston, M.P., &c, &c, &c* (London, 1854)

Kingsmill, J., *Roman Catholic Chaplains to Gaols. A letter to the Rt. Hon. Viscount Palmerston, M.P., Secretary of State for the Home Department, on this Subject; occasioned by a letter of the Rev. Frederick Oakley, M.A., entitled, 'The Religious Disabilities of our Catholic Prisoners considered, with a view to their removal'* (London, 1854)

Stephen, G., *Magisterial Reform suggested in a letter to Viscount Palmerston, &c, &c* (London, 1854)

[Anon], *Palmerston for Premier! The claims of Lord Palmerston to fill the post of Prime Minister of England considered* (London, 1854)

Wilks, W., *Palmerston in Three Epochs: a comparison of facts with opinions* (London, 1854)

Authentic Report of Kossuth's Speeches on the War in the East and the Alliance with Austria, at Sheffield, June 5, and at Nottingham, June 12, 1854. Published by Himself (London, 1854)

Urquhart, D., *The War of Ignorance: A Prognostication* (London, 1854)

Urquhart, D., *'Limitation of the Supply of Grain by the Past Action of British Diplomacy'. Report of the Sub-Committee of the Newcastle-on-Tyne Association for Watching the War* (Newcastle, 1855)

Urquhart, D., *The Home Face of the 'Four Points* (London, 1855)

PUBLISHED JOURNALS, LETTERS, SPEECHES AND WORKS

Bagehot, W., *The English Constitution* [1867], ed. P. Smith (Cambridge, 2001)

Benson, A. C. and Esher, Viscount (eds), *The Letters of Queen Victoria: A selection from Her Majesty's Correspondence Between the Years 1837 and 1861*, 3 vols (London, 1907)

Bolitho, H. (ed.), *The Prince Consort to his Brother: Two Hundred New Letters* (London, 1933)

Bourne, K. (ed.), *The Letters of the Third Viscount Palmerston to Laurence and Elizabeth Sulivan, 1804–1863* (Camden 4th ser., vol. 23, 1979)

Bright, J. and Thorold Rogers, J. E. (eds), *Speeches on Questions of Public Policy by Richard Cobden, M.P.* (London, 1880)

Cabinet Reports by Prime Ministers to the Crown: A reproduction of the series of manuscript letters preserved at Windsor Castle (Hassocks, 1978, microfilm)

Campbell, George Douglas, Eighth Duke of Argyll, *Autobiography and Memoirs* ed. Dowager Duchess of Argyll, 2 vols (London, 1906)

Carlyle, T., *On Heroes, Hero-Worship, and the Heroic in History* (1841; Oxford, 1935 edn)

Cobden, R., *Reminiscences of Richard Cobden* (compiled by Mrs Salis Schwabe) (London, 1895)

Cobden, R., *The Political Writings of Richard Cobden*, 2 vols, 4th edn (London, 1903)

Connell, B. (ed.), *Regina v. Palmerston: The Correspondence between Queen Victoria and Her Foreign and Prime Minister, 1837–1865* (London, 1962)

Dickens, C., *Little Dorrit* (1857; Oxford, 1982 edn)

Benjamin Disraeli Letters, vols III–V (1838–41; 1842–47; 1848–51), M. G. Wiebe, J. B. Conacher, J. Matthews and M. S. Millar (eds) (Toronto, 1987; 1989; 1993); vol. VI (1852–56), M. G. Wiebe, M. S. Millar and A. P. Robson (eds) (Toronto, 1997)

Disraeli, B., *Lord George Bentinck: A Political Biography* (London, 1905 edn)

Gladstone, W. E., 'The Declining Efficiency of Parliament', *Quarterly Review*, 99 (1856), 521–70

Gooch, G. P. (ed.), *The Later Correspondence of Lord John Russell, 1840–1878*, 2 vols (London, 1925)

Greg, W. R., 'The Expected Reform Bill', *Edinburgh Review* (Jan. 1852), 213–80

Greville, C. C. F., *The Greville Memoirs (second part): A Journal of the Reign of Queen Victoria, from 1837 to 1852*, ed. H. Reeve, 3 vols (London, 1885)

Greville, C. C. F., *The Greville Memoirs (third part): A Journal of the Reign of Queen Victoria, from 1852 to 1860*, ed. H. Reeve, 2 vols (London, 1887)

Guedalla, P. (ed.), *Gladstone and Palmerston: Being the Correspondence of Lord Palmerston with Mr. Gladstone, 1851–1865* (London, 1928)

Hobhouse, J. C. (Lord Broughton), *Recollections of a Long Life*, ed. Lady Dorchester, 6 vols (London, 1910–11)

Jennings, L. J. (ed.), *The Correspondence and Diaries of the Late Right Honourable John Wilson Croker*, 3 vols (London, 1884)

Leader, R. E. (ed.), *Life and Letters of John Arthur Roebuck* (London, 1897)

Lewis, G. F. (ed.), *The Letters of the Right Hon. Sir George Cornewall Lewis, Bart.* (London, 1870)

Malmesbury, Lord, *Memoirs of an Ex-Minister, An Autobiography*, 2 vols (London, 1884)

Maxwell, H., *The Life and Letters of George William Frederick Fourth Earl of Clarendon*, 2 vols (London, 1913)

Parker, C. S., *Life and Letters of Sir James Graham, Second Baronet of Netherby, 1792–1861*, 2 vols (London, 1907)

Russell, Earl, *Recollections and Suggestions, 1813–1873* (London, 1875)

Snell, F. J., *Palmerston's Borough: A Budget of Electioneering Anecdotes, Squibs and Speeches* (Tiverton, 1894)

Stewart, D., *Lectures on Political Economy*, ed. Sir William Hamilton, 2 vols (Edinburgh, 1855)

Sudley, Lord (ed.), *The Lieven-Palmerston Correspondence, 1828–1856* (London, 1943)

Taylor, M. (ed.), *The European Diaries of Richard Cobden, 1846–1849* (Aldershot, 1994)

Vincent, J. R. (ed.), *Disraeli, Derby and the Conservative Party: Journals and Memoirs of Edward Henry, Lord Stanley, 1849–1869* (Hassocks, 1978)

Secondary sources

BOOKS AND ARTICLES

Airlie, Countess of, *Lady Palmerston and her Times*, 2 vols (London, 1922)

Anderson, M. S., *The Eastern Question, 1774–1923* (London, 1966)

Anderson, M. S., *The Ascendancy of Europe, 1815–1914*, 2nd edn (Harlow, 1985)

Anderson, O., *A Liberal State at War: English Politics and Economics during the Crimean War* (London, 1967)

Ashley, E., *The Life and Correspondence of Henry John Temple, Viscount Palmerston*, 2 vols (London, 1879)

Aspinall, A., *Politics and the Press, c. 1780–1850* (London, 1949)

Aydelotte, W. O., 'Constituency Influence on the British House of Commons, 1841–1847', in Aydelotte, W. O., *The History of Parliamentary Behaviour* (Princeton, NJ, 1977), pp. 225–46

Bartlett, C. J., *Defence and Diplomacy: Britain and the Great Powers, 1815–1914* (Manchester, 1993)

Battiscombe, G., *Shaftesbury: A Biography of the Seventh Earl, 1801–1885* (London, 1974)

Beales, D. E. D., *England and Italy, 1859–60* (London, 1961)

Beales, D. E. D., 'Parliamentary Parties and the "Independent" Member, 1810–1860', in R. Robson (ed.), *Ideas and Institutions of Victorian Britain* (London, 1967), pp. 1–19

Bell, H. C. F., *Lord Palmerston*, 2 vols (London, 1936)

Bell, H. C. F., 'Palmerston and Parliamentary Representation', *Journal of Modern History*, IV (1932), 186–213

Bentley, M., 'Party, Doctrine and Thought', in M. Bentley and J. Stevenson (eds), *High and Low Politics in Modern Britain* (Oxford, 1983), pp. 123–53

Bentley, M., *Politics Without Democracy, 1815–1914* (London, 1984)

Best, G. F. A., 'Popular Protestantism in Victorian Britain', in R. Robson (ed.), *Ideas and Institutions of Victorian Britain* (London, 1967), pp. 115–42

Billy, G. J., *Palmerston's Foreign Policy: 1848* (New York, 1993)

Bindoff, S. T., 'The Unreformed Diplomatic Service, 1812–1860', *Transactions of the Royal Historical Society*, 4th ser., 18 (1935), 143–72

Blake, R., *Disraeli* (New York, 1987 edn)

Blake, R., *The Conservative Party from Peel to Thatcher* (London, 1985)

Boot, H. M., *The Commercial Crisis of 1847* (University of Hull Occasional Papers in Economic and Social History, no. 11, Hull, 1984)

Bourne, K., 'Lord Palmerston's "Ginger Beer" Triumph, 1 July 1856', in K. Bourne and D. C. Watt (eds), *Studies in International History* (London, 1967), pp. 145–71

Bourne, K., *The Foreign Policy of Victorian England, 1830–1902* (Oxford, 1970)

Bourne, K., *Palmerston: The Early Years, 1784–1841* (London, 1982)

Bourne, K., 'The Foreign Office under Palmerston', in R. Bullen (ed.), *The Foreign Office, 1782–1982* (Frederick, Maryland, 1984), pp. 18–45

Boyce, D. G., 'Public Opinion and the Historians', *History*, 63 (1978), 214–28

Braithwaite, R., *Palmerston and Africa. The Rio Nunez Affair: Competition, Diplomacy and Justice* (London, 1996)

Bridge, F. R. and Bullen, R., *The Great Powers and the European States System, 1815–1914* (London, 1980)

Briggs, A., 'David Urquhart and the West Riding Foreign Affairs Committees', *Bradford Antiquary*, 39 (1958), 197–207

Briggs, A., *Victorian People* (Harmondsworth, 1965 edn)

Briggs, A., *The Age of Improvement, 1783–1867* (Harlow, 1979)

Brockliss, L. and Eastwood, D. (eds), *A Union of Multiple Identities: The British Isles, c. 1750–1850* (Manchester, 1997)

Brown, D., 'Compelling but not Controlling?: Palmerston and the Press, 1846–1855', *History*, 86 (2001), 41–61

Brown, D., 'The Power of Public Opinion: Palmerston and the Crisis of December 1851', *Parliamentary History*, 20: 3 (2001), 333–58

Brown, L., 'The Treatment of the News in Mid-Victorian Newspapers', *Transactions of the Royal Historical Society*, 5th ser., 27 (1977), 23–39

Brown, L., *Victorian News and Newspapers* (Oxford, 1985)

Bullen, R., *Palmerston, Guizot and the Collapse of the Entente Cordiale* (London, 1974)

Bullen, R. (ed.), *The Foreign Office, 1782–1982* (Frederick, Maryland, 1984)

Bulwer, H. L., *The Life of Henry John Temple, Viscount Palmerston*, 3 vols (London, 1870–74)

Burrow, J., 'Sense and Circumstances: Bagehot and the Nature of Political Understanding', in S. Collini, D. Winch and J. Burrow, *That Noble Science of Politics: A Study in Nineteenth-Century Intellectual History* (Cambridge, 1983), pp. 161–81

Cannadine, D., 'The Context, Performance and Meaning of Ritual: The British Monarchy and the "Invention of Tradition", c. 1820–1977', in E. Hobsbawm and T. Ranger (eds), The Invention of Tradition (Cambridge, 1992 edn), pp. 106–64

Carr, R., *Spain, 1808–1975* (Oxford, 1982)

Carr, W., *A History of Germany, 1815–1985*, 3rd edn (London, 1987)

Chamberlain, M. E., *Lord Aberdeen* (Harlow, 1983)

Chamberlain, M. E., *Lord Palmerston* (Cardiff, 1987)

Chamberlain, M. E., *'Pax Britannica'?: British Foreign Policy 1789–1914* (Harlow, 1988)

Chamberlain, M. E., 'Who founded the Liberal Party?', *Inaugural lecture delivered at the University College of Swansea, 26 November 1990* (Swansea, 1991)

Charlot, M., *Victoria: The Young Queen* (Oxford, 1991)

Colley, L., 'Britishness and Otherness: An Argument', *Journal of British Studies*, 31: 4 (1992), 309–29

Colley, L., *Britons: Forging the Nation, 1707–1837* (New Haven and London, 1996 edn)

Collini, S., 'The Idea of "Character" in Victorian Political Thought', *Transactions of the Royal Historical Society*, 5th ser., 35 (1985), 29–50

Colls, R., and Dodd, P. (eds), *Englishness: Politics and Culture, 1880–1920* (London, 1986)

Conacher, J. B., 'Peel and the Peelites, 1846–1850', *English Historical Review*, 78 (1958), 431–52

Conacher, J. B., *The Aberdeen Coalition, 1852–1855* (Cambridge, 1968)

Cook, E., *Delane of the Times* (London, 1915)

Cox, G. W., *The Efficient Secret. The Cabinet and the Development of Political Parties in Victorian England* (Cambridge, 1987)

Cunningham, H., 'The Language of Patriotism, 1750–1914', *History Workshop Journal*, 12 (1981), 8–33

Dasent, A. I., *John Delane, 1817–1879*, 2 vols (London, 1908)

Dreyer, F. A., 'The Whigs and the Political Crisis of 1845', *English Historical Review*, 80 (1965), 514–37

Droz, J., *Europe Between Revolutions, 1815–1848* (London, 1985 edn)

Eastwood, D., 'The State we were in. Parliament, Centralization and English State Formation', in R. English and C. Townshend (eds), *The State. Historical and Political Dimensions* (London, 1999), pp. 18–43

Edwards, R. D., *The Pursuit of Reason: The Economist, 1843–1993* (London, 1993)

Eyck, F., *The Prince Consort: A Political Biography of Prince Albert* (Boston, USA, and Cambridge, 1959)

Feuchtwanger, E. J., *Gladstone*, 2nd edn (London, 1989)

Finn, M. C., *After Chartism: Class and Nation in English Radical Politics, 1848–1874* (Cambridge, 1993)

Fitzmaurice, Lord Edmond, *The Life of Granville George Leveson Gower, Second Earl Granville K.G., 1815–1891*, 2 vols (London, 1905)

Fulford, R., *The Prince Consort* (London, 1966)

Gash, N., 'Peel and the Party System, 1830–50', *Transactions of the Royal Historical Society*, 5th ser., 1 (1951), 47–69

Gash, N., *Sir Robert Peel: The Life of Sir Robert Peel after 1830* (Harlow, 1985 edn)

Gash, N., *Reaction and Reconstruction in English Politics, 1832–1852* (Oxford, 1965)

Goldfrank, D. M., *The Origins of the Crimean War* (Harlow, 1994)

Gooch, B. D., 'A Century of Historiography on the Origins of the Crimean War', *American Historical Review* (October 1956), 33–58

Grant, J., *The Newspaper Press – its origins – progress – & present position*, 3 vols (London, 1871–72)

Grenville, J. A. S., *Europe Reshaped, 1848–1878* (London, 1976)

Guedalla, P., *Palmerston* (London, 1937 edn)

Hanham, H. J. (ed.), *The Nineteenth Century Constitution* (Cambridge, 1969)

Hardie, F., *The Political Influence of Queen Victoria, 1861–1901*, 2nd edn (Oxford, 1938)

Hawkins, A., *Parliament, Party and the Art of Politics in Britain, 1855–59* (Basingstoke, 1987)

Hawkins, A., 'Lord Derby and Victorian Conservatism: A Reappraisal', *Parliamentary History*, 6 (1987), 280–301

Hawkins, A., '"Parliamentary Government" and Victorian Political Parties, *c.* 1830-*c.* 1880', English Historical Review, 104 (July 1989), 638–69

Hawkins, A., *British Party Politics, 1852–1886* (Basingstoke, 1998)

Hearder, H., 'Queen Victoria and Foreign Policy. Royal Intervention in the Italian Question, 1859–60', in K. Bourne and D. C. Watt (eds), *Studies in International History* (London, 1967), pp. 172–88

Hearder, H., 'Clarendon, Cavour, and the Intervention of Sardinia in the Crimean War, 1853–1855', *The International History Review*, 18: 4, Nov. 1996, 819–36

Henderson, G. B., *Crimean War Diplomacy and Other Historical Essays* (Glasgow, 1947)

Herkless, J. L., 'Stratford, the Cabinet and the Outbreak of the Crimean War', *Historical Journal*, 18: 3 (1975), 497–523

Hinde, W., *George Canning* (Oxford, 1973)

Hinde, W., *Richard Cobden: A Victorian Outsider* (New Haven and London, 1987)

Hindle, W. H., *The Morning Post, 1772–1939: Portrait of a Newspaper* (London, 1937)

Hogan, J., 'Party Management in the House of Lords, 1846–1865', *Parliamentary History*, 10: 1 (1991), 124–50

Hollis, P., 'Pressure from Without: An Introduction', in P. Hollis (ed.), *Pressure from Without in Early Victorian England* (London, 1974), pp. 1–26

Houghton, W. E., *The Victorian Frame of Mind* (New Haven, 1957)

Howe, A., *The Cotton Masters, 1830–1860* (Oxford, 1984)

Howe, A., *Free Trade and Liberal England, 1846–1946* (Oxford, 1997)

Humpherys, A., 'Popular Narrative and Political Discourse in *Reynold's Weekly Newspaper*', in L. Brake, A. Jones, L. Madden (eds), *Investigating Victorian Journalism* (London, 1990), pp. 33–47

Hyamson, A., 'Don Pacifico', *Transactions of the Jewish Historical Society*, 18 (1958), 1–39

Jenkins, T. A., *The Liberal Ascendancy, 1830–1886* (Basingstoke, 1994)

Jenkins, T. A., *Parliament, Party and Politics in Victorian Britain* (Manchester 1996)

Jones, A., 'Local Journalism in Victorian Political Culture', in L. Brake, A. Jones and L. Madden (eds), *Investigating Victorian Journalism* (London, 1990), pp. 63–70

Jones, A., *Powers of the Press: Newspapers, Power and the Public in Nineteenth-Century England* (Aldershot, 1996)

Jones, R., *The Nineteenth-Century Foreign Office: An Administrative History* (London, 1971)

Jones Parry, E., 'Under-Secretaries of State for Foreign Affairs, 1782–1855', *English Historical Review*, 49 (1934), 308–20

Karsten, P., *Patriot Heroes in England and America. Political Symbolism and Changing Values over Three Centuries* (Madison, Wisconsin, 1978)

Kennedy, P., *The Realities Behind Diplomacy: Background Influences on British External Policy, 1865–1980* (London, 1981)

Kitson Clark, G., 'The Repeal of the Corn Laws and the Politics of the Forties', *Economic History Review*, 2nd ser., 4: 1 (1951), 1–13

Koss, S., *The Rise and Fall of the Political Press in Britain: Vol. I The Nineteenth Century* (London, 1981)

Krein, D. F., 'War and Reform: Russell, Palmerston and the Struggle for Power in the Aberdeen Cabinet, 1853–1854', *The Maryland Historian*, 7: 2, No. 2 (1976), 67–84

Krein, D. F., *The Last Palmerston Government* (Ames, Iowa, 1978)

Le May, G. H. L., *The Victorian Constitution: Conventions, Usages and Contingencies* (London, 1979)

Longford, E., *Victoria, R.I.* (London, 1967 edn)

Lucas, R., *Lord Glenesk and the 'Morning Post'* (London, 1910)

Lyall, A., *The Life of the Marquis of Dufferin and Ava* (London, 1905)

Maccoby, S., *English Radicalism, 1832–1852* (London, 1935)

McCord, N., 'Cobden and Bright in Politics, 1846–1857', in R. Robson (ed.), *Ideas and Institutions of Victorian Britain* (London, 1967), pp. 87–114

Magraw, R., *France 1815–1914: The Bourgeois Century* (London, 1983)

Mandler, P., *Aristocratic Government in the Age of Reform: Whigs and Liberals, 1830–1852* (Oxford, 1990)

Martin, K., *The Triumph of Lord Palmerston: A Study of Public Opinion in England before the Crimean War* (London, 1963 edn)

Matthew, H. C. G., *Gladstone 1809–1874* (Oxford, 1986)

Middleton, C. R., 'The Foundation of the Foreign Office', in R. Bullen (ed.), *The Foreign Office, 1782–1982* (Frederick, Maryland, 1984), pp. 1–17

Mitchell, L., *Holland House* (London, 1980)

Mitchell, L., *Lord Melbourne, 1779–1848* (Oxford, 1997)

Monypenny, W. F. and Buckle, G. E., *The Life of Benjamin Disraeli, Earl of Beaconsfield*, 2 vols (rev. edn, London, 1929)

Moore, D. C., 'Social Structure, Political Structure, and Public Opinion in Mid-Victorian England', in R. Robson (ed.), *Ideas and Institutions of Victorian Britain* (London, 1967), pp. 20–57

Morley, J., *The Life of Richard Cobden* (London, 1903)

Morley, J., *The Life of William Ewart Gladstone*, 2 vols (London, 1908)

Morley, T., '"The Arcana of that Great Machine": Politicians and *The Times* in the Late 1840s', *History*, 73 (1988), 38–54

Munsell, F. D., *The Unfortunate Duke: Henry Pelham, Fifth Duke of Newcastle, 1811–1864* (Columbia, 1985)

Newsome, D., *The Victorian World Picture: Perceptions and Introspections in an Age of Change* (London, 1997)

Nicholls, D., 'The English Middle Class and the Ideological Significance of Radicalism, 1760–1886', *Journal of British Studies*, 24 (1985), 415–33

Parry, J. P., *Democracy and Religion: Gladstone and the Liberal Party, 1867–1875* (Cambridge, 1986)

Parry, J. P., *The Rise and Fall of Liberal Government in Victorian Britain* (New Haven and London, 1993)

Parry, J. P., 'Disraeli and England', *Historical Journal*, 43, 3 (2000), 699–728

Parry, J. P., 'The Impact of Napoleon III on British Politics, 1851–1880', *Transactions of the Royal Historical Society*, 6th ser., 11 (2001), 147–75

Partridge, M. S., 'The Russell Cabinet and National Defence, 1846–1852', *History*, 72 (1987), 231–50

Perkin, H., *The Origins of Modern English Society, 1780–1880* (1969; London, 1985 edn)

Platt, D. C. M., *Finance, Trade and Politics in British Foreign Policy, 1815–1914* (Oxford, 1968)

Prest, J., *Lord John Russell* (London, 1972)

Quinault, R., 'Westminster and the Victorian Constitution', *Transactions of the Royal Historical Society*, 6th ser., 2 (1992), 79–104

Read, D., *Cobden and Bright: A Victorian Political Partnership* (London, 1967)

Read, D., *Peel and the Victorians* (Oxford, 1987)

Ridley, J., *Lord Palmerston* (London, 1970)

Robbins, K., *John Bright* (London, 1979)

Robbins, K., *Nineteenth-Century Britain: Integration and Diversity* (Oxford, 1988)

Robbins, K., *Great Britain: Ideas, Institutions and the Idea of Britishness* (Harlow, 1998)

Roberts, D., 'Lord Palmerston at the Home Office', *The Historian*, 21: 1 (1958), 63–81

Rose, J., 'Workers' Journals', in Vann, J. D. and Van Ardsel, R. T. (eds), *Victorian Periodicals and Victorian Society* (Toronto, 1994), pp. 301–10

Sainty, J. and Cox, G. W., 'The Identification of Government Whips in the House of Commons, 1830–1905', *Parliamentary History*, 16: 3 (1997), 339–58

Salt, J., 'Local Manifestations of the Urquhartite Movement', *International Review of Social History*, 13 (1968), 350–65

Scherer, P., *Lord John Russell: A Biography* (London, 1999)

Schmitt, B. E., 'Diplomatic Preliminaries of the Crimean War', *American Historical Review*, 25: 1 (Oct. 1919), 36–67

Searle, G. R., *Entrepreneurial Politics in Mid-Victorian Britain* (Oxford, 1993)

Shannon, R. T., 'Gladstone, Canning and Bulgaria', *Etudes Balkaniques*, 4 (Sofia, 1977), 78–88

Shannon, R. T., 'David Urquhart and the Foreign Affairs Committees', in P. Hollis (ed.), *Pressure from Without in Early Victorian England* (London, 1974), pp. 239–61

Shannon, R. T., *Gladstone, Vol. I 1809–1865* (London, 1982)

Shattock, J. and Wolff, M. (eds), *The Victorian Periodical Press: Samplings and Soundings* (Leicester, 1982)

Smith, F. B., *Radical Artisan: William James Linton, 1812–97* (Manchester, 1973)

Smith, P., *Disraeli: A Brief Life* (Cambridge, 1996)

Smith, P., 'Disraeli's Politics', in C. B. Richmond and P. Smith (eds), *The Self-Fashioning of Disraeli, 1818–1851* (Cambridge, 1998), pp. 152–73

Southgate, D., *'The Most English Minister ...': The Policies and Politics of Palmerston* (London, 1966)

Southgate, D., *The Passing of the Whigs, 1832–1886* (London, 1965)

Steele, E. D., *Palmerston and Liberalism, 1855–1865* (Cambridge, 1991)

Stewart, R., *The Politics of Protection: Lord Derby and the Protectionist Party, 1841–1852* (Cambridge, 1971)

Strachey, L., *Eminent Victorians* (London, 1986 edn)

Stuart, C. H., 'The Formation of the Coalition Cabinet of 1852', *Transactions of the Royal Historical Society*, 5th ser., 4 (1954), 45–68

Swartz, M., *The Politics of British Foreign Policy in the Era of Disraeli and Gladstone* (1985)

Taylor, A., 'Palmerston and Radicalism, 1847–1865', *Journal of British Studies*, 33: 2 (April 1994), 157–79

Taylor, A. J. P., *The Trouble Makers: Dissent over Foreign Policy, 1792–1939* (Harmondsworth, 1985 edn)

Taylor, M., 'The Old Radicalism and the New: David Urquhart and the Politics of Opposition, 1832–1867', in E. F. Biagini and A. J. Reid (eds), *Currents of Radicalism: Popular Radicalism. Organised Labour and Party Politics in Britain, 1850–1914* (Cambridge, 1991), pp. 23–43

Taylor, M., 'John Bull and the Iconography of Public Opinion in England, c. 1712–1929', *Past and Present*, 134 (1992), 93–128

Taylor, M., *The Decline of British Radicalism, 1847–1860* (Oxford, 1995)

Temperley, H. W. V., 'Stratford de Redcliffe and the Origins of the Crimean War', *English Historical Review*, 48 (1933), 601–21

Temperley, H. W. V., 'The Alleged Violations of the Straits Convention by Stratford de Redcliffe between June and September 1853', *English Historical Review*, 49 (1934), 657–72

Temperley, H. W. V., *England and the Near East: The Crimea* (London, 1936; Repr. 1964)

Temperley, H. W. V., *The Foreign Policy of Canning, 1822–1827*, 2nd edn (London, 1966)

Thompson, F. M. L., *The Rise of Respectable Society: A Social History of Victorian Britain, 1830–1900* (London, 1988)

Vernon, J., *Politics and the People: A Study in English Political Culture, c. 1815–1867* (Cambridge, 1993)

Vincent, J. R., *The Formation of the British Liberal Party, 1857–68* (London, 1966)

Vincent, J. R., 'The Parliamentary Dimension of the Crimean War', *Transactions of the Royal Historical Society*, 5th ser., 31 (1981), 37–49

Vincent, J. R., *Disraeli* (Oxford, 1990)

Wadsworth, A. P., 'Newspaper Circulations, 1800–1954', *Transactions of the Manchester Statistical Society* (1954–55), 1–41

Walpole, S., *The Life of Lord John Russell*, 2 vols (London, 1889)

Webster, C., 'Urquhart, Ponsonby and Palmerston', *English Historical Review*, 62 (1947), 327–51

Webster, C., *The Art and Practice of Diplomacy* (London, 1961)

Webster, C., *The Foreign Policy of Palmerston, 1830–1841*, 2 vols (London, 1969)

Weintraub, S., *Albert. Uncrowned King* (London, 1997)

Williams, R., *The Contentious Crown: Public Discussion of the British Monarchy in the Reign of Queen Victoria* (Aldershot, 1997)

Winch, D., 'The System of the North: Dugald Stewart and his Pupils', in S. Collini,

D. Winch and J. Burrow, *That Noble Science of Politics: A Study in Nineteenth-Century Intellectual History* (Cambridge, 1983), pp. 23–61

Woodward, L., *The Age of Reform: England, 1815–1870*, 2nd edn (Oxford, 1992)

Worden, B., 'The Victorians and Oliver Cromwell', in S. Collini, R. Whatmore and B. Young (eds), *History, Religion, and Culture: British Intellectual History, 1750–1950* (Cambridge, 2000), pp. 112–35

Wyatt Tilby, A., *Lord John Russell* (London, 1930)

Ziegler, P., *Melbourne* (London, 1976)

UNPUBLISHED THESES

Berridge, V. S., 'Popular Journalism and Working Class Attitudes, 1854–1886: A Study of *Reynolds Newspaper, Lloyds Weekly Newspaper* and the *Weekly Times*' (unpublished PhD thesis, University of London, 1976)

Dreyer, F. A., 'The Russell Administration, 1846–52' (unpublished D.Phil thesis, University of St Andrews, 1962)

Gatrell, V. A. C., 'The Commercial Middle Class in Manchester, *c.* 1820–1857' (unpublished PhD thesis, University of Cambridge, 1971)

Jenks, M. H., 'The Activities and Influence of David Urquhart, 1833–56, with Special Reference to the Affairs of the Near East' (unpublished PhD thesis, University of London, 1964)

Keeling, R. M., 'Palmerston and the Pacifico Debate' (unpublished PhD dissertation, University of Missouri, 1968)

Short, S. H., 'British Attitudes to the Schleswig-Holstein Question, 1848–50' (unpublished PhD thesis, University of Edinburgh, 1969)

Smith, D. A., 'Cabinet and Constitution in the Age of Peel and Palmerston' (unpublished PhD dissertation, Yale University, 1966)

Taylor, A. C., 'The House of Commons and Foreign Policy, 1830–1867' (unpublished B. Litt thesis, University of Oxford, n.d.)

Taylor, A. D., 'Modes of Political Expression and Working Class Radicalism, 1848–1874: the London and Manchester Examples' (unpublished PhD thesis, University of Manchester, 1992)

Index